The
YEARS
of the
WIZARD

Also by Rachel Morris

The Museum Makers: A Journey Backwards

THE YEARS OF THE WIZARD

The Strange History & Home Life of Renaissance Magicians

RACHEL MORRIS

septe mb er

First published in the United Kingdom by September in 2025
September, an imprint of Duckworth Books Ltd
1 Golden Court, Richmond, TW9 1EU, United Kingdom
www.septemberpublishing.org

Illustrations on pages ix and 273 © Isabel Greenberg, 2025

A catalogue record for this book is available from the British Library

Book design by Danny Lyle
Typesetting by PDQ Media
Sun motif Shutterstock

Printed and bound in Great Britain by CPI Ltd, Croydon, CR0 4YY

The authorised representative in the EEA is Easy Access System
Europe, Mustamäe tee 50, 10621 Tallinn, Estonia

Hardback ISBN: 9781914613968
eISBN: 9781914613975

CONTENTS

For Stephen, Isabel and Imogen

The Many Dreams
of Robert Boyle,
Scientist

I t is Midsummer Night on the Irish estate and on this short night – a night so short that it has hardly begun before it is over – Robert Boyle, the earl's son, lays down his long body and closes his eyes. He is about the height of a good-sized grandfather clock and being a motherless boy he is (and always will be) prone to drinking and ranting and quarrelling. That night he dreams that God is writing the world like a vast novel and that out of God's huge brain there flows the loves and hopes and dreams of his vast cast of characters, the lords and shepherds and milkmaids and soldiers and lovers, all of whose comings and goings are perfectly plotted. Among all these characters there are the magicians, of whom Robert Boyle is one, whose task it is to discern the patterns – for nothing is random in the world of God-the-novelist, all is deftly and exquisitely plotted and everything makes sense if only we could see it. And in this most perfect of stories every ending will be both surprising and yet inevitable, and as one story ends so the novel will flow on past that ending and another story and then another one will begin, until finally God will put down his pen and yawn and stretch and say: 'Enough of writing', at which point this most perfect world will melt away into nothingness.

All things were believable back then – wizards, alchemy, fairies, even a god who wrote us all into existence. This is the story of those magical times.

PART ONE
THE WIZARDS

INTRODUCTION
HOW I FELL IN
LOVE WITH MAGIC

I would never have gone there but for a book that I found on my shelves. It concerned Dr John Dee, mathematician, alchemist, astrologer, angel talker and all-round Tudor wizard, and it told the strange, true story of how, in the sixteenth century, John Dee took his young wife Jane and all their children, as well as his scryer (which is to say, his medium) Edward Kelley, to Prague, which was then the occult capital of Europe. Here, the melancholy and poetic emperor Rudolf II ruled over a city of artists, poets, astronomers, astrologers and would-be magicians. Dee and Kelley wanted to talk to the angels to discover what God's intentions had been on the day that the world was born – and believed that they would find answers to their questions in Prague where there was magic on every street corner.

John Dee's home was Mortlake, a village on the River Thames a few miles west of the City of London. Here, he pursued his obsession with alchemy, and with summoning up spirits and talking to the angels. He also had a huge library, the biggest in England, which was full of books on magic. He lived at a time when grown men and women believed in fairies, when kings and queens kept alchemists, when the heavens were filled with angels and demons, and it was widely believed that the end of the world was imminent. The sight of strange comets in the sky was thought to mean that Christ would soon be with us, that the Turks would be overthrown, and that a great new king would appear in Europe. Witches were considered so dangerous that they had to be killed wherever they were found. The world itself – the physical world in which we live – was surrounded by spheres, one inside the next, each made up of an exquisite, transparent element called the 'quintessence', an element so perfect that medieval alchemists had been searching for it for years. The earth, the sun and the stars all shared in the world soul and the planets were alive and dancing a dance called the 'Music of the Spheres', the steps to which God had laid down at the beginning of time. Everywhere, people believed that they were connected to the universe, that the universe had a soul and that just as they felt for the universe, so the universe felt for them.

This was John Dee's magic-saturated world, which I came across in the first year of the Covid pandemic when nothing surprised me – though everything astonished me.

It was a time when we were all panicking and making pacts with Fate and there was deal-making and magical thinking everywhere – please don't let me catch the virus; please don't let my children die; please let me die before them. It was the virus's invisibility that so unnerved us. I had never before been threatened by something I couldn't see. My hair grew long over my eyes. I forgot how to talk to my partner. It was as if we hadn't breathed out for months. I got so used to a magical strangeness that I was amazed when the world obeyed its everyday laws, when I saw someone walking up ahead of me and blinked and looked again and saw they were still there.

That first pandemic spring, though harsh, was also strangely beautiful, one sunlit day after another. Out on Ally Pally hillside the trees were so thick with blossom they looked like they'd been upended and dipped in milk. We hadn't seen an aeroplane in weeks and a strange quiet had fallen on the city. On cold spring nights, I took a drink outside into the garden and sat on the stone wall or stood under the pear tree and looked up through its bare branches into the purity of the quintessence and tried to imagine what it would be like to believe we live in a snow-globe world, that the earth and the heavens are encased in crystalline spheres, that these spheres move because angels push them, and that when they do, everything in the heavens sings out to celestial music. Out in the garden during that first pandemic spring, I thought of John Dee's life and wondered what it would have been like to have lived in those magical years.

It made me remember those times when I was five, six or seven and had believed in magic, not a rabbit-out-of-a-hat magic but the magic of fairies and witches and time travel and strange transformations, such as girls into swans and grandmas into wolves. After that had come the middle years, when there were many Me's, but all of them practical, pragmatic, sceptical, not believing in magic at all; those were the Me's that went out to work to pay the mortgage.

But then, along came the pandemic and after that everything changed. After that I was no longer one hundred per cent sure of things. My world had been enchanted, in a dark sort of way.

I remembered the beautiful but alarming fairy stories of my childhood when anything could happen, a girl could turn mute or wander by mistake into fairyland or watch her brothers turn into swans and fly away, never to return unless she could sew the magic shirts for them. I thought of the magical world of Renaissance Prague and the melancholy emperor and John Dee's belief that he could talk to angels, and I decided that I was prepared to believe in strange glitches in the order of the universe, odd happenings and bumps and wrinkles in the flow of time. I wouldn't say I believed in them, but neither did I disbelieve them quite so strongly.

And of course, a part of me *wanted* these beliefs to be true, because the pandemic had made us all so jumpy, and because it is lonely living in a dead universe and because I wanted the zest and sparkle that comes from granting that the planets dance and the universe has a soul.

There are no stars in London now – the city lights have hidden them – but back in Tudor times the stars poured across the night sky in a vast and slowly moving river.

It was because of all these reasons – the pandemic, the story of John Dee, the memory of the fairy stories I read in my childhood – that I went in search of Renaissance magic and occult thinking.

•

And so, as soon as the world opened up after Covid, I began to seek out the spaces that these people built – their houses, libraries and churches – and to stare at the things their minds had encompassed and their fingers had made. I went to art galleries and gazed at Renaissance paintings, admiring the painted angels, and wondered, did men and women really, *really* believe in angels?

And I started haunting the Warburg Library in London, which specialises in Renaissance history and particularly Renaissance magic. Every library has its own personality, its own ghosts that inhabit it. The Warburg is at the southern end of Gordon Square near Euston station and was the creation, 100 years ago, of Aby Warburg, a member of the German banking family. To this day it has a more 'foreign' feel than, say, the Institute of Archaeology, which looks across at it from the northern end of the square. The Warburg's quirky, un-English feel is accentuated by its distinctive layout. The books are grouped into four categories: Image, Word, Orientation and Action. A category system is like a net through which you see the books – and this one casts an odd light on the collection.

I wrote most of this book in the Warburg Library during its recent building works and some days it seemed as if I (and the builders) were the only people in the entire four-storey building. When I turned a corner and met someone, I jumped from sheer surprise. And yet, on its silent shelves there are books that tell fantastical and tumultuous stories of a time when world views fought each other, when men and women believed in dragons and when angels and witches were everywhere. The Warburg has always been haunted by scholars of Renaissance magic. Drifting along its bookshelves is like drifting through Aby Warburg's head.

Next, I went to Oxford and gazed at the portrait of John Dee in the Ashmolean Museum. In it, he wears long magus robes and a black skull cap and he gazes back at you with his clever, wary eyes. Then from here I went to the History of Science Museum, also in Oxford, and upstairs to their collection of early scientific instruments, which is a gorgeous gathering of astrolabes, quadrants, spheres, sun dials and orreries. Astrolabes were based on scientific principles and were used by navigators to orient themselves by the stars, but they were also beautiful objects, as were all scientific instruments back then. John Dee was widely believed to be a magician, but he was also a scientist in our sense of the word, and he owned several astrolabes.

At Chetham's Library in Manchester they have five books that once belonged to Dee and which still carry his signature. I sat at the table where he is said to have called down the devil (there is a mark in the shape of a hoof burnt into the top of the table) and leafed through his books and admired his doodles. John Dee was an inveterate book-doodler, though back in the sixteenth century there was nothing reprehensible about this. On the contrary, doodling was a sign of your love for your books and a way of connecting you, through a bibliographic camaraderie, to all the readers who came afterwards. The Royal College of Physicians has John Dee's copy of *The Works of Cicero*, on one page of which he has drawn a beautiful full-bellied, three-masted sailing ship tossed on the ocean's billows. In Chetham's Library there is another book – the *Thesaurus Euonymi Philiatri de remediis secretis* written by the Swiss naturalist Conrad Gessner – with a section in Latin concerning the elixir of youth and it was here I found a doodle in the margin – apparently by Dee himself – of a naked and beautiful young woman. Oh, I think, so *that's* what it was all about?

•

Sometimes in the very early Covid mornings when all was quiet outside in the London streets, I lay awake and watched the light come sifting through the folds in the bedroom curtains and pictured the characters of those times. In my mind's eye I saw

John Dee, the magus and mathematician with his charismatic and obsessive temperament; Edward Kelley, John Dee's scryer, with his astonishing visions; the other wizards (Dee was not the only one) such as the wayward, scornful wizard Giordano Bruno and the dreaming wizard Tommaso Campanella. I also saw the magician-astronomer Johannes Kepler; the melancholy emperor Rudolf II, who was in love with magic; the women like Anna Maria Zieglerin who tried to find a place for themselves in this world (and were severely punished for it) and many, many more.

By now I was reading John Dee's diaries, the survival of which is a story in itself (we'll come back to that), and from these I could see how so much of what we know of the wizards' stories has come down to us through the eyes and voices of prosperous men. So where, I wondered, were the women's viewpoints – Jane Fromond, who married John Dee, and Edward Kelley's wife Joanna? And where were all the minor characters in the story of Renaissance magic (although to themselves they did not feel minor at all) – because it is not only the women whose stories have been forgotten – the stories of the young (such as John Dee's children), the poor (such as John Dee's servants) and the very old have also been lost to time.

Much of what we know about John Dee comes from his diaries. Like all diary writers John Dee never sets out to describe himself. He assumes that this being a private diary it will never be read. And so, the John Dee that flits across its pages – a clever, sociable, gullible, obsessive, egocentric man – is entirely unself-conscious, and yet often very vividly conveyed: and at least he has a voice. History has been far less kind to Jane Dee and Joanna Kelley, Joanna even more so than Jane. Just as women back then had relatively little agency to carve out their own lives, they also had very few ways by which to leave their stories behind. The majority of sixteenth-century women were illiterate; their voices have vanished, as have all those other people who were judged to be bit-part players in the lives of prosperous men. We simply do not know what these people thought and felt.

And so, I had to imagine them. In those early pandemic mornings, I imagined anxious, elderly fathers with wayward teenage daughters who were falling for the magic of love; worried daughters fearful their mother might be taken for a witch; girls who wanted to learn alchemy from their brothers; small children who couldn't read entranced by books; smart-arse young women alchemists; and a gang of London ragamuffins sitting on a garden wall waiting for a wizard to return.

There was something else as well. Those early morning Covid dreams, which brought me the women's and the children's stories, also reminded me that there are many ways in which the world is magical, that magical realism is more than a literary device, there is such a thing as everyday magic and it brings with it those brief moments when – through love or beauty – you feel yourself touched by the feather wings of Otherness. The wizards' wives and daughters, the old women and the servants, the elderly fathers and the ragamuffin children – none of them could perform magic, but all of them would have known everyday magic.

This is the story of Renaissance magic, told through the life, death and afterlife of John Dee and his extraordinary library – an entirely true, though utterly improbable, story. This is also the story of the women and the children, the old and the poor of that time, and the magic they might have known, and because their stories have not survived, I have imagined them for you. The final part of this book examines how this world finished and asks the questions: what is magic? Why do we crave it? How come it is so, well, magical? And to what extent has it really ended?

Chapter One
The Wizards

There were two kinds of magic in the sixteenth century. The first was the magic of the Renaissance wizards, of whom John Dee was one. They were early astronomers, mathematicians, scientists and philosophers, but always had a strong streak of magic and mysticism running through their thinking.

Theirs was a high-class, bookish magic that derived from the ancient world and was written in many languages – Greek, Latin, Arabic, Hebrew and Aramaic. They called themselves natural philosophers or magi (which meant learned magicians) and thought of themselves as men who understood the forces of the universe and – more than that – men who could control these forces, whether for good (which made them practitioners of white magic) or for evil (which made them malevolent demons). If they were white magicians, they were also – always – believers in God. Heinrich Cornelius Agrippa was a wandering German scholar who wrote extensively on magic at the beginning of the sixteenth century and was himself believed to be a magician. He said, 'The word "magician" does not among learned men signify a sorcerer or one that's superstitious or devilish, but a wise man, a priest, a prophet.'

John Dee was not the only Renaissance wizard. The wizards were a Europe-wide phenomenon. They included the rebellious Italian Giordano Bruno, who was run out of Oxford for claiming that the earth went round the sun; Heinrich Cornelius Agrippa, just mentioned; the Swiss Paracelsus, part-doctor, part-magician and always angry; and the dreamer Tommaso Campanella, who was sentenced to life imprisonment in Naples for sedition. And along with these there were many more men, such as the astronomer Johannes Kepler, and even Isaac Newton, who – although we think of them as scientists – still shared many of these magical beliefs. From our point of view the wizards' convictions seem to slip back and forth across the very clear boundary that we draw between reality and fantasy, but things looked different then. The wizards never thought of themselves as charlatans (although this was an insult they may have applied to their competitors). They believed in their own powers, as did many of the people around them. In a world where nothing was fixed and few things were understood wizardry made as much sense as anything else.

The second kind of magic in England at this time was rural in origin and belonged to all the social classes. This was the magic of fairies, witches, brownies and goblins, magic that infused the stories told in taverns on dark nights, magic that belonged to farmers and servant girls, in fact, to all the poor and the book-less. This magic was part of the oral, not the literate, world and was deeply embedded in European culture. No one knows where and why fairy beliefs began nor how old they are, other than that they certainly date back hundreds, maybe even thousands of years. By contrast, the magic of the wizards had only arrived in Europe relatively recently. Its origins were in classical Greece, particularly in Plato's writings, and its journey to sixteenth-century Europe had been via ancient Alexandria, then Constantinople, capital of the Byzantine Empire, and also through the Islamic world.

The wizards were modern (notwithstanding that their magic could be traced back to Plato) whereas the fairies were ancient. The wizards were also mostly men and often very powerful whereas fairy magic felt like it belonged to the underdog and often seemed quite female, especially if we count in the witches (though never totally so, there were male as well as female fairies). Elizabethan England was deeply hierarchical and so the two kinds of magic didn't often meet – although just occasionally they did.

•

John Dee was highly educated. He had been a mathematical prodigy and a fellow of St John's College, Cambridge, where he studied arithmetic, perspective and astronomy – as well as many other subjects that we would now find much stranger (but people back then did not) such as alchemy and angel magic. Alchemy was widely believed in; even William Cecil, 1st Baron Burghley, Elizabeth I's hard-headed chief adviser, kept books on the subject in his library.

When Dee was still at university he put on a production of Aristophanes' *Peace* and as part of the play built a giant beetle that at one point appeared to take flight, with an actor on its back, and settle in the eaves above the stage. This was the beginning of John Dee's reputation for magic. It was also a reflection of a time when people loved mechanical objects and automata with moving parts, which is perhaps what the beetle was. Hundreds of years of clockmaking had produced craftsmen who were highly skilled in the clockwork arts. Now, all the great rulers of Europe had roomfuls of automata and gardens full of water organs and mechanical fountains.

In 1547, Dee went to Louvain in the Netherlands where he met the mathematician Gemma Frisius and the cartographer Gerardus Mercator. It was through these associations that he came to understand, as very few people then did, the mathematics that lay behind journeys to the New World. When Queen Elizabeth I came to the throne, she took him under her wing – he became her favourite astrologist – though there was nothing peculiar about this, since everyone believed in astrology at that time.

As well as astrology, John Dee could also advise the queen on the mathematics behind sea voyages to the New World, a very useful talent when the territory was just beginning to be fully discovered. The queen even visited him at his house in Mortlake, which was a great and unusual honour, coming by carriage or boat down the river from her palace at Richmond.

Yet as Dee grew older, he became gripped by another obsession. He became more and more consumed by the possibilities of angel magic, the idea that you could communicate with God and discover the secrets of his universe by talking to his angels. Angels are everywhere in the Bible, where they act as God's messengers. They were believed to have sat at God's side since the Garden of Eden. If you believed in the truth of the Bible, as everyone in the sixteenth century did, you would believe in angels. And, if like Dee, you wanted to understand the history of the universe and God's purpose in creating it, you would obviously want to speak to the angels because of all they knew. The challenge was how to learn their language.

Dee's ideas seem very strange to us, in fact bordering on the deranged, but they would not have seemed so strange to people at the time. Another area of magic he pursued was alchemy and the philosopher's stone. The latter was a magical substance that could turn base metals into gold (amplifying the quantity as it did so). It could also grant you the elixir of life, which provided unending youth and immortality. Alchemy was the science that would help you reach the philosopher's stone. To us all this seems like a fairy tale but back then the existence of the philosopher's stone was entirely logical because it chimed with the widespread idea that the world is endlessly changing and transforming into something else. Alchemy, the science of transformation, was God's magic.

Dee's method of angel talk was by means of shew stones, one of which was a crystal ball 'as big as an egg, most bright, clere and glorious' and another of which was a black obsidian mirror that probably originated in Mexico. When consulting the angels, Dee placed these shew stones on a wax seal which he then placed on his Holy Table, a wooden table made according to instructions from the angels and whose surface was painted with mystical emblems and the letters of a magical, angelical alphabet, all in reds, blues and golds. (After John Dee died the obsidian mirror found its way into Hugh Walpole's collection. One of his crystal balls and the mirror are now in the British Museum.)

The wizards were optimists. They believed that men have the power and the agency to change the world. They also believed that the universe brims with purpose and meaning but that these meanings were buried deep and hard to fathom; it was their job to act like codebreakers and decipher the world.

•

The wizards mainly lived wandering, nomadic existences. They were the counterculture of their times, rebellious, mercurial fast-talkers who sometimes had the ears of kings and queens, though they were just as likely to swing downwards into disaster as they were to swing upwards to glory. They wandered because they passionately wanted to learn things and in a world with scarcely any forms of communication, one way to discover new things was to go out into the world and find things out for yourself. They also loved to meet and talk with fellow intellectuals.

The world that they stepped into, although very beautiful, was also unstable and often dangerous. Great changes in belief were sweeping across Europe. One of these shifts was the Reformation, the schism in Christendom which sent most of northern Europe towards Lutheranism and Calvinism. The Counter-Reformation was the Catholic backlash against this. New worlds were being discovered – literally the New World on the far side of the Atlantic (though this was mysterious because it wasn't mentioned in the Bible so how could it even exist?), and other worlds, like the long-lost worlds of classical Greece and Rome. New technologies like printing were emerging, innovations that could spread new ideas further and faster than they had ever been spread before (though such were the times that people assumed the printer Johannes Gutenberg must be using magic, because how else could he make every copy of every book identical?).

With hindsight, we can see that the sixteenth century was the beginning of what we would call science, and yet magic still appeared everywhere. Magic was also viewed with ambivalence since it was believed to come in two forms: bad, black magic and good, white magic. Even John Dee's mathematical prowess was considered dangerously magical to some of his contemporaries, as mathematics was believed to be close to conjuring (a dubious form of magic), since it enabled you to discover a truth about something without recourse to the five senses.

The most dangerous profession at that time, however, was astronomy. It was still widely believed that the heavens were God's realm and that they were therefore pure and unchanging, with the earth at the centre and the sun and stars circling it in a stately procession. Most of the magicians, Dee included, were passionately interested in astronomy, but those who tried to overturn this earth-centric view were considered to be heretics, conjurors and mad men, and many were punished for it.

Both the Reformation and the Counter-Reformation condemned early science, and ferociously denounced magic. (It was often difficult to distinguish between the two.) The government set watchers to guard ports on the eastern side of England and check which books were coming in from the Continent. Those that carried heretical, magical ideas were regularly censored or burnt. When Edward VI swung the government towards Protestantism, he had his men ransack and destroy the university libraries in Oxford and Cambridge. In Antwerp, where the Catholic Spanish king was in charge, the printer Christophe Plantin risked his life by secretly printing at night the quietist philosophy of a sect called the Family of Love who refused to side with either Protestants or Catholics. Poets, philosophers, astronomers, printers – in fact anyone connected to the book trade was considered to be dangerous.

This was the wizards' precarious world. Some were driven into exile, others were tormented by the Church, most led wandering lives, and Tommaso Campanella spent twenty-seven years in gaol for allegedly conspiring against the Spanish authorities in Naples in an attempt to build a better world.

CHAPTER TWO
MORTLAKE

John Dee was different. He had a domestic side to his nature. He married a woman much younger than himself called Jane Fromond (she was twenty-three to his fifty-one) and was by all accounts an attentive, even husbandly man, although also wilful, obsessive and gullible. They had eight children together and lived in the house that Dee had inherited from his mother in the hamlet of Mortlake, which was on the south bank of the Thames, some ten miles west of the City of London.

Mortlake in those days would have consisted of not much more than a church, farms and farm buildings, a huddle of domestic houses and perhaps a ferry boat that would take you across the river. The house that John Dee inherited – now long since gone – was a ramshackle affair, but it had an orchard and garden, and a river gate at the bottom of the garden where boats could be tied up. Here in Mortlake, John Dee built a vast and magical library, as well as rooms for his scientific instruments, which included sea compasses, astrolabes and early magic lanterns. He also had a cabinet of curiosities (the name for an early museum) which was filled with rarities that he had picked up on foreign travels. Outside in the gardens, he built outhouses to take his alchemical stills, also called alembics, in which you could selectively boil a liquid containing several different substances in such a way that you could separate out the substance you wanted, then turn it into vapour and condense it down to its purest form. (This was one of the skills needed to make the philosopher's stone.)

Inside the house, in the most secret part of his library where visitors rarely went, Dee would have kept his crystal ball, his obsidian mirror and all his other magical apparatus for talking to the angels. Years later, the botanist Nicholas Culpeper got hold of Dee's crystal ball and claimed in alarm to have seen a spirit emerging from it.

John Dee loved his children. His diaries (many of which have survived) are full of references to their childish adventures. On 22 January 1582 he notes, 'Arthur Dee and Mary Herbert, they being but 3 year old the eldest, did make as it wer a shew of childish marriage, of calling each other husband and wife.' On 5 August 1590 he writes, 'Rowland fell into the Tems over head and eares about noone or somewhat after.' (Rowland lived to tell the tale.) And on 27 June 1591 he notes, 'Arthur wounded on his head by his own wanton throwing of a brickbat upright and not well avoiding the fall of it again.' He also loved his wife Jane, though her furious temper sometimes alarmed him: 'Jane most desperately angry in respect of her maydes,' he writes on 15 November 1593.

It was Jane Dee who would have managed the gardeners who built the gardens at Mortlake. Elizabethan gardens were both beautiful and functional. In summer the orchard at Mortlake would have been heavy with fruit, the kitchen garden full of vegetables and herbs, such as thyme and lavender, and the flower garden deep in lilies, pinks, fritillaries, anemones and roses. On fine summer mornings with the dew on the orchard grass, and on summer evenings with the birdsong and sounds of children playing, Mortlake would have been a beautiful place.

•

Mortlake was outside London and yet it had one great advantage – it was beautifully situated on the river-road which linked the queen's many palaces, from Richmond in the west via Hampton Court, Westminster and Whitehall, down to Greenwich in the east. The queen was always on the move – and the river was one of the ways by which she got around. She passed Mortlake many times and sometimes stopped off to pay her best wishes to the Dees. In July 1583 she paused on her journey from Greenwich to Syon House and in the spring of 1583, she was journeying on horseback from Richmond to Greenwich and stopped off at Mortlake where she offered her hand for the wizard to kiss.

John Dee had charm and energy. He was also sociable and very well connected and he loved to talk, but also to listen, and wherever he went he liked to meet up with like-minded people. He had once been a tutor to the Dudley children, including Robert Dudley, who grew up to become the Earl of Leicester and the queen's favourite. Since then, Dee had stayed close to all of the Dudley clan. Mortlake was also near the country house of the queen's adviser Sir Francis Walsingham, as well as to the vast country estate of Syon House, which in the 1590s belonged to the earls of Northumberland. Henry Percy, the ninth earl, was known as the 'wizard earl' for his occult interests. It was said at the time that a circle of poets, scientists and free-thinkers, all of them interested in alchemy, liked to meet at Syon House. They included Henry Percy; the explorer Walter Raleigh, who even when he was later imprisoned in the Tower of London kept his own alchemical laboratory; Dee himself, by now an old man with a long, white beard; and Thomas Harriot, the mathematician, who during his life was accused of conjuring and asserting that heaven and hell were merely stories designed to enforce our obedience. The Syon House circle were mostly young, rebellious and subversive. They were called the 'School of Atheism', with atheism then being considered a particularly shocking and scandalous belief.

Dee's lifestyle was expensive. A man on the make in those days needed servants, fine clothes, a well-appointed house, a carriage and horses. And magic too was expensive, requiring books, equipment and technology. Many alchemists said that they needed a speck of gold to get the process going. They also needed furnaces and an array of glass containers, including alembics or alchemical stills. Alembics had glass flasks with long necks that curved downwards (reminiscent of a pelican's beak) to aid in the process of distillation. Using glass equipment meant that the magician could see the substance changing colour, which signalled that he was getting closer to the philosopher's stone, but all this equipment had to be of the highest quality, especially the glass, and this was a problem because there were very few glassworks in early modern England and so glass was expensive. Books were also expensive and yet crucial, because in them was stored all the semi-secret knowledge of the alchemists.

Nor could a magician afford to look poor – 'Why can't he magic up some money?' his audience would have asked.

Like all magicians, Dee needed wealthy patrons. He was always angling for a paid position at court as the queen's philosopher, but he also offered various services for pay, such as dream interpretation and astrological readings. As well as this he was full of knowledge that a government might find useful, especially about geology, mining, map making and sea routes. The world was expanding, the Elizabethan state wanted to claim the sea routes to the New World and Cathay and John Dee had the knowledge. He taught the sailors Martin Frobisher and Christopher Hall how to use the most up-to-date navigational equipment (Frobisher was organising expeditions to find the Northwest Passage) and Dee frequently went to the headquarters of the Muscovy Company in Seething Lane in the City to advise on northern sea routes and sea journeys to Cathay.

Mortlake was always busy with comings and goings. The house was open to friends, students, patrons and protégés. Francis Walsingham, Robert Dudley and Dudley's nephew Philip Sidney all came to Mortlake, as did Lady Sidney, the sister of the Earl of Leicester, who came to learn about alchemy but also once nursed Dee when he was ill. The map maker Abraham Ortelius visited, as did the explorer Humphrey Gilbert and his brother, Adrian Gilbert.

•

By day, John Dee read, talked, lectured and built networks, but by night he and his brilliant young pupil Thomas Digges spent many hours together, mapping the stars in the night sky. It is easy to forget how astonishing the heavens must have looked back then on summer nights, when every inch of the sky was filled with stars, each one jumping with radiance and seemingly alive and possessed of intelligence, governing the lives of those men born under its aspect. When John Dee looked up at the stars he would have perceived them as collectively imbued with meaning and portent if only he could interpret them.

The heavens have always attracted magical thinking, perhaps because people thought of them as the abode of God and therefore particularly rich in His magic. In those days, astronomy and astrology had equal status, the former being the study of celestial objects like the moon, the stars and the planets and the latter being the study of their effects on us. Astrology was believed to work because it was thought that the stars and planets all emitted rays. As the stars moved across the sky their rays touched different parts of the earth with varying strengths – and because like appeals to like, as it was believed back then, the stars particularly touched people born under their star sign.

This was a very old concept which acknowledged that we are connected to the great movements of the stars; that the stars are in us as we are in them. (Or, as the third-century philosopher Origen of Alexandria put it most beautifully, 'Understand that you are another world in miniature and that you have within you the sun, the moon and the stars.')

•

When John Dee wasn't outside studying the stars, he would have been in his library, working with his favourite scryer/ medium Edward Kelley, attempting to summon up spirits. Scrying meant seeing the future, usually by invoking spirits in some kind of reflective surface, such as a crystal or a mirror. Kelley was a tall young man, running to fat, whose ears had been lopped off for some previous misdemeanour and who arrived in Dee's life in 1582, introducing himself as Edward Talbot (it was only later that Dee discovered his real name was Edward Kelley). Scryers were often peculiar people, typically being lowborn but literate, and sometimes outcasts and fugitives as well. Scrying was illegal and had been so since the 1541 Act against Conjurations, Witchcraft, Sorcery and Enchantments. It was as if all the oddities of scryers were proof of their scrying capabilities. Edward Kelley, who believed that he could see the angels and hear them talking in the shew stones, was exactly this kind of person.

Before the scrying sessions could begin, John Dee and Edward Kelley had to carry out certain rituals. First, they made sure the library doors were closed so that no one could interrupt them, including the children, and then they washed, put on clean clothes, shaved, made confession, read from the scriptures, and said their prayers to north, south, east and west. The practice of alchemy was essentially a religious rite and so the alchemist would have turned towards his equipment – the furnaces, the glass vessels for distillation – and bowed his head as if before an altar. All this was necessary because it was believed that your attitude during the scrying session could affect the outcome. After that, the session could begin.

And it is here (from reading John Dee's diaries) that we realise something extraordinary, that John Dee never felt that he himself could see or hear the angels, and yet he passionately believed and trusted that his scryer Edward Kelley could. It was Dee, as the magician, who led the rituals and believed he was summoning up the spirits and angels, but it was Edward Kelley, as the scryer, who looked into the crystal and saw and heard and spoke the spirits' words aloud. And so, what Dee is unquestion-ingly reporting in his diaries are the visions that another man claims to be having. The twenty-first-century reader is baffled. Was Edward Kelley knowingly tricking John Dee with his talk of angels? And if not that, then what? Was he taking drugs? Was he mentally deranged? Did he really believe that he could see spirits? The diaries tell us a great deal but of these fundamental questions we can make no sense.

What is clear is that Kelley had an astonishing imagination. If the spirits were his invention – as they presumably were – they were an extraordinary creation (and it may be that Kelley, although he invented them, believed in them as passionately as Dee). All the spirits had names and their interactions, their comings and goings, were all as complicated as a huge novel, and yet they were all carried in Edward Kelley's head, to be endlessly extended and embroidered whenever John Dee demanded that he call them up. There were, amongst others, the archangels Michael, Gabriel, Raphael and Uriel; the spirit Murifri; the wicked spirit Lundrumguffa; three or four 'spiritual creatures like labouring men, having spades in their hands and their hair hanging around their ears'; and Galva, an old woman in 'a red petticoat, with a red silk upper bodice, her hair rolled about like a Scottish woman'. Yet Kelley's greatest creation was a pretty seven-year-old spirit girl called Madimi, whose long hair flowed down her back and who liked to play on the mantelpiece, though you could never see her reflection in the mirror. Kelley claimed that she liked to ask, 'Am I not pretty?' Dee's diaries vividly capture the way a small child plays and remind you that Kelley himself had a small stepdaughter. Given that Madimi was only seven, it is remarkable how willing Dee and Kelley were to obey her instructions.

It seemed that Kelley both channelled the spirits' words (like a direct voice medium) but that he also stood back and described what he was seeing. The words we read in the diaries – written down by John Dee but presumably quoting Edward Kelley – are often vivid, arresting, even beautiful, which no doubt added to their magical power in John Dee's eyes.

It was as if Kelley was acting out a drama that he was inventing as he went along, and yet never contradicting himself. This complex drama went on for years. Madimi even had a back story: 'I am the last but one of my mother's children,' she said. 'I have little baby children at home.'

But if the spirits were a play it was also a stormy and tempestuous one. Edward Kelley frequently painted apocalyptic visions of furious angels who shouted and stormed and spewed out flames and threatened hurricanes and the end of the world. It must have been exhausting to be Kelley, which would explain his volatile moods. Once, he shouted out that the spirits were attacking him, that they had nipped him and broken his left arm by the wrist and that John Dee had to help him defend himself against them. At this point, Dee grabbed a spade and started laying about him, following Kelley's shouted instructions. Another time, Kelley claimed that the spirits were demanding John Dee hand over all his writings to be burnt – which, astonishingly, Dee did, apparently all twenty-four volumes of them, though it turned out the spirits did not destroy them.

•

So, this was John Dee's home at Mortlake. The roiling, boiling turmoil of the spirits as they were summoned up in the library was one side of the coin; the other side was Mortlake's bucolic beauty by day, the stars by night and the everyday details of his domestic life with the woman he loved and the children whose games he recorded in his diaries. Soon, word spread of the extraordinary goings on there and Dee quickly acquired a reputation, locally, nationally and internationally, for being a magus or a wizard, the master of strange things, but also for being a man that it was very useful to know. He was honoured by rich and powerful men but was also envied and resented by people who believed he had found the secret to making gold and would therefore never have to work again. The scholar Elias Ashmole, who wrote about him a century later, said that Dee's great ability in 'Astrologie, and the more secret parts of Learning (to which he had a strong propensitie and an unwearying Fancie) drew from the Envious and Vulgar, many rash, lewd and lying Scandalls'. The pursuit of magic not only prompted envy, it was also illegal and sometimes severely punished. All this, then, planted a precariousness at the heart of John Dee's life.

And yet, despite all this, Dee gradually made Mortlake the centre of English magic.

CHAPTER THREE
MAGICAL LONDON

Although John Dee lived in Mortlake, London was his city (sometimes he signed himself 'Joannes Dee Londiniensis') and he would have visited London again and again, to buy books, to meet friends and patrons and to present himself at court. He would probably have travelled there by boat, this being the easiest way to get around in Tudor England, disembarking at one of the numerous water steps that led up from the river's edge to the city's many alleyways.

Tudor London was – by our standards – tiny. It covered an area of just over a square mile, stretching from the Tower of London in the east to Fleet Street in the west and from the Barbican in the north down to the banks of the Thames. To the west of London, beyond the fields and market gardens of Charing Cross and Covent Garden, was the second city of Westminster, which consisted mostly of the palace, abbey and gardens. To the north of this second city were more woods and fields, this time of Kensington and Knightsbridge.

The City of London was still edged with city walls and had seven spectacular gates that were closed at night when the curfew came into force and were then guarded by soldiers until the morning. The wide, cold Thames ran beside it, teeming with fish, and the wild, wooded hills of Hampstead and Highgate looked down on it from the north. Inside its walls were more than 100 church spires, towers and steeples that rang the hours by day and night. To any onlooker coming up the river the city would have looked, within its walls, as spiky as a hedgehog. When night fell, there would unfold overhead the nightly drama of the heavens, ten thousand quivering, shivering stars wrapping the heavens in a gauze of starlight.

To some extent the city walls were notional, London flowed out beyond them. The rich built fine houses along the Strand to the west of the city and James Burbage built his theatre out in the hamlet of Shoreditch to the north (when playhouses were banned within the city walls). When the historian John Stow was little, he was sent to buy milk from a farm just outside the city walls, and movement flowed the other way as well. Country people moved into London and brought with them their customs and beliefs. We know of Maypole celebrations with a maypole in Fenchurch Street and giant puppets and festivals celebrating the Lord of Misrule.

And yet, the city walls also kept their meaning. This, they said, is the capital city of England. The gates were spectacular, some of them three storeys high, with turreted and crenellated tops, archways for carriages to pass through and fine windows above. A Londoner, walking north out of the city one evening, would have passed sheds, allotments, orchards and market gardens but would soon have come to woods and fields, would have heard the sounds of birds settling themselves into sleep, would have seen the moon rising and the city walls receding behind them – and would have marvelled at how very different the countryside was.

Tudor London had no grand Renaissance piazzas. It had some fine streets – Cheapside, Goldsmiths' Row, Leadenhall and Bishopsgate were some of them – and some fine buildings, such as the Guildhall, but mostly within its city walls was a compact network of narrow streets and alleyways. In those days the houses were not numbered. To find your way around you first had to find the right parish and parish church and then look for house names, other landmarks or the signs that might be swinging from signboards or painted on the facades of houses. Your instructions might be: 'Turn left by the Sign of the Ship, then it's five houses on from the Sign of the Bear.'

This was a world in which people made things and so, London was a city of craftsmen. Within its walls there were haberdashers, soap-makers, glassmakers, clock-menders, brewers, jewellers and metal workers, alchemists, salt-makers, carpenters, goldsmiths, apothecarists, gardeners and scientific instrument makers.

Just outside the city walls on the west there were already printing presses in Fleet Street. They were close enough to St Paul's to profit from the booksellers that huddled in the open space in front of the cathedral (called St Paul's Churchyard). Some of these booksellers sold their books from trestle tables and market stalls. Others occupied bookshops – such as William Sears's shop, which was signalled by the sign of the Hedgehog. (Other bookshop signs included a sun and a Bible.) John Dee would have had many friends amongst the booksellers and St Paul's Churchyard must have fizzed with talk and with dissent. The authorities knew quite well that books carry trouble – the bishop of London and the privy council kept the right to censor those coming into London – and their agents would have been here amongst the crowds. Tudor England was highly controlled. It was often at war and always felt under threat from the great Catholic powers of France and Spain and so, in response, Elizabeth encouraged Sir Francis Walsingham to set up a spy network to track dissent of all kinds. Books were one of the many things that were supervised.

London was also a city of museums. For decades now the ships had been coming upriver, bringing with them vast numbers of strange artefacts from the New World, and it may have been this phenomenon that prompted the appearance of private museums – then called 'kunstkammers' or 'cabinets of curiosities'. Out to the west of London when Kensington was still woods and fields, Walter Cope built a country house and a museum, called Cope's Castle, which was famous in the sixteenth century. Richard Hakluyt, who visited it, talked of its contents: 'the many beastes, birds, fishes, serpents, plants, fruits, hearbes, rootes, apparel, armours, boates and such other rare and strange curiosities, which wise men take great pleasure to reade of, but much more contentment to see...'

Downriver in Greenwich, where the air was said to be especially sweet, Queen Elizabeth extended and modernised Greenwich Palace and kept within it a collection of strange and wondrous artefacts. They came from the New World and included globes and a salt cellar modelled on an indigenous North American, inlaid with precious stones and ornamented with feathers. John Dee had his own museum collection in Mortlake, and in Lambeth, just south of the Thames and outside the city walls, the Tradescants, father and son, built another famous museum (a little later, in the time of James I) which they stocked with plants and artefacts that they brought home from all over the world. These cabinets of curiosities were personal museums, built by men – it was almost always men – to delight and impress their friends, to wonder at the world and to try and explain it.

London at this time also had its own historian, a man called John Stow. He was born in 1525 in the London parish of St Michael's, Cornhill. His father had been a candle-maker and Stow was a passionate and largely self-taught historian who lamented the way that the London of his childhood kept on vanishing. It was this that drove him on – in a melancholy kind of way – to continue walking the streets of London and recording in his survey of the city everything he saw, for – who knew? – a church, a house, a wall, a gate that was here today might be gone tomorrow.

•

Tudor London was a magical place. Back then, everyone ascribed magical power to objects and most people would have had an amulet or a charm to keep them safe. Witches' bottles were common, and some have survived, such as a sixteenth- or seventeenth-century witch's bottle which is now on display in the Old Royal Naval College Visitor Centre in Greenwich. Witches' bottles were planted in the walls of houses or at their front doors, to catch witches before they could come in. The Greenwich witch's bottle still contains traces of urine and human hair.

This London contained many magicians. Some were rich and well connected, some far poorer. Names that have been passed down to us include the astrologer Simon Forman, who lived in Philpot Lane and who was famous for his sexual appetite (and who was also implicated in a murder); Cornelius de Lannoy, an alchemist and a Lowlander who persuaded the queen to keep him in some style in Somerset House in 1565 and 1566 in return for his promise that he would make her gold (he was said to be 'stout beyond all measure and speaketh words every inch of a foot and a half long'); Francis Moore, an astrologer who lived in Lambeth and wrote an astrologer's almanac; John Dee (of course); John Lambe, an astrologer and quack physician who was accused of black magic and stoned to death by a mob; and William Wycherley, a tailor, accused of conjuring up a spirit called Scariot who knew the location of stolen goods.

There were many more London magicians practising their trade whose names we don't know. Amongst the most popular services they offered were treasure hunting and foretelling the future. Thomas Shakilton of Aldersgate Street, Christopher Morgan, a plasterer of Beche Lane, and Mrs Crox of St Giles were all accused of practising the 'sieve and shears', which was a form of divination in which you held up a sieve between the two blades of a pair of scissors and watched to see which way the sieve turned when you asked it a question. The Church did not approve of these magical activities; later in the sixteenth century, women like Mrs Crox were defined as witches and the Church launched a systematic campaign of repression against them.

Scandal tends to cling to memories of the London magicians – sometimes it's all we know of them – accusations of murder and black magic – though it would be wrong to think of them all as scoundrels. John Dee, as we will see, though certainly gullible, was no scoundrel. We don't know if the magicians of London ever spoke to each other, although they certainly knew of each other. We also know that William Cecil, 1st Baron Burghley, the queen's adviser, met a Venetian merchant and alchemist called Giovanni Battista Agnello in the parish of St Helen's Bishopsgate one winter's day in 1577 (this was the parish where twenty years later Shakespeare lived). Cecil was interested in alchemy and occult matters, kept an open mind about the powers they might possess, and if they existed he wanted to keep those powers for the queen. Agnello wrote a book on magic that John Dee kept on the shelves in his huge and remarkable library.

If you ever had the opportunity to look down onto Elizabethan London on a moonlit night, you would have seen it crouched on the plain between the river and the hills, its high walls enclosing it tightly, its church spires shooting heavenwards and the whole thing looking as neat and dinky as a model that you could hold in your hand.

And there was another way in which Tudor London was magical. At this time, there was a widespread belief in the connections between the microcosm of the world below and the macrocosm of the heavens above. London was the centre of English power – this was where the queen had her palaces and from where she governed the country. When the queen's barge came floating down the Thames it would have been announced by sackbuts, cornets and trumpets, the sounds of which would have floated across the water and seeped into the city's narrow alleyways. Royal power was magical (the king's touch could cure illnesses) and when all was right with the world and when every man and woman was in their allotted place, including the king or queen, then there was a magical and harmonious affinity between the earth below and the heavens above. As above, so below, as the alchemists used to say. Disorder in the heavens – unexpected comets and eclipses – was a sign of turmoil on earth, whilst the overturning of the social order – for instance, the overthrow of a king or queen – would be pre-announced by the disruption of the heavens.

What was desired above all else was harmony, that everything on earth and in the heavens was so harmoniously combined that when the planets moved, they created the Music of the Spheres. This was John Dee's magic-saturated city.

CHAPTER FOUR
MASTER PLATO

To understand the bookish, learned magic that John Dee practised we need to go backwards in time, to explore how it arrived in Renaissance England. One beginning (there were many) was a day in the early summer of 1439 when the last emperor (but one) of Constantinople and his retinue came to Medici Florence.

The emperor's name was John VIII Palaeologus and he had come to ask for the Florentines' help in his war with the Ottomans. His empire had shrunk, his capital city was surrounded and it seemed only a matter of time before the Ottomans overran it. The emperor arrived riding on a white horse, a bow and arrow in his hands and a vast retinue of soldiers, bishops, poets and philosophers stretching out behind him. He was a Christian, but of the Eastern branch of the Church. Now, he needed military help, but he couldn't form an alliance with Florence until the two sides had ironed out the doctrinal differences between them – because the Easterners wore beards, which was clearly ungodly, but the Westerners (also called the Latins) used unleavened bread in the eucharist and this too was ungodly. The two sides argued over whether the souls of the dead travelled through purgatory or round it and disputed the nature of the Holy Ghost and whether it came from the Father and Son (as the Westerners argued) or from the Son alone (as the Easterners argued).

The emperor had brought all his manuscripts with him, partly because he couldn't bear to be parted from them – his father is said to have said of him (as fathers are wont to do), 'I am afraid the decline of this house may come from his poems and arguments' – but also because he needed to consult his books so as to win what he foresaw as the many theological arguments ahead of him. His books included many that were copies (and copies of copies) of ones that had been written in ancient Greece and Rome.

Also in the emperor's train was the Byzantine philosopher George Gemistos Plethon, a tall, bearded old man, though still very good-looking, who was reputed to be (much to the shock of the Florentines) a self-styled pagan and lover of Zeus. Plethon brought with him a passionate love for Plato and a defiant advocacy of Plato against Aristotle, the latter having been far more popular than Plato in medieval Europe. Plethon must have been an astonishing orator for he was soon stirring up passionate debates about Plato amongst the scholars of Florence. By the standards of the time, Plethon was very old (he was in his seventies when he came to Florence) and he must have known that, just as his own life was ending, so Constantinople, the thousand-year-old city, the great creation of the Hellenes, the capital of the empire, was coming to an end as well. He talked with all the passion of a man who knows that his world is finishing.

And with Plato came the magic that the Renaissance wizards fell in love with.

Plato propounded the mystical belief that the world we live in is not real, that everything in our world is but a shadow of another world that is more beautiful, more real, more true than ours, a world that lies beyond the veil. In Plato's other world there are eternal truths called the 'Forms', of which the truest of all is the 'Form of Beauty'. Everything beautiful in our world is but the faintest shadow of this Form. Thus, Plato dissolved the solidity of this world, gave it a tremulous unreliability and made men believe that the world they can see and touch isn't real at all. To fifteenth-century ears this idea, although beautiful, trembled on the edge of magic, but for Plato, the more beautiful an idea the more likely it was to be true – which is in itself a very beautiful belief.

Plato also wrote about love, most scandalously in a book called the *Symposium*, in which a group of men gather together to drink and praise gay love whilst affirming the idea that a man may begin by loving the body of a beautiful young man and rise from there, via that love, to the love of God. For Plato, love was the force that held the universe together. It was also a daimon, a spirit that mediated between heaven and earth, carrying our prayers and sacrifices to the gods, and returning their commands and repayments for sacrifices. Present at this drinking session in the *Symposium* was Aristophanes, the Greek comic writer, who put forward the idea that we are all born as one half of a lost whole, and that all our lives are spent in searching for our other halves. Who hasn't felt the loneliness of being one and yearned instead to be one half of two? It is probably the most seductive and influential idea ever conceived about love and it was Plato's *Symposium* that brought it to the West.

The Florentine scholars were astonished at these long-robed, black-bearded book lovers and amazed that all of Plato's *Dialogues* had survived in Constantinople (where Plato had been taught as part of the higher civil service exam). For a long time in the West, only one of Plato's dialogues – the *Timaeus* – had been available, and that was only in an incomplete Latin translation (though even if Plato's books had survived in the West very few people knew enough ancient Greek to be able to read them). Instead of Plato, the Middle Ages had looked up to his pupil Aristotle (most of whose books had survived), and who had been a more practical, less mystical thinker than his teacher. (Aristotle had refuted Plato's central belief, the theory of the Forms.) It's not that Plato had been entirely forgotten in the West – it is very hard to lock an idea away entirely; some part of it will always get out – but Plato had mostly been known second-hand, through what other people said about him.

In the early fifteenth century, copies of Plato's works started to slip out of the Byzantine Empire, first in a trickle and then in a flood. They were believed to have been lost and yet here they were, each dialogue as fresh as paint, still in the original Greek and introducing ideas that were, for the West, quite amazing.

•

Plato arrived into a world that was already soaked in magic. According to the old medieval worldview, everything below the moon was liable to change, decay and corruption, whereas everything above the moon was pure and eternal, and neither came into being nor faded and died. All things in the universe had a home to which they belonged and to which they were irresistibly drawn – hence stones fell to earth. Overhead, the stars were alive and by their life force exerted power over everyone below, whilst the planets were spaced out proportionately to each other so that the distance between (for instance) Earth and Mars, or Venus and Jupiter, corresponded to the harmonious intervals of chords, which was why, as the planets rotated, they created heavenly music.

Magic – or at least astrology – was already an academic subject in the medieval universities. It was taught to would-be doctors, because there was believed to be a magical connection between the stars in the sky and the illnesses that affect parts of our bodies (for instance, the zodiac house of Leo controlled the heart and upper spine, Pisces ruled the feet and Aries ruled the head). Astrology was therefore permitted, though other forms of magic, such as ceremonial magic (the calling down of spirits), was bitterly condemned by the Church as black magic.

And then Plato arrived, and his philosophy helped to create the magi or magicians – men like John Dee – bold and ambitious enough to want to change the world. Their writings turbocharged medieval magic until the early modern world jumped and shimmered with strangeness. In the Renaissance, magic could shrink to the size of a spell on a page or a charm in a book or grow so huge it became a philosophy by which a man could live – or die.

There was something dark and heady, as well as melancholic and very alien, about Plato's beliefs. His writing is always beautiful, but his attitudes are often brutal. He believed that in the perfect city, poetry would be outlawed because it was dangerous and that men should share their wives in common and no man should know his children from any others. He said that each man had his own daimon who took care of him (we would say a guardian angel) and spoke of Socrates listening to his daimon, and the fifteenth century heard this as a 'demon' and instantly suspected black magic. Plato also believed in reincarnation and the transmigration of the soul, which the Church thought was heresy.

The closer Western scholars looked at Plato and his ideas the more uneasy they became.

In the spring of 1439 the two delegations in Florence, Greeks and Latins, had many things to discuss concerning war and survival, but they still managed to find time to argue furiously over religion and philosophy and who was better – Plato or Aristotle (with the Latins backing Aristotle and the Easterners, led by George Gemistos Plethon, backing Plato).

For this brief moment – and at a time of great danger for Europe – philosophy, it seems, was the very height of fashion. The Byzantine delegation stayed four months and argued with the Florentines every day, but no agreement could be reached on various matters of doctrine and in the end the Easterners went home and twenty-five years later – without the support of the West – Constantinople fell to the Ottoman sultan.

Yet, the Easterners had left something behind and that was a love for Plato's *Dialogues*.

CHAPTER FIVE
MARSILIO FICINO

P lato's *Dialogues* fell into the hands of a man called Marsilio Ficino, who lived in Florence in the early fifteenth century and was a protégé of Cosimo de Medici. Marsilio Ficino was a slight, lanky, curly-haired stammerer who was both gentle and charming. He believed himself to be a philosopher and a magician and that he could deliver high, learned, white magic (good magic we would call it). He also believed that melancholy people (he himself was one of them) made the best philosophers and, vice versa, that philosophy made you melancholy. And yet he couldn't stop himself. He was addicted to philosophy.

He taught the children of the rich in the villas and gardens round Florence. He was particularly entranced by the idea of Plato's Academy, the school for philosophy that Plato had created in Athens back in the fourth century BCE. For Ficino, there was nothing better than to talk philosophy with friends. It defeated all the loneliness of being alive and so he came together with the people he most loved, to discuss poetry and philosophy in an echo of the first Platonic Academy, versions of which then sprang up wherever the Renaissance spread across Europe – men and women (though more the former than the latter) coming together to talk about poetry, art, classical literature and the meaning of life with as much wit and passion as they could muster. You can picture Ficino in one of those Florentine gardens where the Academy sometimes met, where the cyprus trees and their shadows make lines both vertical and horizontal, crossing and criss-crossing each other in a chequerboard of light and shadows. And stepping across this chequerboard is Marsilio Ficino, philosophising as he goes...

Ficino's talent for reading ancient Greek was rare in those days, and so Cosimo de Medici commissioned him to translate Plato's *Dialogues* from the old Greek into Latin.

He also commissioned Ficino to translate another group of manuscripts that had recently come to light, because Plato's *Dialogues* had arrived at the same time as set of manuscripts written by a group of philosophers in Roman Egypt. These philosophers, who lived 500 years after Plato had died, were obsessed by Plato but had also been touched by the Jewish and Egyptian mysticism of ancient Alexandria and so they developed a strange and distinctive version of Platonism. They are known to us as the Neoplatonists.

They wrote in Hellenistic Greek and they heightened Plato's mysticism and emphasised what seems to us his singularities. They believed that there is a God, whom they called the One and from whose being everything that exists pours forth like the rays of the sun, never ceasing and never diminishing. We humans, like the whole of the cosmos, even the rocks and the stars, are alive because we are continually being dreamt into existence by the One. When time began, the One gave birth to the nous, which is thought or reason, and from the nous came the world soul, which breathes life into everything. Then, from the world soul came all our individual souls. The Neoplatonists also believed that there is a web of unseen divine forces and spirits that knit the universe together and that the greatest of these is love. Man is at the centre of this web of love and is also the bridge between heaven and earth.

(The idea that the world is alive goes back to Plato. 'Thus then,' he wrote, '...we must declare that this Cosmos has verily come into existence as a Living Creature endowed with soul and reason.' It is the most enticing of all the Neoplatonic beliefs.)

Plotinus, who was educated in Alexandria, was the first of the Neoplatonists. After him came his disciple Porphyry and then the philosophers Iamblichus and Proclus, both of whom embellished and extended their predecessors' ideas. And so, on and on the ideas flowed out of the Neoplatonists, in a stream that dazzles us even now.

One of the Neoplatonists' preoccupations, which seems very strange to us now, was the question of 'ensouled' statues and whether it is possible to draw life down from God into statues and whether, once 'ensouled', these statues could then communicate oracles and prophesies. Back in ancient Alexandria, Neoplatonists like Plotinus took these questions very seriously, as did Marsilio Ficino in Renaissance Florence hundreds of years later, when he wondered out loud (in Book Three of the *Three Books on Life* (1489)) whether it is possible to animate statues (for which speculation, as we'll see, he incurred the wrath of the Church). The thinking here was that 'in a universe in which every single thing was deemed to be alive' – or potentially so – 'magic was the discipline in charge of animating objects, such as moving or speaking statues'. The question of 'ensouled' statues is one of those moments when I think you have to have been born into ancient Alexandria and to have sat at the feet of the Neoplatonic philosophers to *really* understand how anyone could have produced this idea.

Marsilio Ficino, the little Florentine philosopher, took on all these ideas. For him, love was the force that knitted the universe together, keeping the planets on their courses and the stars dancing. Love made connections between all things in the universe and it was these living, sympathetic relationships that enabled magic to flow across creation. 'Why do we think of Love as a sorcerer?' wrote Ficino. 'Because in Love there is all the power of enchantment. The work of enchantment is the attraction of one thing by another because of a certain Similarity in their natures.'

Marsilio Ficino had a young, good-looking, aristocratic disciple called Pico della Mirandola, who leaps flamboyantly into this story. Pico and Ficino were very close, both men being learned and studious, but whilst Ficino was mild-mannered and charming, Pico was wild and rebellious. He came from a noble family and studied Latin in Ferrara and scholastic philosophy in Bologna. He also knew ancient Greek and Hebrew. Like Ficino, he was a Neoplatonist – he said that nothing in this world is devoid of life and that nothing in the universe dies, that all is change but never death.

He was only twenty-three when he proposed a huge public debate around 900 propositions concerning philosophy, magic and religion that he held to be true. The Pope put a stop to that discussion and the Church banned his books and had them burnt. Portraits of Pico della Mirandola have survived – there is one in the Uffizi in Florence – showing his long, brown, curly hair and his poet's cap. It takes no imagination at all to transpose him to the counterculture of the 1960s – say to the Isle of Wight festival in 1968. He ran off with the wife of a tax collector, fled to France, was arrested and brought home, and then escaped to Florence where he died at thirty-one, possibly poisoned, though he had already changed the world.

Despite the many differences between them, the Renaissance wizards all shared an obsession with the mystic side of Plato. To us, Plato's thinking is the very height of respectability – he is simply an old, white, male philosopher from thousands of years ago – and so it takes an effort of imagination to understand how dangerously subversive he seemed to some people during the Renaissance. It's a sign of Plato's counterculture status that every ambitious Renaissance wizard would have been familiar with his ideas and, in the case of John Dee, certainly had Plato's books on his shelves.

The wizards had great faith in themselves, great egos you might say. Such self-confidence, such faith in the huge, innate powers of human beings, the belief that we are not mere worms that crawl along the ground but beings who can touch the angels, these were all signs of the times. When the wizard Giordano Bruno writes boastfully (of himself, in the third person), 'Behold now standing before you the man who has pierced the sky, wended his way amongst the stars and overpassed the margins of the world, who has broken down the imaginary divisions between the spheres – the first, the eighth, the ninth, the tenth, what you will – which are described in the false mathematics of blind and popular philosophy', his words ring out like a shout across the centuries.

Chapter Six
The Corpus Hermeticum

One summer when Covid was retreating and we were just out of lockdown, I visited an old house in Amsterdam that looks out onto the quiet end of the Keizersgracht canal. In it is a library that goes by the name of the Embassy of the Free Mind and which was created by a Dutch businessman called Joost R. Ritman. Born into the Rosicrucian brotherhood, Ritman grew up to become a collector of books and art. He was particularly obsessed with Christian mysticism, Neoplatonism and other related ideas. On the shelves of the Embassy of the Free Mind is a fifteenth-century book called the *Corpus Hermeticum*, whose strange and subversive contents helped to change the course of Renaissance history.

The *Corpus* came to Florence in the fifteenth century but originated in the magical world of Hellenistic Alexandria during the second century CE, alongside Neoplatonism, with which it shares many ideas. It consisted of philosophical and religious dialogues on the nature of God, as well as alchemical and astrological thinking, and was thought to be the magical wisdom of an Egyptian, a half-man, half-god called Hermes Trismegistus.

The book begins with the words of a god called Pimander. What it describes is almost another religion – a stranger, but also a softer and more loving religion than fifteenth-century Christianity, and with a peculiar genesis myth, in which man's soul is said to have floated down from the heavens, passing the stars, who are man's brothers and sisters, until he reaches earth. Here, nature smiled with love at man's beauty and wrapped herself round him and they had sex. For the *Corpus Hermeticum*, this world is beautiful and happiness is attainable here, a concept the gloomy Christian Church did not believe. In the harsh and turbulent fifteenth century, the Church considered all this talk of love heretical. It was the kind of belief for which the Church might burn you at the stake.

The day I visit the Ritman library – a soft, damp, hazy Amsterdam day – the librarian brings me a couple of very early editions of the *Corpus*. One of them, printed in Mainz in 1503, catches my eye because of its beauty. The ink is still dark and strong on the page and the margins are generous enough for the sixteenth-century scholars to have included their notes. The 's'es are written like 'f's, the punctuation floats strangely above the lines and the first page is laid out like a triangle (because the idea that text should be laid out in rectangles had not yet become a God-given fact). The first words of the first chapter make this bold pronouncement: '*Mercurii Trismegisti, Liber de Potestate et Sapiencia dei, e Greco in Latinum traductus a Marsilio Ficino Florentino ... Pimander incipit.*' (Which is to say, 'By Hermes

Trismegistus, the Book of the Power and Wisdom of God, translated from Greek into Latin by the Florentine Marsilio Ficino ... Pimander speaks the first words.')

Pimander incipit. The Lord Pimander speaks. And so, it begins. I pick up the book and feel its weight. It is a light and slender thing – lighter than my notebook, lighter than my mobile phone and yet it helped change the course of the sixteenth century. (Sometimes, all this sparkling, magical thinking reminded me of the *Da Vinci Code.* And sure enough, I discovered later that Dan Brown often used to visit the library of the Embassy of the Free Mind.)

Where the Corpus journeyed after it left Alexandria and who brought it to Italy remains obscure. All we know is that when the world of Greek Alexandria ended it was saved and preserved within the orbit of the Byzantine Empire by Byzantine scholars (who edited it into the volume that we have today) and that when that empire fell it was saved again and brought West.

The *Corpus Hermeticum* astonished fifteenth-century Florence. It was believed that the book had been written down in the time of Moses, was the first example of Platonism and long predated Plato himself, and so it was even more important in the history of thought than Plato. Thus, it seemed that here at last was the road back to the beginning of history and to God himself. Cosimo de Medici rated the book even more highly than the works of Plato. He gave it to Marsilio Ficino to translate and Ficino was entranced.

Ficino fell utterly in love with Plato, the Neoplatonists and the beliefs in the *Corpus Hermeticum*, but other scholars at the time were doubtful about the Corpus and suspicious of Plato – they thought Plato was heretical and his ideas repellent, especially those praising gay love. Some, like the scholar George of Trebizond, thought that Plato's ideas were so repugnant that they were responsible for the fall of Greece and the decline and fall of the Roman Empire.

•

Plato's ideas also alarmed the Christian Church. By the end of the fifteenth century, a populist preacher called Girolamo Savonarola had appeared in Florence. He was an ascetic Dominican friar with a gaunt, bony, big-nosed face that looked out on the world from under a preacher's black hood. Savonarola preached what he claimed was a pure form of Christianity. He encouraged the people of Florence to burn all their luxuries, including their books, and amongst the books he condemned were the *Dialogues* of Plato, about which he said in a sermon in 1498, 'It is to be wished that Plato should be Plato, Aristotle Aristotle, and not that they should be Christian ... there is as great a distance between Plato and a Christian as there is between sin and virtue.' And so, the friar had all of Ficino's translations burnt, particularly in the great bonfires which blazed in the Piazza della Signoria in Florence in February 1497. Savonarola was adept at sowing discord between friends. He persuaded Pico della Mirandola, Ficino's young, wild disciple, to come over to his side, much to the grief of Ficino, who loved Pico like a son.

Yet it was too late to stop Plato's ideas spreading. Neoplatonism was never an organised religion but more like a set of beliefs, about which there was something revolutionary and disquieting, as well as beautiful, melancholic and playful. These ideas spread like a scent through the universities and royal courts of Europe, turbocharged by the new art of printing.

These were elite ideas – debated by philosophers and kings and captured in books – but they were no less seductive and powerful because of it.

They reached the court of the gloomy, mystical Holy Roman Emperor Rudolf II in Prague, who was gathering up alchemists, artists, poets, astrologers and astronomers to aid his search for the world beyond our own and the road between them. They even came to the Thames and the village of Mortlake and John Dee's house with its orchards and gardens that ran down to the river, because Dee was almost certainly a Neoplatonist. His library contained a 1532 edition of Marsilio Ficino's translation of the works of Plato, probably printed in Florence and called *Omnia Divini Platonis Opera* (The Complete Works of the Divine Plato). Ben Jonson and John Milton also had copies of Ficino's translations.

Books, like ideas, are great travellers. They go everywhere.

Neoplatonism perfumed the lives of the Elizabethan literati with a woozy melancholia that contained an echo of Marsilio Ficino's grief from 100 years before.

In fact, Ficino misunderstood the *Corpus Hermeticum* and eventually – in 1614 to be exact – the French scholar Isaac Casaubon proved that the Corpus had not been written in the time of Moses, as Ficino proposed, but much later, in the first centuries CE. The truth, however, came too late. Plato, the *Corpus Hermeticum* and the Neoplatonist writings had mingled together and spread like a scent through Europe, and thus became part of Renaissance occult thinking.

According to John Mebane, during the Renaissance, 'magic became the most powerful manifestation of the growing conviction that humankind should act out its potential in the free exercise of its powers'. There have been many definitions of magic. For Malinowski, 'The purpose of magic is to ritualise human optimism.' For Chris Gosden, the essential characteristic of magic is that it gives you a feeling of kinship and participation, of connection with a universe that feels a connection back to you and so is what human beings have always yearned for. For me, in the darkness of the midwinter Covid pandemic, it was a daydream of freedom, of lightness and flying away on feathered feet from this cold earth.

STORY ONE
THE EASTERNERS

It was generally agreed in the neighbourhood that the Tortelli family had been cursed by love.

The first victim of this curse was Beatrice Tortelli and the misfortune happened during the reign of Cosimo de Medici, in the year that the Easterners came to Florence. All winter the outrunners had been arriving. They came in ones and twos and tens and twelves and thronged the streets in their beards and long robes and walked four abreast down the narrow alleyways. They turned up at parties uninvited and talked about magic and paganism and challenged the old men of Florence to games of chess (which they always won), playing them at tables on street corners under the apricot trees. All the Easterners were tall and black-bearded, and some of them had brought pet birds, and one even brought a tame cheetah. They liked to stretch their long legs out under the tables and with their good looks scatter thoughts of love in all directions.

But these were merely the forerunners. Early one summer morning, the main delegation came, the emperor and the noble families at its head and behind them a vast, slow procession moving across the fields towards the city gate and containing monks, scholars, philosophers and soldiers on horseback and on foot, as well as young men in long robes and with thick, black beards.

Two sisters stood on a rooftop and watched. They were Francesca and Beatrice, the daughters of Giuliano the bookseller, who ran the smallest shop in the street of booksellers. Beatrice was seventeen with a beautiful forehead and straight eyebrows and a pure and fierce profile, all milk and gold. No one knew whom she took after. Francesca was ten, long as a pole and with a wandering way of talking. She kept breaking off her sentences in mid-flow due to her amazement at the world. She liked to stand close to people so she could eavesdrop on what they were saying, because how else would she know what was going on?

'Who are they?' asked Francesca, pointing to the young, black-bearded men, and Beatrice said, 'Oh, those are artists and poets, those kinds of people.' Francesca was a one-woman bringer of news. 'Mama, Mama,' she would call out, 'the paper-makers are in town, the cat has caught a rat, the family on the corner have had their baby.' Now, she set off at a run, down the steps and along the alleyway to her parents' shop, to round them up and chivvy them on to the rooftop from where they could watch the procession.

There were so many Easterners in Florence that year they had to sleep wherever they could find a bed. The wealthy Easterners slept in the big palazzos but the younger ones – the poets and artists and other poor, good-looking ones – slept on the floors of private houses, or anywhere really where they could find a bed. One of them, Michael Tzimeskes, came to sleep in the back room of the bookseller's house. Francesca kept watch for him outside in the street – 'Mama, mama, he's coming,' she called and then there he was – standing in the doorway – a young man, stern and proud looking, with black, brilliant eyes on either side of a broken nose and with a scar in the dip of his throat where he claimed a Mohammedan's sword had nicked it.

Later, Katerina, the maid, reported that in his bag he had a silk jacket with a white trim, a poet's cap and a long, black scholar's coat lined with scarlet – because all the Easterners loved fashion. Also hidden in the bottom of this bag was a dog-eared, battered quire of Homer's *Iliad*, hundreds of years old, that Michael Tzimeskes had acquired in Araby from a scholarly Muslim man who had acquired it God knows where. It was said that Cosimo de Medici himself yearned for this quire. It was written in old Greek so that no one could read it, except Michael Tzimeskes.

Soon, stories about him flew around the narrow alleyways. Francesca heard them with her sharp ears and brought them home: that Michael Tzimeskes spoke five languages; that he was a book hunter by trade, commissioned by rich men to recover lost and ancient manuscripts in remote monasteries; that he had worked for the Holy Roman Emperor and had been to Edirne, the sultan's capital, and had lived in Cairo, the heart of the Mohammedan lands, and had been imprisoned in Baghdad.

You would think that they heard all this from Michael Tzemiskes's own mouth – except that he was taciturn and prone to silence around the house.

Florence was a city of magic that year. All through the late spring and early summer the locals laid on jugglers and jesters and carnivals and processions because they would not be out-magicked by the tricksy Easterners. One time, the big men of the city held a masque in the Duomo, dressed up their own children as angels and suspended them from wires so that they could float overhead, playing flutes and plucking harps. The children laughed but their mothers wept to see their children hanging so high up amongst the pillars.

Meanwhile, in the fine palazzos the delegations argued over matters of doctrine and on street corners the Easterners gave lectures to anyone who would listen; their mouths open, the ideas flowing forth like musical notes – on love, magic, philosophy, revolution and the strange man, Plato, who had contended that this world isn't real and that what we see are nothing more than shadows. That year, everyone in Florence wanted to be a philosopher, except for the old men who cried out, 'Who is this Plato?' and 'What have we done to deserve him?'

One night, Michael Tzimeskes read aloud to them from his quire of Homer's *Iliad*, running his fingers along the lines, translating fluently from the old Greek into Italian as they listened. He told them of the old man Priam, King of the Trojans, and how he had knelt before Achilles, who had murdered his son Hector, and kissed the manslaughtering hands, begging for Hector's body back until Achilles also began to weep for his own old father, Peleus, whom he would never see again. Each word fell bright and magical into Francesca's head. Even her mother stopped her sewing and sat with her needle raised, transfixed. Afterwards, they all said to each other how surprised they were that such a man as Michael Tzimeskes, so proud and taciturn, should be so moved by an old man's grief. 'Maybe he has an old-man father somewhere,' their mother said. Everyone agreed that Michael Tzimeskes was a man of stories and that if you opened up his bag too fast, the stories would fly out and you would have to throw yourself down on top of them to stop them flying away.

'I want to learn Greek,' said Beatrice to her mother. They were in the kitchen where her mother was baking bread. The oven was spewing out clouds of white flour and scarlet flames.

'Whatever for?' asked their mother, wiping her floury forehead. 'The Mocenigo girls are learning Greek.'

'They are the nobility. You are working girls. We cannot afford their airs and graces. We have the shop to run. And anyway, the Mocenigo girls are little bratty things.'

'I still want to learn it,' said Beatrice, stubbornly.

'I want to too,' said Francesca.

'What have I done to deserve this?' cried their mother, but still she gave in and Michael Tzimeskes was paid to teach them Greek. They sat in the back room that looked out onto the little courtyard whilst the canary sang in its cage and their mother sat in a corner, embroidering a tablecloth and chaperoning them.

For months now, Beatrice had been growing more beautiful so that she and Francesca could scarcely set foot outside the door without knots of men on street corners looking up and staring at her shamelessly. Francesca shrank closer to her sister's body, but Beatrice put her nose in the air and marched on regardless. Francesca knew what Beatrice was thinking. She was dreaming of her glorious future when she would be a pale, beautiful Greek scholar, so beautiful that all the male scholars would throw themselves down on the ground in front of her.

In the big palazzos the delegations argued bitterly over the meaning of words, with each side claiming that their documents were the true ones, whilst the other side's were forgeries. And in Beatrice and Francesca's house, Francesca saw – but doesn't see – and only truly remembers fifty years later when she herself is an old woman how, during Greek lessons, Beatrice's long, straight, level stare kept collapsing – with a crash of her eyelids – into blushing embarrassment and a look of dazzled bashfulness kept settling on Michael Tzimeskes's face.

By July the talk of an alliance between the two cities had come to nothing. Neither side could agree on the meaning of the leavened bread and the Holy Ghost. The Easterners said that they would rather rely on magic and the Holy Virgin to protect their city than give way on matters of doctrine, to which the old men of Florence said, 'Mad, quite, quite mad.' And so the Easterners left, first the formal delegations and then the outrunners and hangers-on and, finally, Michael Tzimeskes, gone one morning when they woke up and with him, Beatrice.

The first Francesca knew of it was when she woke to a sudden flood of light and a scream that echoed once, twice, three times through her head. Confused, she reached out to feel Beatrice's warm body but there was nothing, just a sheet underneath her fingers and air above them. Alarmed, she opened her eyes. The bed curtains had been flung aside and there was her mother's face with her mouth open, a scream emitting forth, whilst behind her in the doorway was her father's panicked expression. She turned her eyes from right to left but there was no sign of Beatrice, though the window was wide open and outside was a May morning, the air was pouring in and it was all as salad fresh as the first morning of the world.

They had left from a wharf downstream from the city, a place of wild orchards and poor gardens run to seed. On that quiet morning, before even the fishermen were awake, amidst a lattice-work of birdsong, they had boarded a boat downriver to Livorno. From there no one knew where they had gone. The boats from that city fan out across the world, from Cadiz in the West to Antioch in the East. They could be anywhere in this huge world.

The main delegation left behind a set of books for Cosimo de Medici. These books contained all of Plato's *Dialogues*. What

Michael Tzimeskes and Beatrice left behind were empty rooms, as huge as the world, through which Francesca kept wandering, looking for her sister.

•

All families have their stories. Fifty years later, Isotta remembered the story of how the Easterners had come to Florence in the time of Cosimo de Medici and how her great-aunt Beatrice, her grandma's sister, had fallen in love. Now it was the time of Cosimo's grandson, Lorenzo de Medici, and the day before Lent in the season of the book burning and all afternoon the people of Florence had been building up the pyre. Isotta and her family heard shouts of excitement as the book-burners went from door to door demanding all the things the people loved – their mirrors and books and playing cards and slippers and musical instruments. When they knocked on the Tortellis' door Isotta should have been afraid but instead she was excited. She opened it a crack. 'Give us Marsilio Ficino's books,' they demanded. Her grandfather came up behind her. 'Give it to them, Isotta,' he said grimly, so she gave them his copy of *De Amore*. 'What? Only one?' they clamoured. Her grandfather was old, but his voice was strong. 'Only one, you bastards,' he shouted and he slammed the door in their faces.

After that they watched through a slit in the shutters as the pyre grew taller and taller. Soon, it wasn't so much a pyre as a mountain. Small children scrambled up its sides, carrying the city's valuables to the top. It grew so fast it was as if the objects were flying there of their own accord. When night came the shouts turned to screams and there was a bang. Trumpets rang out and the bells tolled and the people in the square started up a hymn whilst a red glow appeared on the sides of the Palazzo Vecchio, and that is how they knew that Savonarola had started burning books.

Isotta's grandparents, who were very old, sat huddled round the stove and, because it was clear that this was no longer their world, they began to trace the steps in their downfall. Isotta's grandmother said that if there was one thing the book-burners couldn't stand it was kindness and love, but really she had to allow them this, that there had been too much love in Florence these last fifty years, ever since the Easterners had come to Florence when she was little.

Isotta's grandfather kept getting up to stand anxiously by the window. He was a publisher and a bookseller and it hurt his heart to know that books were being burnt. When he heard Isotta's grandmother say this he turned on her angrily and said that she was an old woman and should stop talking nonsense. Still, he said after a pause, he did agree that the children of Florence had stopped obeying their parents and that many sorrows had flowed from this, but for his money the cause of it lay far closer to home. It was, in fact, the fault of the Medicis, both Cosimo and Lorenzo ('God help us, even though they were good friends to us') but especially Cosimo, who had had all the books in old Greek translated into Latin so that every well-born child in Florence could read them. (And at this Grandma nodded along and said, 'It's true, in those days we were all besotted with books.')

Her grandparents looked very small the night of the book burning, as they huddled round the stove, but Isotta and Elizabetta ran round the house, checking the shutters and the bolts on the doors and bringing pans of water from out of the kitchen in case there was a fire. Elizabetta was Isotta's little sister; she could scarcely reach up to the bolts, but she never wavered for one moment. Isotta shouted up the stairs: 'Grandpa, we must bring the paper in from the outhouse. It will only take a torch tossed over the wall and it will all go up in flames.'

They lived in a tall, narrow house on the corner of the Via dei Librai. Their grandfather talked about books and their grandmother ran the business. All kinds of people came into the shop – book lovers of course, but also scribes, poets, artists, illustrators, type-face makers, bookbinders, manuscript hunters, sellers of paint and gold leaf and makers of parchment and paper. Out the back in the workshop it was all 'We need another quire of paper' and 'Where's the ultramarine?' but outside in the street, at the front where the book lovers gathered, it was always 'Our divine Homer' and 'What manuscripts have they found now?' Sometimes, when their grandfather shouted in the workshop, the gold-leaf artists shook their heads in mute panic that the gold leaf would float away.

When Isotta was nine, she began to look clear-eyed at her grandparents and to see them for what they were; that her grandfather was volatile and quick-tempered and that her grandmother didn't think long enough and so did everything too fast. Isotta's parents had vanished, and her grandfather never stopped grieving for the son and heir he never had. Sometimes he looked at Isotta and Elizabetta through narrowed eyes as if he was thinking, 'They are girls. What am I to do? How can they work in the business?' But other times he forgot and took them to work anyway.

Their grandmother was in and out of the publishing house all day, handing out the orders, but their grandfather loved nothing better than talking about books and so he often left work in the afternoon to play chess with his scholar friends and talk about politics and publishing. And chief amongst his friends was

Marsilio Ficino. In the winter they liked to talk in Grandpa's study – and then Marsilio brought his slippers and his latest manuscript, and the maid lit the brazier and the cat crept in and Isotta and Elizabetta brought them glasses of wine and plates of cakes, which they put down on the desk amongst the scholar's muddle of maps and globes and manuscripts.

Uncle Marsilio was a great talker. He often arrived talking before the maid had even opened the door and he loved to be loved, even by small girls, so he always enquired how they were. 'Show me your book.' (Isotta always had a book in one hand.) 'Ah yes, a Latin grammar, and can you read Latin yet?' 'Not yet but soon...'

One thing he loved to talk about was Plato, whose writings were saturated with talk of love. 'Love is a wondrous thing,' said Marsilio to Isotta one day (though she was only nine), 'and to be human is glorious. For through love we humans can apprehend God. It is our love that lifts us up to God and it is not only God we love, it is also our love for each other that makes us divine.'

All this talk of love made the atmosphere in their grandfather's study feel like a church, very dark and airy and prickly and holy.

When their grandmother got to hear of it, she first challenged their grandfather. 'You don't understand,' he said, 'Marsilio is a very loving man. He believes in a good love.' Next, she challenged Marsilio over supper. 'No, no,' said Marsilio, smiling his sweet smile at her, 'Plato's love is not the love of the body, it is love of the mind and the soul. Plato tells us to leave bodily love behind.'

'Perhaps,' said their grandmother, 'but I am sure he talks a great deal about bodily love in order to get there' (with a look on her face as if to say, What does this old man know about love anyway?).

And then their grandfather shouted, 'Can we stop talking about love in front of our granddaughters,' at which their grandmother looked at him in surprise because she didn't know if he was criticising Marsilio or herself. Their grandfather often switched sides in an argument and always with great vehemence. You never knew which side he would come down on.

On the night of the book burning Isotta and Elizabetta came back to the dining room to find their grandparents in a state of silence that meant they had only just stopped bickering. Grandma said, 'Shush,' but Grandpa roared, 'Don't tell me what to do, woman, the children know we love them, but their mother should never have done it. I will say it plainly, love led her astray.'

'What, so you would rather your daughter was unhappy?' asked Grandma, who could change sides as rapidly as Grandpa.

Their mother was the story they were told when they were little – or rather the story Grandma told – Grandpa only made grim allusions to it, but Grandma told it often and in many different ways. She would sit sewing by the fire in the evenings and, thus occupied, she would say: 'In those days when this house was new and business was good and the poets tell us that angels were commonplace and could be seen on every street corner (not that I ever saw one) – well, we lived quite a life did your grandfather and I. We had new marble flooring in the dining room – pink and white marble squares, they were the very height of fashion, and embroidered pillow slips and putti over the mantelpiece. And we had one child – that was your mother – and she was so pretty, everyone said so. She had beautiful golden hair and when we crimped it' – here she made a squiggle with her fingers – 'it zigzagged like gold wire. She was a little thing. It was George who had the height' – (George was their father) – 'but people could never stop gazing at her. Your grandfather thought we could marry her into the nobility because she was so pretty, although I always had my doubts because, despite her looks, she had a headful of poetry and art and books and what man – even in Florence – wants a wife who cannot cook but spends her days reading Plato?'

Grandpa nodded grimly.

'She was beautiful,' said Grandma. 'Everyone said so.'

'The boy had no money,' said Grandpa – he meant their father – 'and he didn't even know it. Thought the world owed him a living.'

'He had charm,' said Grandma.

'Charm. What's that worth?' cried Grandpa.

'He came from a good family.'

'He was the youngest son,' said Grandpa. 'They are always penniless.'

Grandma said (as if they hadn't heard it all before), 'He came from an old Constantinople family – they'd been in exile since the day their city fell. Your father was born in Mystras in the Morea and lived all his childhood in big houses on the charity of the other old families, all of them exiles. When Mystras fell, his family came even further west, first to Corfu and then to Florence. There were many Byzantines here in those days – all of them book lovers so they were excellent for business. And he had charm, whatever your grandpa says, and he always beat him at chess' – 'No, he didn't,' said Grandpa sulkily – 'and he could speak many languages, although he was terribly disputatious. Of course I chaperoned them, but to me they always seemed to be quarrelling. They could quarrel over anything. God help me, I even told her to stop contradicting him. I should have known from the way they were always talking. It's always a sign,' she added sadly.

This was the story that their grandma told, though sometimes she dwelt longer on her memories of their mother as a little girl (her dresses, how quick and sharp and bright she was) and sometimes on their mother when she was older (how beautifully she spoke Latin) and then, when she was feeling very bitter, on how they ran away – slipping unnoticed one afternoon from a picnic outside the city walls.

'You were too soft on them,' said Grandpa. 'You should have watched them better.'

Grandma's voice wavered but still she went on, 'They went to Ravenna and then to Venice' – 'Always an excellent place for two lovers to get lost in,' said Grandpa sardonically – 'but she never wrote to us. I would have forgiven her, but I had no address to send a letter. We knew they were in Venice, we heard that from people who saw them, and so we sent servants to find them, but Venice is a city that likes to keep its secrets, and all Venetians are liars and so each time the servants came back knowing even less than when they left.'

'It was always going to end badly,' said Grandpa. 'They had no money, what could they have lived on?'

'It might not have done,' said Grandma stubbornly.

Isotta knew how it ended, that she was born in Bologna ('Always a godless place,' said Grandma) and Elizabetta was born two years later in Padua and then, when Isotta was five and Elizabetta was three, their mother died of the plague. 'Did she think of us when she was dying?' asked Grandma tearfully – 'Woman,' shouted Grandpa – but somehow Grandpa found out where they were and came to take his granddaughters home.

No one ever told Isotta and Elizabetta what happened to their father. Sometimes when Isotta imagined him, she saw the little boy he had been back in the Morea, a beautiful, precocious, self-assured little boy coming down to breakfast by himself in a stranger's house and much fussed over by the older women because, surely, he had learnt his charm early in life? Other times, she would picture him the year he came to Florence, always smiling, always talking, always listening – to Grandma talking about cooking and to Grandpa talking about books, always disputing with their mother.

The night of the book burning, Grandma and Grandpa talked about love and Isotta could see that Grandma wanted to talk more about their mother, telling and retelling their mother's story, as she always had done and always would do until the day she died, but Grandpa didn't want to and so they sat in silence.

'Granddaughters,' said Grandma after a while, 'there is always sewing that needs to be done', and so they took out their embroidery and bent their heads over the stitches. Isotta thought of her great-aunt Beatrice, who had run off with a Greek when the Easterners first came to Florence, and she thought of her own mother, who had done the same, and she thought, 'Grandma likes to keep us busy in case we are struck by the curse of the runaway daughter. But I tell you, it's too late and all the God-fearing, righteous families in this city who would never let their sons marry Elizabetta or me for fear that the Tortellis' wildness runs in our blood – well, I tell you' – and here she burned with silent satisfaction – 'all those same sons can look at us as longingly as they like, but they cannot have us because we are shamed.' But sometimes she says to Elizabetta, as fiercely as she can, 'Take no notice. That shame we are meant to feel – I promise you, it weighs no more heavily on me than a dried-out old leaf.'

•

That night, Grandma lay in bed in the dark with the old man in his nightcap propped up on pillows beside her. First, she saw her own lost self, the young Francesca, skinny as a pole, bright as a painting, but very, very small in the darkness of the past. And then she saw Florence in its youth, before they paved the roads and built the dome on top of the Duomo. 'Those were better times,' she thought, 'before we all got rich.' Then, the memories came back in a torrent and she remembered Beatrice buying fish in the market – stretching out one white hand – and how all the men stared and how she, Francesca, crept up close against Beatrice's body. And she remembered how Beatrice blushed when Michael Tzimeskes looked at her and the day they ran away on a morning so fresh there were swans out on the Arno.

'Whatever happened to my sister,' she thought, 'with her beautiful, straight eyebrows? Where is she now? If she's still alive she'll be an old woman like me.' Then she thought of the book-burners and how much they hated love. And she pictured the business ledgers and those two debts that she cannot get back. And she thought of her two granddaughters, Isotta and Elizabetta, and how pretty they were but who would marry them because they are cursed by love and the blood of the unknown Easterners that flows through their veins? And she thinks of the old man breathing heavily beside her and what he was wearing the day they were married (did ever a man have such fine legs as his?) and what will she do when he dies? And she thinks, 'It was brave of him to marry me – he must have feared the family curse – and as it happens, he would have been right to, although it was not his wife who ran off but our daughter.' And that makes her think of her dead, runaway daughter, a weight she has to carry and a pain so sharp it stops her heart. 'It will kill me,' she thinks.

'Love,' she thinks, and she thinks of how, that very night, when the book-burners had gone to work outside, they had sat indoors in silence and the girls had sewn, and everything had gone quiet and they had even heard an owl shriek, until suddenly she herself had cried out – in a voice as strong as an ox – 'Stupid man, that book burner. What does he call himself? Savonarola? He thinks he can put an end to all our books but I tell you, the books have already left this city, they have travelled over the mountains, they are already in Paris and Berlin and Frankfurt, they have even travelled over the sea to London, they are breeding like rabbits' – 'Woman,' shouted Grandpa, 'don't talk like that' – 'and love,' said Grandma, 'has gone with them and once you let it out, it will never go back.'

CHAPTER SEVEN
JOHN DEE'S LIBRARY

John Dee, the English wizard who lived beside the Thames in Mortlake, loved his books so much that he sometimes dreamt about them. On 6 August 1597 he noted in his diary, 'This night I had the vision and shew of many bokes in my dreams, and amongst the rest was one great volume, thik, in large quarto, new printed ... And many other bokes methowght I saw new printed...' And on 24 November 1582, he noted that 'I dreamed that I was deade and after my bowels were taken out I walked and talked with ... among others ... Lord Thresorer who was com to my howse to burn my bokes when I was deade...' And another time (7 July 1600) he notes that – like all writers since the world began – 'this morning as I lay in my bed it cam into my fantasy to write a boke...'

In the late 1540s and early 1550s, when he was in his early twenties, Dee studied at the university of Louvain and then lectured on Euclid in Paris. He also studied under the instrument-maker Gemma Frisius and became friends with the cartographers Gerardus Mercator and Abraham Ortelius, both of them Lowlanders. Back in London, he met the mathematician Girolamo Cardano on a winter's day in Southwark and they talked about how to create that most mysterious of things, a perpetual motion machine. This was a machine that could work indefinitely without any source of energy. It is – as far as science can establish – an impossible dream, though that has not stopped men trying to achieve it.

In the early 1560s Dee went abroad again to Louvain, Zurich and Antwerp. All the time he was buying books. When he moved into Mortlake he immediately began to create his library. We are not talking here about an extravagant baroque library with a high painted ceiling showing clouds and angels and putti. Nor are we talking about a stately early Renaissance library such as in the abbey of San Marco in Florence, with its tall stone arches and pillars. Instead, you should picture a series of rooms with low ceilings built of timber and plaster, with fireplaces, mantelpieces and candlesticks (though probably unlit for fear of what fire could do to his books), and with brown wooden floorboards underfoot and book shelves and book cupboards, the latter covered by painted cupboard fronts, which were in fashion at the time. (For hundreds of years, books had been kept in trunks and cupboards; shelves were a relatively new invention that were just becoming fashionable.) The windows would have had small windowpanes and looked out onto the green Mortlake garden.

At any rate, this is what an outsider would have seen. What John Dee would have seen was a magical structure containing within it the entire history of the world, its meanings and God's intentions from the beginning of time. Dee's library was the largest private library in England, bigger even than the libraries of the Oxford and Cambridge colleges, and its size must have been because John Dee realised that whilst a man cannot grasp the enormity of God's creation by his own brain alone, maybe – just maybe – with the help of a library and the work of all those other brains, he might. A library as big as the world might give a man a ladder to reach up to the mind of God. According to Frances Yates, the twentieth-century Renaissance scholar who did so much to revive the reputation of John Dee and the other wizards, there was contained within Dee's library the entire Renaissance.

John Dee lived only a hundred years or so after the invention of printing and the wonders it brought were still fresh and astonishing. At that time, the world was huge and very hard to traverse and yet books, packed into the holds of ships or on the backs of mules, could travel far more easily than humans. Whereas before there might have been only half a dozen manuscript copies of a book, now there might be hundreds, even thousands, of printed copies. Books were messages in bottles from other worlds – worlds that would have felt as far removed from Mortlake as the moon feels from us – and yet, books could connect these worlds, spreading ideas further and faster than ever before. Books could jump through time, carrying ideas from the deep past. When you opened a book, an entire world would spring into being, with ideas that felt like they had been formulated just for you, as if the author was your dearest friend even though he lived a thousand miles away or had lived hundreds of years before. Books responded to a hunger for reading, for imagination, for ideas, for companionship, for the friendship of people far away. They could also carry subversive ideas; they made revolutionary movements possible and had the power to change the world. When Caliban, the servant of the bookish magician Prospero in Shakespeare's *The Tempest*, is working up a revolution against his master, he shouts: 'Remember first to possess his books, for without them he's but a sot as I am, nor hath not one spirit to command, they all do hate him as rootedly as I. Burn but his books.'

We know that John Dee liberally annotated his books (and his notes are proof that he not only owned books but read them as well, unlike some book lovers). In those days, books were printed with wide margins so that scholars like Dee could use them for notes. When the books moved on to new owners, so too did the ideas in the margins, which was another kind of magic.

Dee owned between three and four thousand manuscripts and printed books, a vast number for the early modern period. They were written in many languages – including French, Italian, Arabic, Latin, Greek and Hebrew – and on subjects such as astronomy, astrology, angel magic, optics, geography, mathematics, horology, perspective, alchemy and Neoplatonic philosophy. He owned books by Plutarch, Pliny, Cicero, Plato and Aristotle. He had a complete set of the works of Marsilio Ficino, including his translations of Plato and Plotinus. Amongst his many books on magic were the works of the Spanish mystic Ramon Llull, Johannes de Burgo's *Treatise on Magic*, all the books by the Swiss alchemist Paracelsus, the Jewish Kabbalah and *The Book of Soyga*, a book of spells and incantations (which has recently been rediscovered in the British Library).

To accommodate all these books, Dee first built an outer room where the majority of his books and his scientific equipment resided; then he built several more rooms to house his official papers, his alchemical stills and the marvels and rarities that he had collected on his travels (in other words, a kind of museum); and finally, an inner, very private room containing his magical equipment, his confidential writings and his most secret books. He may have also had a scholar's desk – with its top set at a pitch so that it was like the roof of a house. That way he could write standing up with his books stored within easy reach on shelves by his knees.

We don't know exactly how John Dee grouped his books within each room, only that he must have had some kind of organisational principle inside his head – because otherwise he would never have been able to lay his hands on the book he wanted. He was a librarian to his fingertips and the impulse towards order was fundamental. He was also an Elizabethan and so would have believed in the power of microcosms, particularly when it was an accurate reflection of the macrocosm – 'As above, so below', as the alchemists used to say. Part of the magical power of a library was that it was a microcosm of the entire universe.

John Dee may have divided his books into bound and unbound, then laid them on their side and perhaps with their spines against the walls. It was not until the sixteenth century that books began to be printed with titles on their spines. Before that, their titles were often painted on the edge of the pages facing outwards.

In effect, John Dee also had a museum. This would have contained his scientific instruments, probably including a magnet (considered very magical in those days), a five-foot quadrant, a ten-foot cross staff (for measuring the location of the stars), a sea compass, a watch clock and a terrestrial and a celestial globe given to him by the map- and globe-maker Gerardus Mercator. Celestial globes had a double orb, the inner orb being the earth itself, and the outer, transparent orb being painted with the constellations.

The outer orb was movable. You, the watcher, looked down on the earth as if you were God, moving the outer orb and seeing how the constellations passed across the earth's surface.

He also owned several astrolabes, one made by the instrument-maker William Boroughs, and all of which would have been exquisitely constructed from the finest metals so that they glittered beautifully in the candlelight.

Dee was a man of his time and liked to think in two ways: with his hands, through the objects he explored, and with his head, through the words on a page. There is a very old association between museums and libraries; they were different but had complementary ways of thinking about the world. (The British Museum and the British Library, for instance, were only finally separated in the 1970s.)

Yet, possessing books was also dangerous. They could carry subversive ideas and so were always censored by the government and the Church. Henry VIII publicly burnt Martin Luther's books in May 1521 and issued a list of banned books in 1526. Likewise, magic was illegal – in 1542 Henry VIII made it a capital offence – although in practice there was some leeway. Much depended on who you knew, and John Dee knew many powerful people who could protect him. Even so, there would have been many books on John Dee's shelves which hovered on the fringes of legality and so he would have had to be very careful who he allowed into his library. Its outer rooms would have been open to readers (so long as he approved of them) but very few people would have seen the innermost rooms, which were his most secret and private of sanctums.

John Dee loved his library and always feared its loss and sometimes even dreamt about its destruction. It was because he loved his books that he frequently catalogued them. Over the course of his life he made a number of these catalogues, and one in particular on 6 September 1583 when he was about to embark on a long journey from which he might not return. That catalogue was 172 pages long and was meant to protect against – or at least provide evidence of – a potential loss of his books. As it turned out, Dee was right to be worried. During his long journey abroad, his library was destroyed.

CHAPTER EIGHT
THE BOOKS ON JOHN DEE'S SHELVES

etween 1560 and 1562 when John Dee was still a young man and before he lost his library he went abroad on a book-buying spree. Many of the books he purchased were about the Hebrew language and the Hebrew Kabbalah. The wizards believed that ancient Hebrew was the language that God, Adam and Eve, and the angels spoke in the Garden of Eden and thus that it was closer to the mind of God than all the languages that came afterwards. This explained the wizards' interest in Hebrew. If you wanted to understand the meaning of everything – and the wizards did, passionately – then Hebrew was an important part of it. On a previous trip abroad in 1550, John Dee made a point of meeting a scholar called Guillaume Postel, who was eccentric and deeply learned and had just returned from studying Semitic languages in the Near East. Postel knew Arabic, Hebrew and Syriac.

The wizards' interest in Hebrew led them to a set of ancient, mystical Jewish writings called the Kabbalah. Like Neoplatonism, the Kabbalah tried to explain the creation of the material world from the divine mind. The Kabbalists called the divine mind the Ein Sof and they thought of it as neither male nor female, but infinite and eternal. The conundrum for them was, how could something eternal and everlasting create something finite and temporal like our world?

The Kabbalists believed that Hebrew was a divine language spoken by God, which meant that Hebraic words were not arbitrary, random sounds but were uniquely meaningful and thus able to reveal the essential truth of the things they signified. Being a divine language, Hebrew was also a magical language and so it was believed that the Ein Sof (i.e. God) had spoken the universe into existence at the beginning of time simply by uttering words in Hebrew. Even seeing Hebrew characters written on the page could create magic.

These ideas felt plausible because they echoed the idea, widespread at the time, that there are some words just by the speaking of which we can cause magic to happen. This was a power that everyone believed in – rich and poor, men and women – the power of the spoken word to change the world, whether that was through the prayers the priest spoke in church on Sundays, the prayer that John Dee uttered at the beginning of his scrying sessions, or the spells to bring good luck that the magicians to the poor (of which more later) sold to their clients, or even the magical word 'Abracadabra', which was known at this time and which some scholars believe derives from the ancient Aramaic phrase meaning 'I create as I speak.' We see the power of language at the beginning of Genesis – 'In the beginning was the Word' – and in fairy stories like *Tom Tit Tot*, the Elizabethan equivalent of *Rumpelstiltskin*, where the girl has to say the fairy's true name out loud to save her life.

The Kabbalists also believed that every Hebrew letter had a number and that if you knew which number attached to which letter you could take words from the Bible and by adding up the numbers buried inside them discover secret codes and messages.

One of the many wizards who were obsessed with the Kabbalah was Pico della Mirandola, Marsilio Ficino's young, wild, aristocratic disciple, who had incurred the wrath of the Church by challenging it to a debate about religion and magic. Pico believed that the Kabbalah was evidence of an early religion, the '*prisca theologia*', which he believed was purer and truer than any of the religions that came afterwards. All the wizards wanted to discover the '*prisca theologia*'. Pico learnt Hebrew from a converted Sicilian Jew called Samuel ben Nissim Abulfaraj so that he could read the Kabbalah and many others acquired some Hebrew one way or another, whether at university (Hebrew was taught at both Oxford and Cambridge in the sixteenth century), through a private tutor (perhaps a converted Jew) or through Hebrew grammars and dictionaries, of which there were plenty in Europe at this time.

●

There was another book that was deeply important to John Dee and that he kept in his inner library, his most secret place where he attempted to summon the angels. This was a book in three volumes called *De Occulta Philosophia*, written by a German magician called Heinrich Cornelius Agrippa and published forty years earlier. In its time, *De Occulta* was one of the most famous books on magic ever written.

Agrippa was born near Cologne, went to university in Cologne and Paris, left to become a mercenary soldier and then, in 1509, began to lecture on magic at a university in Paris. From then on, he led the magician's usual wandering, rebellious, provocative and dangerous life. His book, *De Occulta Philosophia*, divided the vast and sprawling subject of magic into three parts: physical magic that took place on the earth and under the moon; celestial and mathematical magic that took place above the moon but under the stars (this included astrology); and religious and ceremonial magic concerning angels and demons that sought to draw down energy from God. *De Occulta* was full of ideas from Neoplatonism, the *Corpus Hermeticum* and the Jewish Kabbalah. Agrippa was also familiar with the ideas of Marsilio Ficino, and believed that man was God-like before the Fall and that they must strive to return to that state.

In 1510 Agrippa came to England at the invitation of John Colet, the humanist dean of St Paul's. Agrippa was only twenty-four, but he already had the dubious but compelling reputation shared by all the wizards. A manuscript copy of *De Occulta Philosophia* was in circulation. Agrippa had written the book in 1507 when he was twenty-one (although it wasn't printed until nearly twenty-five years later). Even whilst he was in London, Agrippa was in the throes of a controversy, issuing tracts to defend himself against his enemies who had accused him of being a 'judaising heretic who introduced into Christian schools the criminal, condemned and prohibited art of Kabala'. To this, Agrippa answered smartly, 'In your ignorance even of the very name of the Cabala and lack of knowledge of the Hebrew teachings you have called me a heretic...' John Colet was curious to meet this young man who claimed to be a magician and who had found a way to use his mind to travel back in time. He was also intrigued by Neoplatonism and owned a copy of Marsilio Ficino's letters, called *The Epistolae*, which had been published in Venice in 1475.

After his trip to London, Agrippa spent seven years in Italy, writing and lecturing on Plato's *Symposium*, and then spent time in Cologne and Geneva, and after that in Lyon and Antwerp. He married and had six children, but his wife died of the plague. Like many of the wizards he did not age well. The 'counterculture' rebelliousness of the wizards' twenties easily turned to a weary, cynical, chippy anger in their forties. Dark rumours gathered round Agrippa's name. It was said that his black dog, Monsieur, was a demon in disguise and the Dutch Jesuit demon hunter Martin Del Rio told the following spooky story about him. He said that once when Agrippa was away, a young man smuggled himself into Agrippa's museum, opened *The Book of Spells* and began to read it. Suddenly, there was a knock at the door and a demon came in, asking 'Why did you call me? What is your command,' and when the young man couldn't answer, the demon ate him. When Agrippa came home and saw the demons dancing and rejoicing over his house, he knew what they had done and summoned them with his usual powers, telling them to enter the body of the victim and thus to 'walk' it away from his house. It was also said that Agrippa paid his tavern bills with coins that, though they appeared to be made of gold, turned into horn afterwards.

The Inquisition tried to stop *De Occulta Philosophia* being published on at least one occasion; another time, Agrippa had to leave town because he defended a woman accused of witchcraft. For Agrippa, 'man's transgression was the sexual act ...

offended by this carnal behaviour the divine light withdrew'. For Tommaso Campanella, who was another wizard – we'll come to him in a moment – the opposite was true: the sexual act, according to Campanella, was not a sin, quite the contrary. As with all countercultures it was either all sex or no sex, and nothing in between.

John Dee never met Heinrich Cornelius Agrippa, who died when Dee was eight, but even so, for John Dee, Agrippa's book would have been an example of book magic, the way a book and therefore the person who wrote it could become your dearest friend, even though they had lived in another country and had died before you were born.

De Occulta Philosophia was a seminal work that no magician would have been without, but it was also the kind of book that you would keep in a private place. In Catholic countries it was always on the Index of Forbidden Books. Even in England, ownership of it was not something that you would want to advertise.

Chapter Nine

John Dee and the Women

S ome time in 1578, John Dee married and brought home to Mortlake his third and final wife, Jane Fromond. It is easy to view the story of wizards as being entirely male. Most, though not all, of the wizards we will meet – John Dee, Giordano Bruno, Henry Agrippa, Paracelsus, Tommaso Campanella – were men; and yet look again and you can see that John Dee's life was also full of women – clever, difficult, demanding women who stand around him like chess pieces, both enhancing and blocking his magician moves.

There were the spirits that Edward Kelley summoned up, many of whom were women. There were his rich female patrons, like Lady Sidney, like the queen herself, each one of whom he no doubt had to tiptoe around. There was his youngest daughter, Katherine, who looked after him in his old age, and there was Edward Kelley's wife Joanna, because wherever Dee went, so too did the Kelleys.

Joanna Kelley is a puzzle. We know very little about her other than that she was born in Chipping Norton in 1563, that she had no wealth nor family status, and that she already had two children, a boy and a girl, by another man when Kelley married her. The evidence from Dee's diaries suggests a troubled relationship; Kelley is often overheard shouting that he hates her. Yet, many scholars now believe that Joanna Kelley's daughter grew up to become the English-Czech poet Elizabeth Jane Weston, who wrote in Latin. Weston, who could speak Czech, English, German, Italian and Latin, wrote poems, odes, epitaphs, fables and reveries, all in a version of Latin favoured by Renaissance humanists. To write at length and so beautifully in Latin and then – as a young woman – to be published was highly unusual and would have required, at the very least, an expensive education. This introduces another puzzle, because that education could only have been provided by her stepfather – whom she speaks of lovingly – and who must have been Edward Kelley. Once we know this, it is tempting – though evidence is sparse – to read back from Elizabeth into her mother Joanna a bohemian intellectualism, evidence of a clever, talented woman living outside the strict social hierarchy of the Elizabethan world, all of which casts a different, much kinder light on Edward Kelley's nature.

But central to Dee's life was his wife Jane.

A married woman in Tudor times was never simply a housewife in our sense of the word. Although her sphere was confined to the house and garden, in practice, this was a very large space indeed. She was in charge of the household and so would have had to cook, clean, bring up the children and manage the servants. In addition, because this was a world in which you had to make what you couldn't buy – and that was almost everything – she would also have made cheese, butter and other agricultural produce (grown in the garden), as well as spun, woven and sewn clothes for herself and her family, and even made shoes, soaps and herbal medicines (since most people had no access to doctors). On top of all this, the home was often a business as well and so she would have had to sell these things too. Tudor women had to be resourceful and very, very hard-working. As Jane Dee's workplace was the home, she would also have helped John Dee with his experiments, managing his apprentices and his alchemical stills.

We know Jane Dee from her husband's diaries and we can see that she was clever, impatient, practical and quick-tempered. She was loyal but often angry with him too – but then who wouldn't be? She was always obliged to play second fiddle to his flamboyant, dangerous magician's lifestyle, to pick up her children and follow him halfway across a dangerous world, to endure alarming bouts of poverty, often in strange countries, when Dee would pawn her jewellery and anything else he could find. We know from his diaries that Dee was still pawning her jewellery in order to survive as late as the early 1600s.

John Dee's diaries are written in a mix of abbreviated English, transliterated Greek and colloquial Latin (Latin still being the international language of intellectuals) and feature an idiosyncratic, personal spelling. Look carefully at these diaries and you can detect the couple's quarrels, which are often about money. On 16 September 1589, for instance, Jane seems to have complained that they were short of money, because he writes in informal Latin (into which he always lapsed when he was under stress) that she was ungrateful (*'ex ingratitudine concepta ex verbis uxoris'*).

But we can also detect their love. In January 1587 when they are abroad, Dee quotes a note that Jane has sent him: 'Sweetheart,' she says, 'I commend me unto you, hoping to God that you are in good health, as I and my children with all my household am here; I praise God for it. I have none other matter to write unto you, at this time.'

It is a rare moment in the diaries when Jane leaps off the pages, unfiltered by the mind of Dee, and I pause my reading to admire how effortlessly these few sentences communicate her love for him. Dee doted on his wife and as far as we know she was, despite everything, loyal to him to the end.

CHAPTER TEN
The Good Wife Faldo's Magic

We know of one other woman in John Dee's life. More than sixty years after his death, an antiquarian called Elias Ashmole came to Mortlake in the summer of 1672. Like John Dee, he was a believer in magic; he was also the founder of the Ashmolean Museum in Oxford. He was researching a potential biography of Dee and fell into conversation with an old woman of eighty who had lived in Mortlake all her life and was known locally as the 'Good Wife Faldo'. John Dee was long since dead, the world had moved on, men now wore wigs and high-heeled shoes with buckles and the magician was just a story lost in time; but even so the old woman had never forgotten him. She had been six years old when she met him; he had invited her and her mother into his house to see how a magic lantern worked. (This fits with what we know of Dee, that he would often make a point of talking to the servants, knowing how much they saw and knew.)

Looking back, she spoke of him very warmly, saying that he had been respected and well-beloved in the neighbourhood, was a very handsome man with a long, pointed beard the colour of milk, and a great peacemaker amongst the people of Mortlake, though the children had run away from him, shouting that he was a conjurer.

We know very little about the Good Wife Faldo except that she wasn't a member of the gentry, that she had lived her entire life in the village and that although she wasn't the poorest of the poor – a vagrant – neither was she rich. She would also have been very familiar with rural magic, the magic of witches and fairies. In fact, she would have lived and breathed it. John Dee's magic was privileged, deeply bookish and philosophical, but fairy magic, which was older than Neoplatonism and the Renaissance, belonged to the oral world and all social classes. It may be that the two forms of magic met that afternoon when John Dee showed his magic lantern to the Good Wife Faldo's mother whilst the little girl looked on.

England was a land infused with rural magic. Charms and amulets could protect you and bring you luck. Poppets and dolls were ways of wreaking havoc on your enemies. Spells spoken aloud could change the course of events, and some parts of the year were particularly magical. On Midsummer's Eve the veils between the worlds grew especially thin and old men would sit outside on church porches and watch to see the ghosts of all those who would die the following year.

The country was haunted by many strange creatures – not only fairies but ghosts, angels, goblins, brownies, black spirit dogs, dragons, mermen and spirit children. There was a huge dog called Black Shuck who haunted the north Norfolk coast, especially on stormy nights. There was a merman who was caught in fishermen's nets off the coast of Orford Ness. There were the two completely green children who had turned up alone in the village of Woolpit in Suffolk in the thirteenth century, speaking some unknown language and saying (when they had finally learnt English) that they had come from a land where the sun never shone. The boy died almost immediately, but the girl lived to be an adult, although she was always forward and badly behaved. They were widely believed to have come from the land of the fairies.

Most people believed in demons. The worlds of demons and humans were thought to be interleaved, like two packs of cards shuffled together, although the demon world was invisible to all but a minority of humans. There were also angels and ghosts who gathered around humans at moments of great fear, such as at the deathbed, when the good angels tried to lead your soul up to heaven and when the ghosts and bad demons tried to lure your soul down into hell.

There was ample room for all of these spirits in sixteenth-century England because it was a land of many wildernesses. Towns and villages were small and far apart and there were forests, marshes, heathlands, fells and moorlands everywhere. The Fens had not yet been drained, roads were poorly constructed – often no more than tracks – and at night the darkness was so utterly black you might as well have been blindfolded. In Scotland, wolves still roamed. And over all this was another magical memory – not much more than a scent – of a mythical past, poignant and powerful though hard to pin down, of giants and King Lud and the knights of King Arthur. It was also a time when the aristocracy were building themselves fine country houses, some so delicately beautiful that if you had come across one of them after walking through forests and marshes you might have thought you had stepped into fairyland.

Then there were the witches. Throughout the sixteenth century and into the seventeenth, there was a rising mania for witch-hunting. In those two centuries, 73,000 men, women and children across Europe were tried for witchcraft and between 40,000 and 50,000 were executed. In 1542 Henry VIII passed a law against witchcraft and conjuring, and though it was repealed in 1547 (as being unfit for purpose) another act was introduced in 1562, the Act against Conjurations, Enchantments and Witchcraft. By 1566 a major witchcraft trial was underway in Chelmsford, Essex, where four women were accused of witch-craft. Two of the women, Agnes and Joan Waterhouse, were mother and daughter. Agnes was hung; Joan, her daughter, testi-fied against her mother and thus escaped hanging herself. News of this trial, which was an escalation in the war against witches, must have reached John Dee in Mortlake. Most of the victims of the witchcraft trials that followed for at least 100 years were herbalists and healers, the purveyors of charms and amulets to protect against ill fortune – in other words, mostly poor, elderly, probably illiterate women.

Fear of witches, and of being identified as a witch's child, must have haunted Tudor childhoods. Sometimes, children were the victims of witchcraft and it was their parents' grief at their deaths that drove the accusations of sorcery. Sometimes, the children survived and testified against the accused. Sometimes, shock-ingly, they accused their own mothers of witchcraft (as did Joan Waterhouse) and so brought about their mothers' deaths, the guilt of which must have haunted them for the rest of their lives. Sometimes they did not fight back and so, astonishingly, were lumped together with the adults and branded as witches. It was commonly believed that witches' children inherited witchcraft from their parents, so you could accuse an entire family of the practice even though the evidence pointed to only one of them. Of all the unlucky fates to befall you in the sixteenth century, one of the saddest must have been to be born a witch's child.

And yet, there may also have been something about witchcraft beliefs that was beautiful. The truth is that it is impossible to know what, if anything, those who were accused of witchcraft believed in. We know that many of the charged were simply illiterate herbalists, but it is possible that others held on to some kind of philosophy, and with that in mind scholars have identified similarities between tenets of witchcraft (in as much as we can guess at them) and those of the Neoplatonists. Behind this belief in witchcraft probably lay the assumption that the world is a living organism, full of powers and able to be manipulated, whilst the Neoplatonists also perceived the world as a living entity over which some men could exercise control by means of magic. There are clear echoes here from one to the other and, interestingly, it may not be a coincidence that the rise in witch trials coincided with an increasing intolerance (on behalf of the Church) towards Neoplatonism. There is something very appealing about the idea that witchcraft is touched, however faintly, with philosophy.

Interestingly, those accused of witchcraft often claimed in court that they had learnt the practice from the fairies, having met them on some dark night or having been seduced by a fairy lover and taken to fairyland. Witches and fairies thus went together. It is hard to know whether the accused were proud of their fairy connections or whether they were making an 'its-not-my-fault' apology or simply trying to explain what had happened.

Chapter Eleven
The Fairies

Fairies belonged to everyone, but especially the poor (as did fairy stories, which were passed down orally and were probably, at least in part, a creation of the poor). Fairies were thus at the service of everyone, including farmers, tinkers, servant girls and shepherds, many of whom claimed to have met them on a dark night. In this way, fairies possessed a democratic kind of magic. As the historian Owen Davies says, 'While learned conjurers with their grimoires commanded demons, spirits and angels to come to their aid, the humbler could instead call on the services of the fairies.' (Grimoires were books of spells. We will come to them in a moment.) Thus fairies were the magic of the poor and the book-less.

You can't just set out to find the fairies. They don't turn up like that. They are mostly too nebulous to be connected with material objects – though in the seventeenth century they were often associated with those remnants of the past, such as flint arrowheads and prehistoric ring forts, that seemed very mysterious to people then. In museums you mostly encounter them in connection with the amulets and charms that people used, either to draw the fairies closer or scare them away, though sometimes they are associated with vessels such as the cauldron in St Mary's Church in Frensham in Surrey, which is said to have once belonged to the fairies. They were sung about as ballads or told of in poems and stories that were connected to certain places, like forests, streams, springs and wells. They and their stories are as insubstantial as mist, though far more powerful. They were believed to be demons or some version of the ghosts of dead people or fallen angels or wild pagan spirits.

Renaissance poets and dramatists loved the concept of the fairies and embellished it constantly. Their inventions have survived through their work. When Shakespeare wrote *A Midsummer Night's Dream* he drew both on the remembered stories of his Warwickshire childhood, but also further developed a set of beliefs that had already been assumed and elaborated on by literate poets.

It is far harder to know how ordinary, non-literate people imagined the fairies because their views have not survived. What we can deduce is that in the Middle Ages, fairies were not elegant and diaphanous, they probably did not have wings and they were not necessarily small. They could have been male or female and the same height as humans. (Merlin's father was said to be a male fairy, good looking and of normal height.) And they were definitely not kind by nature, although occasionally they could be. They were more commonly dangerously capricious and had to be placated. In some parts of the country, such as the Scottish Highlands, they were believed to walk invisibly amongst the population, as co-walkers and doubles.

Because the fairies were so elusive, sometimes it is easier to understand them by means of the 'cunning folk'. This was the name for men and women – mostly as poor as their clients – who offered to navigate magic on their clients' behalf. The cunning folk were the poor man's answer to a magician like John Dee. They offered their clients whatever they most passionately desired – including love charms and potions; the promise of a much-wanted pregnancy; treasure-hunting skills; protection against witches and the evil eye; the chance to be unbewitched and released from a spell; and predictions for the future.

Some of the cunning folk might even own a grimoire, a book on magic that could include instructions on how to make magical objects, how to perform spells and how to summon demons. Grimoires did not contain stories; they were not full of fine passages of prose or poetry. Instead, they were magical directions to the book's owner and were accompanied by many strange (to us) symbols and incomprehensible signs. Before the invention of printing, grimoires were handwritten and sometimes mysteriously illustrated. Books were a luxury at this time and even after printing made them cheaper most of the cunning folk would have considered themselves lucky to own more than one or two of these books at most. (John Dee's personal library, on the other hand, was huge and only added to his magical aura.)

Some of the cunning folk also claimed to have met the fairies and learnt their skills from them. Others 'fessed up in courts of law. The Dorset 'Cunning Man' John Walsh claimed that he would go up into the hills to speak with the fairies, who would tell him which of his clients was bewitched. We also meet fairies in herbals, which were books of medicinal plants, including plants that could ward off fairy magic. In one such herbal, called *The Garden of Health* (1597), William Langham recommended linen soaked in bay oil as a treatment for fairy pinches.

The fairies introduce us to a world that was poor and working class and thus the exact opposite of the worlds inhabited by John Dee and Giordano Bruno. It is only when we put the learned, bookish, Neoplatonic magic of John Dee next to the magic of the fairies that we really notice the gender differences between them. Dee's magic was male and powerful and so women were (largely, though not entirely) excluded from it, due to their not being so well-educated nor owning extensive libraries and because bookish magic was believed to be so powerful that women were obviously kept away from it. Rural fairy magic was different. It existed beyond the doors of John Dee's house at Mortlake. It was the magic of woods and streams and fields, of night creatures and witches and fairies. It was the magic of the Good Wife Faldo and it was noticeably more female (especially in the case of witches) though never entirely so.

There is one fascinating moment when, in March 1582, so not long after Edward Kelley arrived in John Dee's life, he seems to have offered Dee an introduction to the fairies. In his diary, Dee says that 'this learned man after dinner promised to do what he could to further my knowledge in magic ... with fairies'. Over the top of this, Dee then writes, 'A monstrous and horrible lie', and proceeds to cross out the entire sentence. Then, over Dee's writing Kelley seems to have written, 'You that read this underwritten assure yourself that it is a shameful lie for Talbot [the name he then went by] never showed himself dishonest in anything.' And over this, Dee seems to have written, 'This is Mr Talbot ... for his own writing in my book, very unduely as he came by it.' All of which is hard to make sense of, but it seems that in the face of wild, female magic John Dee's reaction was swift and vehement and very prim. He wants nothing to do with the fairies, probably because they are pagan spirits.

There may, however, be a tradition in the history of English magic of powerful men wanting, for whatever reason, to summon beautiful, penniless young fairies. Elias Ashmole (the same seventeenth-century antiquarian who founded the Ashmolean Museum in Oxford) left behind in his papers a spell by which to catch a fairy, which is now in the Bodleian Library. It went as follows:

> First get a broad, square crystal or Venus glass, in length and breadth 5 inches, then lay that glass or crystal in the blood of a white hen, 3 Wednesdays or 3 Fridays in a row; then take it out and wash it with holy aqua and fumigate it; then take 3 hazel sticks or wands of a year's growth, pill them fair and white and make so long as you write the spirit's name, or fairy's name, which you call 8 times, on every stick being made flat one side, then bury them under some hill where you suppose fairies haunt, the Wednesday before you call her, and the Friday following take them up, and call her at 8 or 3 or 10 of the clock, which be good planet or hours for that turn; but when you call be in clean Life and turn thy face towards the East, and when you have her bind her to that stone or glass...

We can't tell from this spell whether Ashmole really believed in fairies or whether he kept it for reasons of antiquarian curiosity. Nor – if it was a question of belief – do we know why a magician would want to catch a fairy, though at first sight, it does look like a question of sexual domination (note 'when you have her bind her'). Either way, Elias Ashmole's spell is an example of the high-class magic of the wizards colliding with the lower-class rural magic of the fairies.

When I was researching this book, I used to wonder what – if they had met – the two kinds of magician – the upper-class magician and the poor, female fairy – would have said to each other.

THE LUCK

It is the night before the party, a warm, dark, furry night in the village of Nockhill Wood in the county of Buckinghamshire in the year of Our Lord 1573 and the old man is brooding in his chair. He is wearing his dressing gown and nightcap. Beside him on his desk is a glass of wine and a plate of sweet biscuits. The old man is a widower and has been so for many years. On the wall hangs a family portrait, of a mother, a father and two little girls in their best frocks, each child as stiff as a board, their ruffs up round their ears, their eyes wide open in astonishment. It was a month between the artist's sketches and the delivery of the final picture and in that month their mother had died. When the artist first unveiled the painting, the old man, who was the father in the painting, had sunk down suddenly on a chair and drawing his two young daughters to his knees had bent his head and wept for everything he had lost. That was fourteen years ago and now he cannot sleep for worrying about his children.

It is Cecily who is worrying him. It is always Cecily. He has just employed a new tutor for her and Cassie, but when he sees Cecily sitting opposite this man all he can think of is the three-year-old Cecily, running straight towards a hole that the gardener has dug in the beds and tumbling hard into it. 'But what were you thinking of?' they ask her, fishing her out, and she wails, 'I wanted to see how deep it was.' She was always like that – always curious, always laughing (except when she'd fallen into a hole a yard deep), never daunted. And now he knows what will happen, that Cecily will sit down with the tutor, who is a good-looking man – he has to admit it – but oh my God, the way he wears his breeches – and really he should have let him go – he's Italian and almost certainly a papist – but then the girls would cry – and so the Italian stays and torments the old man with the image of him sitting close to Cecily and turning the pages of a book they are sharing whilst the madness jumps between them.

He wishes his wife were here to help him, though he also blames her – of course he does – for dying and leaving him. She'd been a Londoner, very bookish, and they had loved to read together. He doesn't remember this thing called 'love'. All he can remember is that the minute he met her he grabbed hold of her tight and never let her go, and that when they were together, they were part of the beautiful, shifting patterns the universe makes as it rolls along, with everything in its allotted place. Now, he pictures her in heaven, lined up with the troops of angels, the seraphim and cherubim, a book in one hand and a holy look on her face, and he has such a yearning to reach out and touch her, he can see his fingers twitching. Without her he doesn't know where to put his worries.

Both girls take after her, always reading, always laughing. 'Oh Papa, stop worrying,' they chorus. They had been out in the garden that afternoon, the sun on their hair, picking sweet pea flowers, some joke flying between them. He had watched them from the study window, Cecily in her white dress and Cassie, the younger one (who, thank God is less impetuous), in yellow, when over the hedge they had seen the tutor coming up the lane with his friend, the wine merchant who is up from London, and both girls had run across to talk to them. The tutor sees the old man watching at the window and waves to him. The tutor is dark-bearded and wears a leather jerkin. He is affable and assured, as if somewhere – wherever he comes from – he too has an elderly, worried father. The wine merchant's name is Henry Kyd and he is tall and diffident-looking – not at all like the tutor – but he brings with him all the London gossip. You know what Londoners are like – they hear everything – and sometimes just to listen to the court gossip, who's in, who's out, after all these years, is wondrous.

It's the talk that he enjoys. He's had some very good conversations with the tutor lately – he's very what you might call 'Italian' – and it can be very hard to find anyone to talk to in these lonely parts – and so they sit up late and talk about Homer and Aeschylus and Rome and Julius Caesar. And now here's yet another yearning, to share his worries with the tutor – man to man – although this makes no sense at all, since the tutor is the cause of them.

The old man goes across to the window. He sees how the lantern by the back door is turning the warm darkness navy blue and is picking out the leaves on the cherry tree. Beyond the tree, he can just about make out the carrots and turnips in their neat rows and the peas and beans climbing up their sticks – a lovely, domesticated night garden. The garden stretches down to the common where the tall trees stand and the crows nest in winter. The old man frowns over his spectacles. He sees the moon coming up over the trees, a full moon, rising so swiftly he can almost see it move. It is silver with a strange orange sheen. The old man shivers. Beyond the patterns that men make lies the wilderness. He does not like the wilderness at all.

That same day, the day before the party, Cecily and Cassie sit back to back on the orchard grass, their skirts spread out around them, their eyes shining and their golden faces lifted up towards the sky. Overhead, the branches are already thick with young apples. Cecily is eighteen, Cassie sixteen and this is their favourite thing, laughing together about everyone and everything.

'Cook's cross with you,' says Cecily.

'What now?'

'She says you were meant to make pies with her.'

'I don't like pies.'

What Cassie loves is to fly around on her light, sixteen-year-old feet, managing the household – putting her nose into everything – 'Is it finished? Shall I help? How did you do that?' – and only about once a day colliding with the mountain that is the cook (with her giving orders to the cook and the cook giving them back) – although once every ten days or so she wakes up and thinks, I'm tired of being sixteen, and then she goes off to play dolls with the little girls who live on the far side of the common – or doesn't get up at all, even though the cook comes up the stairs to shout at her. Today has been a playing-with-dolls day – Cassie rolling around on the floor in the other house, dying of laughter – 'You're tickling me' – and the three little girls clambering all over her – 'Cassie, Cassie, we love you.'

A few weeks ago, she was coming home up the lane with the little girls rolling thick as bees around her when they bumped into the tutor's friend, the wine merchant. He was reaching across the ditch to pick an orange-yellow day lily. He is interested in botany and all the strange plants coming from the New World.

'Mr Kyd,' said Cassie kindly, 'let me do that,' and she jumped deftly across the ditch, picked the lily and jumped back again.

The children had stopped rolling on the ground and now sat up to watch them. Mr Kyd has a sweet smile and beautiful eyes the colour of black treacle. Behind him, the Evening Star was swimming in the purest blue. 'Thank you,' he said, with his air of bemusement.

The evening before the party, after the old man nodded off in his chair, his two daughters crept into his study to tidy up and dust the Turkey carpet and go into the inner bedroom to plump up his pillows and the feather mattress.

On the old man's desk sat a glass cup called 'the Luck', to which a strange story was attached. The old man had inherited it from a distant cousin who lived up north in the county of Yorkshire. When the cousin died, the Luck had been placed in a leather bag, then wrapped up in a blanket and sent on its long journey south, into the hands of the old man, who had taken the bundle into his study and unwrapped it on the desk. His daughters, who were then six and four, had put their noses over the edge of the desk to watch. The Luck trembled in the firelight. 'Be careful, Papa,' they cried. Everyone knew the story behind it, that in their grandfather's time it had belonged to the fairies, who – one riotous night – had been frightened off at dawn and, as they scattered, had left the cup behind, shrieking as they fled, 'Be careful,' because if the Luck was broken or shattered, so likewise would be their fortunes. The Luck is very pretty – its blue glass patterned with threads of glass in reds and pinks and yellows. When Cicely and Cassie went into their father's study to tidy up, they liked to touch it with their fingers to bring themselves good luck, though carefully – very carefully – in case the story was true.

All through the day of the party they get the garden ready. They do not have a banqueting house – they are not (quite) gentry

– but they lay out the tables and spread them with cloths and the old man gives orders to the gardener. He wants the musk rose tidied up, the pots reordered, the paths swept. In the kitchen, the cook and her assistant make rice puddings and snows and fools and possets and syllabubs.

The two old widows, Mrs Macaulay and Mrs Johnson, arrived first. Over the years, they had each pondered marrying the old man but had both hesitated because of his daughters. 'Well, you two will be getting married soon, I expect,' said Mrs Johnson the minute she arrived. 'Oh no,' chorused Cecily and Cassie. 'We don't want to marry. We love Papa far too much to leave him.'

Next came the neighbours with the three little girls – 'Cassie, Cassie,' they shout – and other neighbours from the other side, and after them the tutor, very broad-shouldered and long-legged, whose arrival is attended by the usual zizz of excitement, and with him, bringing up the rear, his friend Henry Kyd.

Cecily falls back, out of the throng. She goes upstairs to her bedroom to fetch a handkerchief and looks out of the window. She sees that the village has fallen into the evening shadows, but that all around it the uplands are still sunlit and that beyond them are the misty, sun-infused horizons so that the hamlet is rimmed with gold. It's as if the village is the world and all the world is encompassed in it. She is having one of those moments – she gets them sometimes – when she falls out of the present and the past and the future melt together and she sees with absolute clarity what will befall them all. She sees Cassie sitting on the bench under the musk rose with the three little girls, making them wreaths of flowers, and she sees how the youngest girl, who has always been sickly, will outlive her sisters; and how the widow, Mrs Johnson, will live another five years; and how Papa

– No, I do not want to know how long he'll live ... and how Mr Kyd can't take his eyes off Cassie and how he yearns for her. And she sees how she will never marry. I will always live with Papa and with Cassie, thinks Cecily. I will live in this house and this garden for ever.

That was the last time they saw Cassie. By next morning she had gone, without a word, leaving only a silence that went on for three months until a letter arrived.

> Dearest Father, I hope you are well and not angry with me, your loving daughter? I am with Mr Kyd in Aldgate near St Bartholomew's Church in London. We are plight-trothed and hope to marry very soon if you will give us your blessing.
>
> You have no idea how glorious is his business. The wine comes from Gascony – he has family there – and even in the court they know of it and have pronounced their approval. Mr Kyd says I can help him with his business. When I come home a married woman with Mr Kyd, we will bring you his best white.
>
> Please give my love to Cecily and say I miss her very much.
>
> Your loving daughter, Cassie.

As he sat there, winded by astonishment, the old man saw the Luck sitting on the desk beside him and somehow the idea leapt into his head that the Luck was to blame, that Cassie had touched it with her long, white sixteen-year-old fingers and the Luck had seen its chance and leapt straight out of itself and into Cassie's head, sowing all this confusion.

That evening at the end of the garden a wrackish moon rose over the trees on the common as Cecily walked to and fro, weeping for the loss of her sister. In his study the old man wept as well, for his wife, for his daughters' childhoods, for everything that would never come again.

Chapter Twelve
Bedtime Stories

I n 1579 the Dees' first child was born and was christened Arthur. Thereafter, babies came thick and fast until there were eight in all: Arthur, Michael, Rowland, Katherine, Madinia, Theodore, Frances and Margaret. The Dee children probably shared one or two beds when they were little and in summer would have gone to sleep when it was still light outside and the birds were still singing. It was probably only the promise of a story that would have got them to bed at all.

The question of the Dee children's bedtime stories brings us to the concept of the 'Ocean of Stories'. In Tudor England few people could read – literacy was low – and so the country still had almost entirely an oral culture in which – for the widespread lack of the ability to write – knowledge had to be memorised and stories passed down the generations by word of mouth. In this oral culture hundreds of stories would have been circulating. Some of these would have been religious, but many would have been myths and legends, origin stories (how England began) and also fairy stories. Some of these stories you would have known by paintings on church walls; others (if you were moderately well-off and a boy) you might have encountered in schoolbooks, but the majority of them you would have known through tellings and retellings by friends, your parents or grandparents, your teachers, servants and nannies or from talk overheard in the kitchen or the tavern. There would also have been travelling storytellers, some no doubt of great artistry, although because they too belonged to this oral culture their names and their stories were forgotten long ago.

This was the Ocean of Stories.

Looking back, we cannot know how old its stories were, nor how many stories circulated within it. What we do know is that everyone could draw upon it – rich and poor (though more the poor than the rich), nurses and nannies, grandparents telling stories to their grandchildren, wives to their husbands, small children to even smaller children and lone children telling stories to themselves with the aid of dolls, puppets and dolls' houses (if they were wealthy). Stories travelled both ways, from the literate to the oral world, but also in the other direction, from the oral world to the literate via servants and working-class nannies who would tell stories of their own childhoods to their high-born charges.

In Tudor England, even those who could read and write would still have kept one foot in this oral world. The further you went into the countryside and the further down the social scale, the more important the Ocean of Stories was in your life, but in Tudor times no one had moved so far from their origins or become so literate that they would have forgotten the Ocean entirely.

John and Jane Dee's stories would have come from many different sources. Some would have come directly from the Ocean of Stories – the myths of old London Town, just down the river, said to have been founded by the Trojan Brutus, or stories of the time before Brutus when England was ruled by giants. Others would have been family stories – John Dee's grandfather had been a Welshman from Radnorshire and so Dee must have been familiar with Welsh myths and legends. John and Jane Dee would also have known stories from the performances of poets at court – the English court had been a place for storytelling since the days of Geoffrey Chaucer – whilst others might have come from the books on John Dee's shelves.

There were no children's books on John Dee's shelves – the concept of childhood as we know it had scarcely been invented – but we do know that he had a copy of Geoffrey of Monmouth's book *The History of Kings of Britain*. Geoffrey of Monmouth was one of the great myth-makers of medieval England and was responsible for some of its greatest and most magical stories – those of Merlin and Excalibur for instance. Did John Dee tell Arthurian stories to his children? The fact that he named his first child Arthur tells us that he was interested in them.

In addition, the children would have had a nanny and perhaps she told them stories about the great River Thames that flowed at the end of their garden?

In all this storytelling, shapeshifting would have been a common theme, since shapeshifting and magic have always gone together. The history of shapeshifting goes back at least as far as Homer's *Odyssey*, in which the gods appear to mortals in many guises, including that of young men. We see shapeshifting in the *Metamorphoses*, a collection of myths originally written down by the Roman poet Ovid, a copy of which John Dee had in his library. We also see it in the Arthurian stories where Morgana le Fay has shapeshifting skills, as well as the ability to fly and to heal the sick. And we see it in fairy tales, such as in the Cornish story about the young girl who meets an old man beside the road on a dark night and he turns out to be a lord of the fairies. Sometimes in these stories the pursued turns into a hare in order to escape, whereupon the pursuer turns into a hound and when the quarry then turns into a fish the hunter turns into an otter, and so on they go, flipping from one form to the next throughout the story until either the pursued escapes or the pursuer eats them.

Writers and storytellers have always loved the concept of shapeshifting because it captures the bewildering quality of being alive and the difficulty in knowing oneself, along with the suspicion that what you see is not what you get. Shapeshifting also chimes with the truths of alchemy and Neoplatonism: that there is no death, only change and endless transformation. Due to its classical antecedents (Ovid, for instance) it belongs to high, learned magic, but also – with its appearance in fairy stories – to low, rural, working-class magic as well.

Many of the stories that the Dee children would have heard would also have been what we would call fairy stories and therefore full of magic and mystery, though the more we try to understand the history of fairy tales the harder they are to pin down.

On the one hand, fairy stories are often extraordinarily beautiful and can evoke a surprisingly consistent alternative world, characterised by the slippage of time and shapeshifting, the hardships of the journey to fairyland, the fate of the captives in fairyland and by the even greater difficulties of returning from there. They are full of dragons, witches and descriptions of fairy-land (although a surprising number of them don't even contain fairies). They are also full of grandparents and grandchildren, grandparents possessing a kind of magic and small children having the eyes to see it. Fairy stories show us where magic was believed to reside. In *Sleeping Beauty* it is in the similarities between sleep and death. In *Rumpelstiltskin* it is the power of speaking the right word out loud.

Yet, fairy stories are also elusive and ahistorical. We cannot attach an author's name to them and their beginnings are impossible to firmly date. Separating them out, one from another, is like trying to separate the trees in a vast, overgrown and tangled forest. They seem to float outside history and it is hard to trace them across time and continents with any certainty. Despite the orderliness of fairy tales, they can also make magic feel like it has no laws nor limits, that anything can happen – that a girl can turn into a swan, a grandmother into a wolf or a frog into a prince.

Fairy tales are some of the great creations of human civilisation but there is fierce debate about their origins, which is divided into two extreme positions and many in betweens. One (extreme) position is that they were entirely the creation of an oral, illiterate society – the poor and the book-less – and were passed down by word of mouth until folklorists, notably the Brothers Grimm at the beginning of the nineteenth century, saved them and wrote them down. They thus represent a way into the minds of illiterate people who otherwise would have left nothing of their ideas behind. The problem with this position, however, is that literacy has dealt a huge blow to the Ocean of Stories and we have, by definition, very little hard evidence for the exact stories inside it, at least in Europe. It is even questionable whether the Brothers Grimm were really collecting their stories from 'the common people' – as they believed.

The other (extreme) position is that many, maybe most, of the stories were the creation of literate writers, many of whose names are now lost, and that these stories passed the other way, into the oral culture and the great Ocean of Stories. Yet this position also seems dubious, because it feels driven by the assumption that there is no creativity in the world of the poor and book-less and that only clever, literate people are creative.

A more likely scenario is an intermediate position, that in the early Middle Ages, fairies (although they were called elves in Anglo-Saxon times) were probably largely the creation of an oral culture. Fairies were believed to inhabit a separate world, but with the ability to enter our world as we could enter theirs. In the fourteenth and fifteenth centuries, the fairy tradition grew more elaborate. The concept of a fairy kingdom with a fairy king and queen emerged, possibly because the tradition was being embellished by literate poets whose writings travelled into the oral culture, just as stories travelled back the other way when working-class women acted as nannies for upper-class children. In other words, the concept of the fairy realm, with all of its beauty, was the creation of both the oral and the literate world and the road between them was always a two-way affair.

Story Three
Take Me with You
When You Go

He left me by moonlight. It was an hour before I realised he was gone and then I searched the barn, the copse, the meadows by the river and the upland pastures. When I found nothing I turned back towards the house, which in my panic I had left with all the doors and windows wide open. When I saw how the night air flowed through the house from front to back as if we were a hundred years hence and the walls were nothing but ruins and rubble, a terrible fear gripped hold of me and I set off running for the village.

The men were drinking in the ale house. They turned out willingly and searched until midnight when the moon went down and then they went home, but I lay in bed and sometimes I considered very coolly how I would cope on my own – how I would manage the farm and everything without him – but at other times such grief overcame me I couldn't breathe. All night I heard whispers and conversation.

At dawn the men came back and resumed the search. They beat down the undergrowth in the copse, looking for his body ('Let him not be dead,' I prayed) and traced the tangled course of the brook for several miles in each direction. They went back up to the high pastures (nothing, just larks singing), went as far as the Standing Stones and searched both the copses again – still nothing. By evening the moon was coming up and the men were losing faith. They kept glancing at me with pity, but also in confusion – how can a man just vanish? – when there came a shout from the hill path and there he was, between two friends, limping slowly towards me.

They took him into the house and laid him out beside the fire. They were as tender as young women. Then they stepped back so that I could kneel beside him. Though they had often disliked me they felt sorry for me in my grief. 'Oh, my love,' I said, but he had closed his eyes and was as cold as ice. I tried to wrap the whole of his long body into my arms. I willed the flames to warm him. He opened his eyes and frowned. He tried to find my hand. 'I wanted to come home,' he said, 'but they wouldn't let me. I thought I might come back to find you dead or married to another.' 'You've only been gone a day and a night, my love,' I said. I was as innocent as a bird. 'I don't think so,' he said, and now his friends bent closer into the firelight in order to hear him better. 'They told me years had passed. It felt like a lifetime.'

And that's how the story started, that my husband had been taken by the fairies, bewitched by fairy time – where one night in our world equals fifty years in theirs. My family has had a long acquaintance with the fairies. Maybe this is why the villagers believed it?

My father was a clergyman and a scholar in the parish of Winterbourne Chase, not far from the Standing Stones. Ours was a little village, just a scattering of houses, very far from any town or city. On all sides of us there were uplands open to the sky, great sweeps of land that fell away at the edges, down into narrow valleys filled with small rivers and strips of meadow and woodland. On winter nights when the villagers went to bed early and only my father stayed up late to work, we were just one speck of light in the vast darkness.

My father was a fairy-scholar of some renown, although always of the Puritan persuasion. He believed that fairies were kinfolk to demons and devils and he often went out at twilight searching for them so that he could berate them. He himself had never seen a fairy, although he said his father did many times. When my grandfather was little, his sister had been stolen by the fairies and a changeling left behind to fool his family. It was a year before the real child came home.

My father wanted to know where the fairy-demons fitted in God's universe. Were they fallen angels? Did they breathe? Did they eat? What were they made of? And did they die? His passion for this subject possessed him. Sometimes, he could go for days without speaking. On a few rare days, he had a kind of contemplative melancholy that was almost sweet, but more often he was angry – and on those days I had to be careful not to step too close to him in case he cut me with his sharp words. Other scholars – mostly men of the Church and, like my father, inclined towards Puritanism – came to consult him on fairy-demon matters. Such was my father's fame that once a bishop came down by carriage all the way from London. It was the talk of the neighbourhood for years to come.

I don't remember my mother. She vanished when I was three. They say she ran off with a fairy lover to punish my father and certainly, if she ran off with any lover it must have been a fairy one because such was the remoteness of our village that there wasn't a young man to love for miles in any direction. People said that after that my father grew even more melancholy and angry.

By the time I was seventeen I was proud and nervous, baffled and burnt by everything that had befallen me – and beautiful, which I mention, not out of vanity but because it was one of the few things I possessed that was mine and so I guarded it carefully.

Once a month, my father led a service in a village five miles down the river where the church sits low down in the shelter of the valley – and it was there that I first saw Matthew. His family were yeoman farmers. Their farm straddled the lowland meadows and the empty uplands. Matthew was the oldest son. He was long and lanky, nearly two yards tall, and only twenty, like a young sapling but already as steady as a rock. I was fourteen and so shy that I couldn't look at him directly. I could only see bits of him: his hands, his white shirt (his Sunday best – I like that shirt, I thought), his throat and then – when I grew bolder – his mouth and then finally his eyes – which were winter grey. I knew at once that we were two halves of one whole.

I was seventeen when we met again – and by this time he knew we belonged together too. He took me to his farm, walked the land with me, showed me the lower meadows, the barn, the copses and the upland fields. He held out his hand to help me jump the ditches though I didn't need it. He was a farmer's boy and so he couldn't read or write, but there were many other things he could do. He had numerous friends and could play the fiddle (he had taught himself) and could sing and he wore his Sunday cap (made of black velvet) at a jaunty angle like the gentry. You could have put him down in the queen's court and no woman would have thought him strange or out of place; every woman would have admired him.

The day he showed me his farm it was spring and the wind was young and green and as sharp as knives. We sat sheltered by a tree close to the stream in the sunshine and he explained the land to me – how the stream flooded in the spring but each year he was deepening its course so that it could hold more water; how the upland meadow had caught the east wind until he had planted saplings along its eastern edge; and how the barley field was stony but year by year he was weeding out the stones. He looked dog tired as he took my hand.

Very soon we were betrothed. His mother bitterly opposed our marriage (his father was already dead). She said that even though I was a clergyman's daughter my strange childhood had besmirched me, but Matthew took no notice. His friends also thought he had married beneath him. Every girl for miles around wanted him. I came from a different village and they thought that somehow I must have bewitched him with my beauty. But I didn't care. I loved him with all my heart, as only an orphan or a nearly orphan can. I thought that I would be a good wife, that we would work together on the farm six days a week and go to church on the seventh, that I would learn to do everything the farmhands did, haymaking and harvesting and helping with the lambing. I would plant the kitchen garden and grow cabbages, onions, spinach and turnips, learn to milk the cow, go down on my hands and knees to weed the spring-sown barley, and when he cut the corn I would bind it.

When my father died word spread that the fairies had killed him as revenge for everything he had written about them. After that, the rectory went to another family and so Matthew and I were married. On our wedding day I saw him outside, in the yard beside the well, getting ready to wash. I saw him draw his shirt – it was his wedding shirt – over his head, his face lost in its folds. I saw the shadows of muscles on his back and his skimpy drawers. And I thought, 'He's mine.'

When Matthew came home from fairyland, I continued to run to and fro, telling the farmhands what to do, helping them with the tasks around the farm, but I also sat up late and held Matthew's hand in case the fairies came back for him. I thought how much I loved him, his eyes, his hands, all of his long person from his head to his feet. I wasn't surprised by his silence and his sadness. I knew it was often like that when a man or woman came home from fairyland. I tried to imagine how it had happened. Had the fairy queen passed this way, across our land, on horseback with her dogs (they would have been greyhounds – very elegant) and seen my good-looking husband singing in the twilight as he finished the day's last tasks – and thought, 'I will have him.' I pictured fairyland, the music and feasting and dancing, the lights and the clothes and the sounds of the lute and the flute and pipes – all the sad, sweet, tawdry glamour of the other world. I wondered if my husband had played his fiddle for her?

But after a couple of weeks, I began to panic. We were only a few days away from the harvest and I knew that I couldn't do it alone, not even with the help of the farmhands. I lay down beside Matthew. 'My love,' I said, 'you have to talk,' and then I saw what he held in his hands – a small doll that he twisted and turned in his fingers. I knew what had happened. He must have got up when I wasn't looking and taken it out of the trunk.

She had been our beloved, born two years after we were married. First, she had smiled, then she had sat, then she had stood and then – the summer she turned one – she had learnt to walk, making a hazy, mazy path across the farmyard and

120

everywhere she went, running away and then running towards us, picking things up and then dropping them down in a sweet, baby confusion. Matthew loved her. He called her 'my love' even more often than he did me. I didn't mind. I made her daisy chains to protect her from the fairies. When we went to church on Sundays, I put her down on her feet beside the wicker gate so that she could run up the path beside us. I was proud of the three of us, how fine we looked, how God had blessed us.

But when she was eighteen months old, she started to sicken. She died slowly from the inside outwards, like a bud that withers before it can blossom. She is buried in his family's grave, along with his mother and father. That was his choice. I would have buried her here in our woods and worshipped at her grave every morning. When she died the rumour started up again that we were fairy-cursed, that my father had offended the fairies and so they had taken their revenge on us.

Now, I twisted the doll gently out of his fingers. He opened his eyes.

'I tried to find her,' he said.

'I know.'

I thought of the long, hard road to fairyland, though the way back is even harder, and how when you get there they say the light is low and the air is always filled with sad music. And I thought of the fairy queen and her terrible jealousy – because surely she desired my husband and so would want to kill me? – and how she already had our daughter and how she must run to and fro on her bare little feet to do the fairy queen's bidding, like a page, always willing. Did she fetch the queen's ribbons and veils and sleep with the queen beside her?

I said, 'Next time ... take me with you when you go.'

Chapter Thirteen
Alchemy

We know that John Dee studied alchemy, which was considered back then to be the lord of all the magic arts. It was also the obsession of every penniless aristocrat in England – and there were great numbers of these – because of its financial possibilities, its claim that via the philosopher's stone it could turn base metals into gold. There were huge financial rewards for anyone who could make alchemy happen. Even the queen, whose finances were always precarious, kept alchemists on her payroll.

For centuries alchemists have had a bad reputation for being either scammers or gullible fools. In fact, their thinking was entirely logical. Alchemy was proto-chemistry – through its techniques, particularly of distilling, people could make paints, perfumes, salt-petre, etc – but the central ambition of alchemy was always to turn base metals into gold. The idea that this was even possible came from the belief that gold and silver are constantly being created under mountains by an ongoing process of purification. This made sense to alchemists because it matched a truth – as they saw it – about the universe, that nothing dies, that Change floods constantly across the cosmos, that everything is always in the process of dissolving and recombining into something else. What's more, this change is never random. The world seeks perfection and so Change tends constantly towards it.

The alchemists set out to mimic these natural processes – and speed them up – by making gold in their laboratories. They believed that the right mixture of mercury and sulphur would make gold, though too little sulphur and you would get silver; too much and you would get copper. Likewise too much mercury and you would get tin or lead. Everything depended on the precise proportions and also the right temperature (though in the days before thermometers even maintaining a steady temperature would have been tricky).

Alchemy was focused around the art of distillation – the process by which you boil a liquid until you are able to separate off the different vapours – and on the magic of fire, which can purify, change and transform. Alchemists believed that when making gold there were twelve steps in this process. They included calcination and oxidation (which included heating); congelation and fixation (making the substance solid); dissolution and digestion (which involved purification); distillation and sublimation (when the vapours rose and condensed); and separation (when the liquid was distilled). One of the last steps was fermentation, when the philosopher's stone became like yeast and able to effect transmutation of base substances. After that came multiplication (when the stone was given the power to transmute many times its own weight in base metal without losing its strength).

Even when making gold alchemy always had an esoteric and spiritual side to it. It was bold and poetic and full of a vaunting ambition to fulfil God's work. Alchemists believed – as many people did then – that the end of the world was coming any moment and that the task of men was to make the world as perfect as possible on the day of its ending. Since it was believed that the cosmos itself was dancing towards perfection this was a moment when the alchemist and the cosmos were at one with each other. For the alchemist it must have felt like that moment when you fall in love and for that short space of time you seem to sing in tune with the universe. Alchemy is an optimistic philosophy that answers to our yearning for spiritual transformation, to the desire to make – or to be – something better, something more beautiful and eternal, and thus to perfect this fallen world. In this way it feels like the creative process, which is why artists, writers and poets have always been fascinated by it.

When alchemists attempted to turn lead into gold they were trying to practise both forms of alchemy – the practical and the spiritual – because gold was both physically and spiritually perfect.

Alchemy has received much mockery down the centuries but if you accept the premise that nothing ever dies but rather is perpetually transformed into something else, then alchemy makes sense – and you too might have been an alchemist.

Some alchemists went even further than all this. If the universe is in flux and nothing ever dies, could it also be that we can cross the ultimate boundary between the living and the dead, or create a living creature out of clay, or bring our own dead loved ones home from the grave? Some alchemists thought this was possible. In alchemical literature the image of the serpent or dragon eating its own tail stands for the moment when the alchemist breaks out of sequential, linear time – one thing after another – and discovers circular time, by which we may return to a golden age of eternal youth. Thus, some alchemists thought that they could prolong life, discover the elixir of youth, even discover immortality.

•

When the story of Renaissance magic began in the fifteenth century, alchemy had already been in Europe for hundreds of years. Its deep roots went back to ancient Egypt and in particular to ancient Alexandria, which for hundreds of years had been a meeting place for Greek and Jewish philosophy as well as ancient Egyptian thinking and so had become a city where scholarship and magic flourished. From Alexandria alchemy spread into the Byzantine Empire and from there into the Islamic world until – in a third great journey – and probably via the Arabic Andalusian kingdoms in Spain – it reached the medieval, Latin world of Western Europe.

By the fifteenth century alchemy was flourishing in England. There were alchemical books in the library of Edward IV and some form of alchemy was probably being practised in the medieval monasteries, even though the Franciscans (in 1272) and the Dominicans (in 1323) explicitly condemned it.

There was also alchemy being practised in every country in Europe. Today, in a tiny, cobbled courtyard just off Totengasslein street in Basel there is an old pharmacy museum. All around it are tall, white-painted houses with green shutters and windows rimmed with ox-red paint, each house growing into the next as they climb the steep hill of the old university quarter with flights of steps running between them. Here in the early fifteenth century, Johannes Frobenius, the humanist printer and publisher, ran his own printing house and – as was often the case with the printing houses – drew to himself many of Europe's intellectuals. Erasmus lived and worked here, as did the doctor-alchemist Paracelsus and the painter Hans Holbein the Younger.

Paracelsus was a Swiss alchemist, born in central Switzerland in 1493. When he was a child his mother died and his father, who was a doctor, managed his education, teaching him medicine, botany, mineralogy, mining and natural philosophy (which would have included Neoplatonism). When Paracelsus was eleven his father took him on a 200-mile journey. They were heading for Carinthia in Austria where silver had recently been found under the mountains and where Paracelsus's father was to become a doctor in the mines. It must have been a spectacular mountain journey, made by horse, by mule and on foot, when the snows had melted in the high valleys, the passes were briefly open and the meadows full of flowers. In those day metals were hardly understood but silver is part of the alchemical quest and maybe it was the memory of that journey across the mountains towards the Carinthian mines that stirred alchemical dreams in Paracelsus, made him dream of all those possible metals under his feet, and formulate the idea that one metal can flow into another and that therefore lead might turn into gold.

Paracelsus became a chemist and a metallurgist, as well as an alchemist and a doctor, bent upon curing people of their illnesses. He was a big man with a rude, bad-tempered tongue and a wizard's wandering ways. He travelled to Russia, Lithuania and Hungary, as well as to Egypt, Arabia and Constantinople before settling briefly as a lecturer in Basel. He believed that 'a doctor must seek out old wives, gypsies, sorcerers, wandering tribes, robbers and such outlaws and take lessons from them. A doctor must be a traveller ... Knowledge is experience.' Whilst he was in

Basel, and because he was always a troublemaker, Paracelsus lit a bonfire and publicly burnt the books of the old medical authorities, men like Galen. He was also an alchemist, though he was not so much interested in making gold as in using alchemy to make medicines. For Paracelsus, 'God was the divine alchemist who created the world by calcinating, congealing, distilling and sublimating the elements of chaos.' John Dee knew about Paracelsus's thinking; he had his books on his library shelves.

•

In 1517, just under sixty years after the *Corpus Hermeticum* came to Italy, Martin Luther publicly protested to his local bishop against the sale of indulgences. He pinned his protest to the doors of Wittenberg Cathedral and so set in motion the violent schism that tore the Christian Church in two. Fifteen years after Martin Luther's gesture of defiance, Henry VIII saw in these events an opportunity to break from Rome, divorce his wife Catherine of Aragon, marry the woman he chose – Anne Boleyn – and sire a male heir to hold his dynasty together. Henry's government was rapidly consumed by a struggle between the conservatives, who espoused a kind of Catholicism without the Pope, and the radicals who were pushing towards full-blown Protestantism. Their bitter, violent struggle destabilised the government, swallowed up the lives of women like Anne Boleyn and spread outwards across the country.

Between 1536 and 1540 the English monasteries and nunneries were closed down. This had the effect of changing utterly the look and feel of the country. During the medieval period in London alone there were many monasteries and convents squeezed inside the city walls or outside and leaning up against them. For the first few years after Henry dissolved the monasteries and before he gave away their land to his favourite ministers, London's monastic churches, cloisters and gardens would have been left empty and would have contributed to the city's abandoned and dilapidated feel.

The Reformation also destroyed the monastic libraries, which had contained many fine books, including Bibles and commentaries on Bibles; philosophy of a spiritual kind written by medieval philosophers like Peter Abelard and Roger Bacon; books on history such as Geoffrey of Monmouth's history; secular literature by Roman poets such as Virgil, Horace and Cicero; and important books on science, medicine and alchemy (which we know because, later, many of these books found their way into John Dee's library). When each monastic house received its commands to shut down, its monks gave back their monastic clothes, ended their rituals, sang their last hymns in their last services and went their separate ways. Many of the monastic books were destroyed, but some had already been taken by the king; others were taken by the monks and thereafter acquired by book lovers like John Dee. About 5,000 books are known to have survived from the monastic libraries.

In the 1540s and 1550s there was another round of book destruction, this time when Edward VI purged the libraries in Oxford and Cambridge, and again some books on alchemy were saved and by one route or another fell into the hands of book lovers and book collectors, like John Dee, and from them, in due course, into the hands of kings and queens and the aristocracy.

The ending of the monastic libraries was a tragedy, but it was also wonderful for book-loving men like John Dee who acquired their books.

STORY FOUR
IN THE RUINS

London was a city of ruins then. On summer evenings – when the streets smelt of old drains and the hollyhocks grew as tall as weeds – the children went out looking for violets and speedwells in the ditches, goldenrod on the fallen masonry and lady's slipper growing out of London's ancient, ruined floors. They sold the plants to the apothecaries who lived on Lime House Lane. It was ten years since the old king had driven out London's monks and nuns and now their buildings were falling into ruin. In some places, the merchants and traders had moved in, storing their wares in the great halls and dining rooms, but really, they were small people compared to the vastness of the ruins, like children trying on big shoes. The monastic gardens were full of weeds. That summer, London was a city of flowers and weeds and ruins and papist ghosts. In the mornings the ghosts went home, and the children came out.

Everyone knew the children. On their mother's side they came from an old London family, the Harwells, working people, never rich, never gentry, but they had lived in this part of London for as long as anyone could remember and in the days of the young king's grandfather had laundered for the Charterhouse monks. The children didn't go home very often but after Dame school played along the city's ancient walls in the west – from the wharf down by Whitehall on the river as far north as the ruined monastery of the Knights of St John not far from Clerkenwell village. The old king had given some of the monasteries to his friends, the big men who ran the country, but there were still many hidden places – orchards and sheds and barns and chantry chapels and kitchen gardens – that went unclaimed and here the children played.

One day, they went so far west they left the houses and the streets behind and came to a place where the woods and fields began. It was a summer twilight. The Evening Star was low down in the sky and looking very holy, the moon was rising opposite and the fields were filled with the hooting of owls and other strange sounds – honks and creaks and croaks – as the birds settled to sleep. The children stared in wonder until they were overcome with panic and then they turned and hurried back to the city, carrying the littlest one between them like a sack of beans.

On the other side of the city wall and close to Clerkenwell Green lived Old Ma, who was their mother's mother. She was a lanky old woman – unutterably tall and unutterably old – she was nearly sixty – who lived in a single room in a house that leant sideways at the top of a lane. She had fallen beside her wits when her husband died and had never got them back. By day she went searching for herbs in the monastery ruins. The children were frightened of her, but her stories entranced them. She told them about laundry days at Charterhouse and how the lay brothers had brought out heaps of clothing – the robes and hoods and socks – and piled them up in the laundry courtyard and how when the water started to flow, she and her brothers had splashed and stamped in the sparkling gutters. Sometimes, the children called out questions in the middle of her stories. 'Where's your daddy?' (They were pitiless.) 'Dead. Don't ask questions.' 'Where's your mummy?' 'What do you think? Don't ask so many questions.'

But at other times, Old Ma didn't want to talk and then she fled from them across the ruins of Clerkenwell Priory and they chased after her until she turned to face them down, at which they scattered like mice, but not for long. Soon, they poked their heads out from behind the fallen walls and started hunting her again. It was her stories they wanted; they craved her stories.

The Harwells had been papists but now the young king burns papists alive. What does that feel like? Once, they each put their finger into the candle flame and turned white with shock at the pain. They still have the scars on their little fingers.

Another time, they went looking for Old Ma in her lean-to old house. The front door was ajar so in they crept, but instead of climbing the stairs to her room they slithered straight through and into the gloomy rear of the house, through one door after another, until they found themselves in a lean-to with the light tumbling down through the broken tiles and more spilling in behind them. By this light they saw – on the floor in front of them – one, two, three great, grave, stone angel heads – like lopped-off flowers – with stone lips and huge eyes and the tips of their stone heads just touching.

'Angels,' breathed all three of the children together.

'Are they alive?' asked the smallest one.

'I don't think so,' said the oldest one doubtfully.

•

'I wouldn't believe everything your grandma tells you,' said their mother, who was small and pale and ladylike. She had come home late from the market that day and turning the last corner had seen, opposite their house, a stranger playing the pipes and three small children dancing. The children's dresses swayed and their hands were interlinked like paper dolls. 'They should be in bed,' she'd thought, before she realised that they were hers. 'Mama,' they cried out as they surged towards her.

After supper, the four of them knelt down to say their prayers and then the children climbed into the single bed that they shared (two at one end, one at the other) whilst their mother seated herself on a stool to commence her stories. She told them how the old king closed the Charterhouse monastery and inflicted the utmost cruelty – starvation and plague and Lord knows what – on the monks of Charterhouse until God sent down an army of angels with golden wings and golden toes and golden trumpets affixed to their golden lips to usher the souls of the old monks up to heaven. Then she told them how there had once been a fine stone church in Clerkenwell Priory, with a great, tall bell tower and stone angels looking down from the rafters until the lord protector had got hold of some gunpowder and blown it up – boom, boom, boom – you could hear the noise right across the city – and then he had used the stone to build his new house on the Strand.

Their mother's father, whom she had dearly loved, had been an educated man, a tailor by profession and so a man of needles and buttons, but with a great interest in what he called 'history'. There was nothing he did not know about London's past and he often told his daughter of the apparitions he had seen on winter evenings – how once he had seen the Saxons overtopping the city walls and another time, two Romans quarrelling on the corner of Leadenhall Street. They had been pushing each other angrily, but when they saw him they set off at a run towards the city gates.

When the tailor had died, his wife – who was Old Ma – had lost her senses, although that, thinks his daughter seated on the stool, has never stopped her own children running after the old woman. Every day she prays for her father's soul, remembers with pain and pleasure the back of his neck as he bent over his work, his long fingers settling the hem of the jacket before he starts to stitch it. She thinks of the demons that haunt Old Ma and of the apparitions her father saw. She herself has never seen the ghost of her father, although she would dearly love to.

Now her children play in London's ruins.

•

'I wouldn't believe everything your mother says,' said their father to them. He was a big man, a waggoner by trade and as ruddy and hulking as their mother was pale and ladylike. He was often away from home and knew every road across the eastern counties from London to Kings Lynn. He had taken up the Protestant cause and had recently been in Cambridge with the king's men, emptying the university libraries of their heretical, superstitious books. He had looked around in horror at the library's dust and cobwebs – 'My wife keeps a cleaner house than this,' he had shouted – and within minutes he was sweeping up the volumes by the armful and flinging them out of the windows, from where they plummeted to the ground like fallen birds and were swept up by other men into bonfires, whilst the librarian, a little man, looked on in shock. The waggoner couldn't read but he was a great arguer. His wife said that when the Last Day came, he would be arguing with the Good Lord himself. 'No, no, that's not true, Almighty God, the Bible says quite the opposite.' He had leant out of the tall library windows and shouted to the heavens, 'There will be no more books on the Last Day when the Good Lord comes, just his own book, the Good Book, the Bible.'

The next morning, the children found their father down on his knees on the riverbank, mending the nets with which he liked to catch fish on his days off. He was brooding on his wife's distaste for him. His three daughters knelt down and watched his busy fingers. 'You shouldn't believe everything your mother says,' he said again, and he looked at them sideways to make sure they had heard, at which point each child's face took on a distant, vacant look. He had come home late from his waggoning and must have overheard their mother's stories. He does not love his wife – although he did once. Her pale, prim, ladylike ways remind him – of all things – of the books on the library shelves.

He makes his way back from the river, with his three young daughters running to keep up with his long strides. By an unspoken agreement the children do not mention Old Ma's angel heads, not now, not ever. They know the angels are outcasts, just as they are outcasts in the world of adults.

CHAPTER FOURTEEN
THE GOLDEN AGE OF ALCHEMY

When the alchemical books slipped out of the monastic libraries after the dissolution of the monasteries, the last great golden age of alchemy began.

Alchemy became the passion of kings and queens, who built fine laboratories and kept alchemists, both because it was the stylish thing to do and because they hoped that if alchemy worked it might repair their bankrupt treasuries. The mournful Emperor Rudolf kept dozens of alchemists on his payroll. King James IV of Scotland supported an alchemist called John Damian, who had a secret laboratory in Stirling Castle and who built himself a pair of wings and attempted to fly from the castle ramparts (he failed). Queen Elizabeth supported and encouraged alchemists, such as Samuel Norton, the Dutchman Cornelius de Lannoy, Thomas Charnock, Richard Eden (the distiller of the royal works) and, chiefly, John Dee of Mortlake, the all-round angel talker. Even William Cecil, Elizabeth I's hard-headed, clear-sighted, cynical chief adviser, kept books about alchemy on his library shelves at Hatfield House.

Elizabeth was fascinated by alchemy. At that time, it was widely believed that the end of the world, which was imminent, would unfold in three steps. First, there would come the last world emperor, who would know the secrets of the philosopher's stone and who would bring with them a golden age. Then would come the antichrist, who would destroy the last world emperor. Finally, Christ would come and destroy the antichrist and put an end to time and to the world. Elizabeth hoped and believed that she was the last world emperor. She kept a distilling house in Hampton Court, another one in Somerset House, presided over by the Lowlander Cornelius de Lannoy, and even had distilling apparatus in her privy chamber, which was managed by a woman called Millicent Franckwell.

Alchemy was expensive and alchemists who tried to advance themselves without money usually struggled to fulfil their dreams. Those who wanted to succeed had to come to London to be near the power and wealth of the court. Thomas Charnock, one of the alchemists who sought Queen Elizabeth's patronage, lived near Bridgwater in Somerset for most of his life. He inherited the alchemical library of his uncle, also called Thomas, who had been Henry VII's confessor and claimed to have learnt the secrets of the philosopher's stone from the prior of Bath. Charnock was usually short of money, always struggling to manage his servants and support his children and perpetually wanting to be left in peace to pursue his studies. Without this peace, he was often gloomy: not every wizard was flamboyant.

One hundred years after Charnock's death, the folklorist John Aubrey visited his house in Combwich. No one had lived there since Charnock's death for fear of the spirits that were said to haunt it and so Aubrey found Charnock's laboratory untouched and with strange alchemical symbols still painted on the walls. Yet, just as often it happened the other way round and the secrecy and illegality of alchemy meant that when workshops and laboratories were abandoned, they were destroyed and forgotten for ever.

It is hard now to find traces of those old alchemical laboratories.

In the Palazzo Vecchio in Florence, just off the great hall on the first floor, there is a beautiful little room with a barrel-vaulted ceiling and paintings along the walls of – amongst other things – alchemists and the god of the *Corpus Hermeticum*, Hermes Trismegistus. Each of the walls represents one of the elements – earth, air, fire and water – from which the world was made. Behind the lower level of paintings were hidden cupboards, in each of which was something rare and curious. Together, the paintings and the objects told the story of the world. That such a huge story could unfold in such a tiny space was part of its power. This was the private studio of the sixteenth-century Medici ruler Francesco I, where he liked to sit and ponder alchemy and the meaning of the world, though it is unlikely that any real alchemical experiments ever took place here. It was far too beautiful a space for that.

Spaces for experiments would have been bigger, plainer and much more functional. One such space was probably the basement of what is now the History of Science Museum in Oxford. The museum's fine seventeenth-century building was constructed to be the first Ashmolean Museum. Its ground floor had a lecture hall, its first floor was where the museum's collection was displayed and its basement was for chemistry

– but almost certainly with a strong strand of alchemy running through it. If you stand in the basement now, you will see no sign of alchemy – though you will notice how solidly and skilfully the walls were built (as if to withstand fire). In 1999, archaeological excavations were carried out at the back of the museum and in the process, crucibles, retorts and flasks were uncovered. Link these to the letters and papers of the first Ashmolean curator, Robert Plot, who believed that he could create the menstruum, or elixir of life (a very alchemical idea), and seems to have even made arrangements to market it, and you have some idea of the kind of experiments that Plot would have been carrying out in the museum's basement.

When it comes to the spread of alchemical knowledge there must have been two opposing tendencies in play. One was to keep your knowledge secret, to hold it close to your chest, whilst the other must have been a desire to talk about the things you love with the people that you considered to be your peers. This second impulse would have expressed itself through conversation, letters and correspondence, through the relationship between masters and apprentices, and – above all else – through the proliferation of books on alchemy, some of which have survived and are often astonishingly beautiful.

We know that John Dee had on his shelves a mid-sixteenth-century edition of George Ripley's alchemical masterpiece *The Twelve Gates* or the *The Compound of Alchemy*. Ripley had been the canon of Bridlington in Yorkshire in the fifteenth century and the most famous alchemist of the early modern era. The twelve gates were the twelve steps towards acquiring the philosopher's stone. As well as this book, we know that Dee had acquired some of Ripley's writings in manuscript form and carefully copied them out in order to keep the latter's wisdom safe.

Ripley's thinking has survived both in the form of books and in the Ripley scrolls, sixteen of which still exist, most of them dating to the seventeenth century, though they were all probably based on something earlier. The scrolls are mysterious things, the text is obscure but the images are often beautiful. They lay out the steps in the alchemical process, depicting them through a series of allegorical pictures, all in pale greens and reds and greys and golds, and featuring sickle moons, a woman with webbed feet and a dragon's tail, lions up on their hind legs and a sun's face with long, pointed flames flowing from it. Artists right up to the twentieth century, such as William Blake and Leonora Carrington, have been inspired by the scrolls, but who the original artists were we do not know. In fact, everything about the Ripley scrolls is mysterious. Who made them? What was their purpose? Who was George Ripley? Did he even exist? The mystery surrounding them is probably deliberate – alchemy was often semi-secret, usually illegal – but their beauty is a testament to the beauty and the hope of alchemy.

Chapter Fifteen
Lady Sidney's Recipes

There was one form of magic that belonged to all women, rich and poor, and that was kitchen magic, the magic of herbs and potions. This was a time when there were very few doctors, when medicine was in its infancy and there were no professionally made medicines. And so, it fell to women to develop the skills by which to keep their households alive. Herbal knowledge grew by trial and error. Most Elizabethan women would have had some knowledge of the properties of herbs – which ones helped healing or relieved back pain or conferred energy or granted peacefulness or worked as love potions – and some women would have known a very great deal about where to find the herbs, how to prepare them and how often to administer them. Many of these women herbalists would have been poor and illiterate, inhabiting an oral world where knowledge was passed on by word of mouth and anonymity reigned and – as with storytelling – no one knew the origin of anything. It was precisely this kind of woman who was most frequently accused of witchcraft.

Herbal knowledge is scientific knowledge, but it has always attracted magical thinking. The herbs themselves were thought of as magical, particularly those with alleged dark powers, such as henbane, hellebore and mandrake roots, and so by extension, were the women who knew about these herbs.

There was another, connected knowledge that women also had that made them particularly well equipped to practise this herbal magic.

Not far from the kitchens of the great country house at Wilton outside Salisbury, Lady Mary Herbert, wife of the second earl (and as it happens a patron of John Dee), would have kept a still room in the sixteenth century. Here, she and her assistants would have made candles, soaps, medicines, laundry recipes and perfumes, as well as preserved food and distilled wine. Still rooms played a crucial role in feeding households and keeping their members alive. All the big country houses – in fact any household that could afford to – had a still room. The connection to alchemy was that when Lady Mary was at work in her still room, she was essentially using the same chemical skills of heating, melting, vapourising and distilling that the alchemists also used. Hence, women's kitchen experiences gave them an unexpected, backdoor way into the magical profession of alchemy.

Kitchen alchemy was a pan-European phenomenon. This was a time when across Europe recipe books were flourishing. Caterina Sforza, the Italian Countess of Forlì, wrote a book called *Experimenti*, which included instructions on how to create everything, from cosmetics to medicines for fevers, coughs, epilepsy and cancer, as well as how to make the philosopher's stone, alchemical gold and the elixir of life. (This mix of the everyday and the momentous, from cosmetics to elixirs of eternal life, seems very strange to us and yet clearly didn't seem so odd at the time.)

Another of these books, *I Secreti*, was a recipe book published in 1561 and was apparently written by an Italian alchemist called Isabella Cortese. In it, she writes, 'If you want to practise the art of alchemy don't follow the teachings of Geber or Ramon (Llull) or Arnaldo (da Villanova)' – all famous male practitioners of magic – 'or any of the other philosophers, because their books are full of lies and riddles.' In that one sentence you can feel her anger that her skills are belittled whilst men's are celebrated.

As always, upper-class women had the advantage of time and money when it came to alchemy but even so, other women sometimes seized an opportunity, women – for instance – who worked in apothecary shops and even some nuns who became apothecarists.

Mary Sidney was sixteen years old when she married the Earl of Pembroke in April 1577, and he was nearly forty. Her father had been Henry Sidney, a scholarly man, but her mother had been Mary Dudley, the daughter of the Duke of Northumberland, who had been beheaded for treason, and her uncle was Robert Dudley, Earl of Leicester, the queen's favourite. Mary was fluent in French, Italian and Latin, and she also spoke some Greek and Hebrew. In other words, she was one of those upper-class girls whose astonishing Renaissance educations (Lady Jane Grey was another one) brought them within touching distance of a magician's knowledge; of the learning of a man like John Dee. Mary Dudley also knew John Dee, as did the entire Dudley family, because Dee had been her uncle's tutor when Robert Dudley was a young boy.

Her husband, Henry Herbert, the second earl, was quite different. The Herberts had been raised up to grandeur by several Tudor monarchs. Mary's father-in-law, the first earl, had built the big house at Wilton with its many chimneys and the cupolas on the gatehouse and had also enclosed the common land for his gardens and hunting grounds. The second earl, Mary's husband, didn't have this energy. Instead, Henry Herbert loved hunting and owned a great many Arab stallions and mares, as well as a huge establishment of hunting dogs. (Although to give him credit, he was also a patron of Richard Burbage's theatre company.)

Mary was not even half his age and yet was as witty and sparklingly clever as her husband was dull. She did not marry Henry Herbert for love. The man she loved, and would always love, was her brother, seven years older than her, the poet Philip Sidney. He had been at Elizabeth I's court in the 1570s but had alienated the queen by giving her gauche and unsolicited advice about a possible marriage and so had to retreat to Wilton House where the pastoral beauty could soothe his moody and melancholic disposition. Meanwhile, Mary was rapidly turning Wilton House into an academy; a Renaissance paradise; an echo of Plato's Academy in Athens.

Mary Sidney did not, as far as we know, attempt to turn lead into gold. The alchemy she pursued, notwithstanding all her kitchen magic, was quite different. She wanted Wilton House to be a place of wit and beauty and learning, of beautiful architecture and poetry and to have a magical Renaissance garden. In other words, she wanted the alchemy of creativity.

Like so many other things at this time, Renaissance gardens were touched by magical thinking. The idea of a garden as a part of paradise had emerged in Italy during the fifteenth century and then spread across Europe. Mary Herbert's garden at Wilton has long since vanished, as have most Renaissance gardens – not even a painting of it has survived – though we can, to some extent, imagine its components: the knot garden (the swirling, geometric patterns made by low hedges), the herbs and flowers that were planted in the islands made by the spiralling hedges, the sanded paths leading to vistas of sundials and classical statues (because this was a period that loved the classical past), the strange new plants from Asia and the New World and the fountains and flowing water created by the mechanical arts that the Renaissance also loved. The patterns made by the knot gardens were often so mathematically complicated that they needed to be drawn up first (or perhaps copied from a pattern book). In those days, mathematics was considered to be a faintly magical art (because how else, except by magic, could we know something without recourse to the five senses?) and perhaps this fact alone would have been enough to lend a whiff of magic to the knot gardens.

Mary Herbert's Renaissance circle included Sir Walter Raleigh, John Dee, Francis Walsingham, the poets Fulke Greville and Edmund Spenser and the adventurer Humphrey Gilbert. Most of them wrote poetry, a pursuit in which both Philip and Mary excelled, at a time when being a poet was both stylish and sexy. Philip and Mary both understood the alchemical and philosophical magic of poetry, as did William Shakespeare, who wrote in Sonnet 33: 'Full many a glorious morning have I seen, Flatter the mountain tops with sovereign eye, Kissing with golden face the meadows green, Gilding pale streams with heavenly alchemy.' Philip Sidney took the same idea and subverted it in his Sonnet 108 where grief and the absence of love makes the alchemical process run backwards and turns gold back into lead in the lover's heart.

What these poets are saying is that there is a magic in sunlight and music and poetry and falling in love – in fact, just being alive – and that there is a magic in the creativity that can capture this everyday magic. All of these are things that poets have always known.

Only Henry Herbert refused to take part in such intellectual, poetic endeavours and he instead stuck stubbornly to his hunting.

Philip Sidney died in the Netherlands in 1586 whilst fighting for the Protestant cause against the Spanish. He was only thirty-one. When the news reached Wilton House, Mary Herbert went into mourning for two years, but after that she emerged as witty and sparkling as ever and went straight to London with a spectacular entourage of eighty servants.

Meanwhile in 1575, as Mary Herbert began to create her poetic and philosophic Platonic Academy, a young German girl called Anna Maria Zieglerin was sentenced to death on charges of alchemy and murder. Zieglerin had spent her childhood in the Dresden court of Augustus, Elector of Saxony. When she was fourteen, she was raped and became pregnant and it is alleged that she secretly brought the baby to term then wrapped it in a cloth and threw it in a river. Within a few years, Zieglerin had married twice, the second time to Heinrich Schombach, a jester at the court of Duke Johann Friedrich II of Saxony. She and Schombach shared an interest in alchemy with a Lutheran pastor called Philipp Sömmering and by the time Anna Zieglerin was twenty-one, all three of them had arrived at the court of Duke

Julius of Braunschweig-Wolfenbüttel and Anna was running her own alchemical laboratory with the help of an assistant. She was very young and must have had huge self-confidence, as well as the kind of vivid imagination that Edward Kelley also had. Zieglerin wanted to create human life and invented a golden oil that she called 'lion's blood', with which she believed she could create gemstones, cure illnesses and, most importantly, speed up the gestation process in the womb so that a mature foetus could be made in only six weeks. Such golden children, born of lion's blood, would be immortal – and because of their perfection would be the most appropriate people to inhabit the earth as the end times gave way to the Second Coming. When it became clear that Zieglerin, Schombach and Sömmering could not make the philosopher's stone, they were put on trial, tortured and charged with murder. They were found guilty and condemned to die by fire, this being the punishment for the most heinous crimes, such as heresy, sorcery, poisoning and sodomy. In 1575 Zieglerin was strapped to an iron chair and burnt alive.

Anna Maria Zieglerin's death horrifies me. She was very young (only twenty-five when she was killed) and part of her crime was undoubtedly to be a young smart-arse know-all and female. Throughout the centuries, many men have disliked clever women.

The situation of all those who practised magic, both men and women, was always precarious. Their survival depended on the beliefs of those around them – but belief is changeable, it comes and goes, grows stronger or weaker from day to day – and anyone will turn on somebody else if they feel that they have been deceived and taken for a fool. Magic, as everyone knew back then, came in two forms: good white magic and bad black magic. Black magic, the magic that cheated and deceived, was widely feared and disliked. It was called 'conjuring' and a man who practised black magic was called a conjurer or a juggler or a necromantic mage. The problem was that the line between white magic and black magic was alarmingly fine, anyone could slip across it.

And so, wizards and alchemists were treated with both admiration and suspicion. If their powers were real, they were potentially dangerous. It was easy to accuse them of hubris and believe them deserving of nemesis.

In this world, a magician could be feted by kings but also die at the stake. As we will see, John Dee ended up a poor and broken man; Giordano Bruno ended worse. Both men flew high and burned bright, but when they fell, they fell fast.

CHAPTER SIXTEEN
BROTHER–SISTER LOVE

In the far north at the end of the sixteenth century, there was another garden of paradise built by another brother and sister who loved each other.

Tycho Brahe was a Danish astronomer in an era before the telescope was invented, but when astronomy was in turmoil. Thirty-five years previously, Nicolaus Copernicus, a Polish churchman, had published *De revolutionibus orbium coelestium*, in which he showed that the earth went round the sun, not vice versa. Copernicus had studied the heavens all his life but held back from publishing his book until he was near death for fear of what the Church would say – the first time he saw a printed copy was as he lay dying. *De revolutionibus* changed the world.

Thirty-five years later, Tycho Brahe, who came from generations of Danish noblemen and who was wealthy, domineering and enormously self-confident, set out to study the stars, for which he needed an observatory. King Frederick II granted him an estate on the island of Hven in the sound between Sweden and Denmark. Hven was tiny, just a couple of miles long, and was rimmed with steep cliffs within which was a patchwork of small fields and hamlets of poor fishermen. Here, between 1576 and 1580, with a combination of his own money and royal funds, Tycho Brahe built an observatory called Uraniborg and next to it an underground facility called Stjerneborg.

In the days before telescopes Brahe mapped the placement of the stars at every moment in the year. This was the first and most crucial step towards understanding their journeys and where, how and why they travelled. Despite working without a telescope, his observations were remarkably accurate. He saw the new star in the constellation of Cassiopeia (also seen by John Dee), tracked the comet of 1577 and wrote books on all these things. He knew that the old Aristotelian model of the unchanging heavens must be wrong, although he could never bring himself to fully accept the new Copernican theories. And, like all the Elizabethan intellectuals, he was well connected; he knew of John Dee in England and sent him a copy of his book.

Tycho Brahe was many other things as well as being an astronomer. He was an alchemist, a follower of the Swiss doctor Paracelsus and was also a Neoplatonist. For him, Uraniborg on the island of Hven was both a celestial and a terrestrial laboratory – a place to study both the heavens and the earth, the two things being connected. 'As above, so below,' as the alchemists used to say, or as Tycho said, 'By looking up I look down.' As well as the observatory, Tycho built an alchemical laboratory, containing sixteen alchemical ovens, and a millhouse that contained workshops for milling, papermaking and parchment production so that he could publish his own books. Finally, he built apartments for the miller and for himself, the latter including a stove with green-glazed tiles.

Uraniborg was, however, also the creation of his youngest sister Sophie whom Tycho loved dearly. She shared his scientific and alchemical interests and he ensured that she learnt chemistry, mathematics, German, Latin, astronomy and classical literature, so she could be more help to him. Sophie married a Danish nobleman, Otto Thott, but she visited Hven frequently and worked there as Tycho's assistant.

The architect responsible for Uraniborg was Johan Gregor van der Schardt, who had worked in Italy on Palladian villas before coming to Denmark. Surviving drawings show that the central building had fantastic pinnacles, domes, towers and cupolas, as well as fine classical statues over the doors. Inside, there were rooms for Brahe and his family, as well as for guests, scholars, students and the astronomical instruments. All around the building were formal and symmetrical Renaissance gardens, inspired by the famous botanical gardens at Padua. The gardens were planted with parterres containing angelica, gentian, juniper, medicinal rhubarb, sweet flag and wormwood, which Sophie Brahe used to make medicinal drinks. Beyond the parterres, the gardens were ringed with apple, plum, pear and cherry trees. Beyond the fruit trees were the earthen ramparts in which there were pavilions for music and meditation.

Four dreams would have made these gardens magical: the dream of the garden as a paradise, a resurrection of the Garden of Eden and Arcadia; the garden as an alchemical metaphor for the processes of life, death and rebirth; the garden as an echo of the gardens on the ancient Greek island of Cythera, believed to be the home of the goddess of love; and the garden as a place that gathered together all the plants of the world and was in fact the world in miniature.

Tycho and Sophie were brought up in the fortress-like castles of the old Danish nobility, but Uraniborg was different. It was open to the sky and breathed a Renaissance optimism. As well as being an astronomer and an alchemist, Tycho was also an accomplished poet who wrote in Latin. Hven was a place where poets, scientists, artists, astronomers, astrologers and magicians could come together to build a microcosm of the heavens in all their beauty, a place that would reveal the gloriously interconnected Neoplatonic universe. It was an echo of the old Platonic Academy, the dream of which Marsilio Ficino had fallen in love with 100 years before.

All this – the observatory with its domes and cupolas, the gardens with their orchards, parterres and herbs – must have looked extraordinary on the short summer days of that northern island.

In 1589 after Sophie was widowed, she fell in love with a friend of Tycho's, a nobleman called Erik Lange, who was also obsessed with alchemy and thus as penniless and full of dreams as alchemists always were. Lange planned to create a great trading company which would amass vast quantities of wealth by discovering unknown countries. By 1590 Sophie and Erik were betrothed, although it was against her family's wishes – only Tycho supported her – and shortly afterwards Erik had to leave Denmark to escape his creditors. For more than a decade he wandered across Europe until, finally, he and Sophie were married in Germany in 1602. Their marriage, like their betrothal, however, was plagued by poverty, creditors and debts. Sophie had to pawn the jewellery her sisters gave her and afterwards Erik pawned the clothes he wore on their wedding day. Poverty was the curse of alchemy; alchemy was expensive and many alchemists bankrupted themselves in pursuit of the philosopher's stone, gambling on the fact that if they discovered it they would be able to pay off their debts.

The love match between Sophie Brahe and Erik Lange has a Renaissance feel to it. Historians have long noticed a tension between marrying for love and being told by your community whom you should marry – a tension that becomes particularly acute in the Renaissance. Romantic love is increasingly discussed (it features often in Shakespeare's plays) and is seen by society as troublesome because it is both wonderful and dangerous. The love affair between Sophie Brahe and Erik Lange perfectly demonstrates this.

Meanwhile, Tycho had fallen out with Christian IV, the new Danish king, and feeling that the atmosphere in Denmark was growing less and less tolerant of Renaissance ideas had left Hven in 1597 and gone to Prague, where he became the emperor's imperial mathematician. In 1601 Tycho died and was buried with great splendour in the Church of our Lady before Týn in the centre of Prague. Twelve years later, Erik died too – and also apparently in Prague. For intellectuals in the sixteenth and early seventeenth century, Prague, with its love of the arts and sciences, its religious tolerance and obsession with the occult, had a never-ending allure.

After Tycho left, Christian IV decided that Hven was too expensive to maintain and so let Uraniborg fall into ruin. By the early 1600s it had disappeared entirely. The paradise on Hven island didn't last; paradises never do. They vanish, though sometimes they leave behind a scent in the air or – in some way – a dream-memory.

•

Sophie Brahe shows us how often the story of magic was a family story, particularly when it came to women who wanted to learn the magical trade. When other routes were closed, daughters could learn it from fathers and sisters from brothers. Astronomy, like alchemy, was high, learned magic that relied on the secrets inside books in libraries and was therefore out of most women's reach. But, if you wanted to pursue astronomy as Sophie Brahe did to understand the meaning of life then brother–sister love, like father–daughter love, was one way by which a girl could leap the walls that kept her out.

Story Five
Everything Rises

The artists came by water. They were dressed in furs and long black robes and their boats rocked and swayed dangerously on the surface of the floods. Girolamo greeted them at the water gate, took them upstairs and warmed them by the fire then plied them with white wine and fruit tarts and marzipan and let them feast their eyes on the tall windows, so luxuriantly filled with glass. The artists had come for Margaret's vermilion, which was famous across the city. Girolamo said, 'Did I tell you that my wife's father is a great magus back in England, an alchemist of heavenly renown from a town called Norwich? From him I learnt many magical things about the secret laws that underpin the transient mutability of the material world.' The artists bowed and smiled but really, they were impatient for their vermilion. They used it for the pink that edged their storm clouds and for the shadows in the Virgin's robes.

Girolamo had white skin and dark eyes and was dressed in black. He moved amongst them like a liquid shadow, filling up their glasses. He was thinking, 'But what's she doing out there? And why hasn't she brought in the vermilion?'

Meanwhile, out in her workshop at the end of the garden Margaret Buckley watched and waited. For a long time nothing happened and the apprentices looked at their nails and listened to the roaring waters, but then quite suddenly, the mercury started to bubble upwards in the glass retorts and the red gases began to form and rise. So, the magical transformation began, which goes from black to white to red, from base metal towards the philosopher's stone. Suddenly they were making so much vermilion that the apprentices couldn't keep up. Hastily, they sat down and began to extract it and wash it and grind it and weigh it on the scales. The artists liked the vermilion fresh with all its powers intact. As fast as they wrapped it, the quicker it appeared under the beehive lids.

It was February, the season of the floods, and outside the spring tides were surging along the narrow waterways. Up rose the water with crashes and bangs as the water gates flew open and the boats bashed against the bridges. And up rose the flames and the bubbling mercury. It was as if everything was rising – not only the water and the gases but also the wood and stone, the palaces and houses and alleyways – even the city's bridges were being lifted up from their stone foundations – all of it rising and floating away into the black and watery air.

But Margaret Buckley is miles away, not here at all. She has known water do this before because she comes from England's Fen country, from a house called Temperley to the north of Norwich, a great brick and timber house, gabled, with steep roofs and battalions of chimneys, and all around it gardens laid out in generous squares. At the foot of the gardens runs the River Meade, though it rarely stays where it belongs but is forever on the verge of surging upwards and flooding outwards to overwhelm them. On stormy winter nights her mother lights the candles in the house's many windows – delicate, tremulous lights – to guide her father, drunk as usual, home from Norwich.

The thought of her father is bothering Margaret. She has been waiting for a month now for a letter from England. The mail boat comes twice a day and nothing, not storms nor floods, ever stops it. So far, however, there has been no letter – and therefore no forgiveness?

This was her father. Sir Robert Buckley. Bart Esq. of Temperley in Norfolk. Two thousand a year in rents incoming, although with outgoings much exceeding that. A man of curiosity. A tall man with a way of stalking on his heron legs and with jackets very fine, with ruffles at the wrists and neck, though they date back in style to the queen's brother's reign or maybe even their father's reign before them. A cautious, dreamy look. A cynical but hopeful nature, always rising. And of course, he was a notorious alchemist with the finest alchemical laboratory in the east of England.

And this was Margaret, a little slip of a thing, quick and slight but ever so authoritative. The summer she was ten, a baking summer in every way, she was in the kitchen daily, watching intently through narrowed eyes at how the cook blended the sugar and butter, then beat in the eggs, folded in the flour and added the strange new dusts (called nutmeg, mace and cinnamon), plus a crumble of some strange white cake, then baked it all in the oven. Whereupon – how does it do this? – it puffs upwards and outwards, takes on an unexpected and floaty lightness and rises like the morning sun.

By the autumn of that year she's vanished, gone down one more flight of stone steps, into her father's alchemical laboratory where things also rise. 'Have you got the child?' her mother shouts angrily down the stairs. 'It's not safe for her down there.' 'You shouldn't be here, child,' says her father, bent over his equations, measuring the angle of the sun to Venus, but he makes no effort to shoo her away and she makes no effort to leave. Instead, she steps around his laboratory, eyeing up the equipment. 'What's this ... and this ... and this?' she asks. Sometimes he puts his hands under her armpits and lifts her onto the table so that she can stand next to the alchemical retorts. She has a talent for alchemy. When she's around the mercury keeps rising.

There's a war between her father and her mother, a long-running, bitter, tricksy war. He has failed her by spending her dowry and putting Temperley at risk and reducing them to penury, but she has failed him by turning old and ugly. If only she would be beautiful again the mercury would start to bubble upwards and the magic take and the cakes rise and the lead turn into gold and they would be rich again. The child takes her father's side. She runs up and down the stairs, bringing him plates of food from the kitchen, and every time her mother sees this it's like a knife in her side. The child knows it and she turns pale and looks remote because it hurts her too, but she cannot stop herself. She's burning up her mother's love as if there's no tomorrow.

And meanwhile, Temperley. A great, hulking house deep in the Fens and the notorious haunt of alchemists. Some years the floods are so bad that the Fen men walk down Norwich High Street on stilts and the family's guests have to row the last ten miles to Temperley in a flat-bottomed Fen man's boat. Other times, the winters are so cold that the Fens freeze over and the guests have to ice skate to the house with a couple of Fen men to guide them.

The locals tell a story that a guest once came to Temperley on a cold winter's evening when the snow was falling and met a sprite on the stairs. She looked about eight years old and was dressed in a white nightdress, with long hair and bare feet. The guest pauses, thinks perhaps she's an alchemical spirit conjured up by his host. He bows low and the sprite pauses. 'Who are you?' he asks politely and the sprite says, proudly, 'I am Margaret Buckley. My father is a magician. I am his apprentice.'

•

Then, she turns sixteen and everything changes and she can hardly remember the alchemical sprite. And nor it seems can her father. When she goes downstairs into his laboratory, he growls at her and shoos her out – 'What are you doing here? Who invited you?' – and sometimes, behind closed doors, she hears her parents talking – marriage talk – *her marriage* talk – of suitors and dowries and alliances of land and estates. In this they share a strange and unfamiliar unity. Her father has not yet found the philosopher's stone but there is more than one way to save a family's fortune. She still wanders through the library – because he has not yet banned her from that, thank God – pulling out books and opening them and taking them to the window seat where she can sit and watch the snow falling. It is winter now and every day the snow falls and Temperley is frozen.

It was on just such a winter's day when Margaret was sixteen that Girolamo came to Temperley, skating between two Fen men, a tall black hat on his head, his cloak wrapped tightly round him, his hands clasped behind his back. He was the Venetian secretary to London and so he was used to water in all its manifestations, although rarely had he known cold this bitter. Sir Robert came out onto the front steps in the falling snow to greet him. 'So, you made it,' he says nastily. He has already taken against the Venetian, Lord knows why.

Margaret, standing in the shadows on the stairs, watches Girolamo step into the hall, hand over his ice skates to the man servant, shed his heavy cloak with its fur-lined collar and put on the velvet-lined slippers that a house maid brings him. 'My God, Sir,' he is saying to Sir Robert (ignoring the nastiness), 'to live in this cold – you have all my respect – tell me you have summers of gentle warmth...'

After supper, Sir Robert and Girolamo meet in the library. A fire has been burning all day and now the room is toasty hot. Sir Robert is in a good mood. He is showing off his books with pride. Lately, he has been experimenting with colour and has found a new recipe for vermilion, which he believes has alchemical powers because it uses sulphur, which is the sun king, the red youth and the fire, but also mercury, which is the moon queen, the maiden, the water and the earth. As everyone knows, the red and the white is at the heart of the search for the philosopher's stone. At any rate, this is what Sir Robert intimates to Girolamo, albeit in the most roundabout way. Sir Robert keeps his recipes in a black notebook with a silver clasp. He is hospitable – he pours the wine – but, like all alchemists, he likes to keep his secrets.

Margaret sits back in the shadows of the library. Close up, she can see that Girolamo has neat features, black eyes, a short beard and a black moustache combed to neat points – which gives him a faintly rakish air. Over all, there is about him a delightful feeling of foreign-ness. She knows the moment that Girolamo catches sight of her because she sees him jump. She opens her eyes very wide – she's very short-sighted – she thinks it helps her see – and Girolamo jumps again in surprise, and as clear as anything she sees enchantment rising in his face. It rises like the waters of the Meade in springtime, like the sulphur and the mercury. She sees how the sight of her gets hold of him and the feelings of disbelief, of terror and delight that it engenders inside him. She knows that he wants to tell her everything he knows, that he wants to listen to her talk, that he is thinking there is no greater alchemy than love.

Three days later, she hurries down the steps to her father's laboratory. She has to hold herself back – she's almost running in her excitement. It's months since she's been down here. Now she looks around in surprise, at the dim, low space and the dust, and the scorched black glass vessels that hold the mercury and at her father in his long, black magus robes and she sees how lonely and stooped and despairing he is. His bitterness catches her unawares.

'Father, I am betrothed to Signor Girolamo,' she says.

Quick as a snake he snaps at her – 'So you are betraying me too' – and for a moment she is shocked, but then she flashes back at him – 'So, you only ever think about yourself, do you?' – because in the end she is her father's daughter.

•

They travelled overland by carriage, a glorious journey, first to Paris and then south to Annecy where they joined a convoy of travellers all waiting to cross the Alps by the Great St Bernard Pass. When the spring came and the snow melted, they went again by carriage, higher and higher, until the vehicle could climb no further and after that they got out and the hired men loaded their luggage onto mules and they continued by foot. Each night they slept in mountain huts and heard the deafening roar of the melting snow, and some nights they also heard the sounds of wolves and Margaret thought there was no way her life could ever be more perfect. From the pass they came down through Aosta and then on to Turin and from there, by a string of papist cities, across the northern plains of Italy to the port of Trieste where they caught a boat to Venice on a Sunday morning when all the bells were ringing out across the islands.

That first winter Girolamo takes out a huge loan to buy a house on the Grand Canal. 'Don't worry,' he says to Margaret as they stand at the window and he points out the watery mists and clouds and all the city's vaporous possibilities. 'Nothing is fixed, everything changes, today we are poor but tomorrow we will be rich.' It is the creed of the alchemists.

In the house, the artists are collecting their vermilion and hurrying to their boats so that they can get back to their work. Out in the laboratory everything goes quiet as well. The flames die down, the red gases sink back, the mercury ceases to bubble, and out on the canals the spring tide has passed its peak and is turning to the ebb. Margaret sits on the stone steps. Beside her is her father's black notebook with the silver clasp and his recipes inside it. She took it from his desk that last morning when her anger was rising. Inside it, in her father's scratchy handwriting, the words are set down as neatly and as tightly as bricks in a wall, and with diagrams like windows. On the first page he has written: 'The Great House, Temperley. On this day, the 31st October 1600, the Lord God Almighty laid down for me the steps in the making of alchemical vermilion. I declare by my life that every word herewith is true.'

Now, she is back in Temperley, lost in the ice and the cold and the library and the fire and the warmth. There is still no letter from her father. Everything rises, she thinks, except her father's forgiveness.

CHAPTER SEVENTEEN
Kepler

There is one last postscript to the Tycho Brahe story. A year before he died, Tycho Brahe met a young German astronomer and mathematician called Johannes Kepler. They met in Benatky Castle outside Prague, and perhaps also at the Sign of the Golden Griffin in Prague's Hradčany (Castle) district. Unlike Tycho, Johannes Kepler was born in poverty. He came from a Lutheran family, his father Heinrich having been a mercenary and his mother's father having run a tavern called The Sun. Kepler had been a small, sickly boy who had been bullied at school but even so, through a mixture of determination and luck, he had won a scholarship to the University of Tübingen. There, he became openly a Copernican, a stance which took courage, especially for a boy with no family to support him.

Thereafter, he would live a life of frequent tragedy. He married twice but at least half of his children died in childhood. At one time he had to leave Graz and take his family with him because he refused to convert to Catholicism. Another time, he was persecuted by the Lutherans for refusing to receive the Lutheran eucharist. Until the end of his life, he had the personality of a waif and stray – getting into verbal fights and swinging between arrogance and humility. And yet, he was also a Neoplatonist and belongs in our story because – with his Neoplatonic beliefs – he was half a scientist, in our sense of the word, and half a magician. Despite the tragedies in his life, he always retained the ability to see the world in playful and magical ways. Like John Dee, he thought with a combination of imagination, mysticism and mathematical skills. 'God is a mathematician', he said. 'I am only thinking God's thoughts after him.'

When Kepler met Tycho Brahe in Prague in 1600 he already had a reputation as a talented astronomer. He was trying to understand the rotations of the planets and wanted to use Brahe's data on stars – because the more data he had the more accurate his conclusions would be. There followed a brief, though quarrelsome and turbulent, partnership between the two men until Tycho died. Afterwards, Kepler inherited his data and replaced Tycho as Imperial Mathematician.

There followed the best years of Kepler's career. He often took measurements of the stars outside, in the gardens of Prague's Imperial Palace high up on the hill. He became the first person to plot the rotations of the planets and to realise that their rotations are elliptical, not circular (though he was slow to realise this because he assumed that surely the rotations of the planets would prescribe perfect circles, a circle having a classic Platonic beauty?).

When he observed that the further away the planets were from the sun the slower they moved he came very close to discovering gravity. And yet, his sense of the universe remained Neoplatonic to the end – he always believed that the universe lives and breathes, the world has a soul, the planets dance to the Music of the Spheres and that astrology is true. He also believed that the universe was finite and so was shocked by Giordano Bruno's concept of an infinite universe (which we will come to).

There is another sad and curious part of Kepler's story, and that is that his mother, Katharina Kepler, was tried for witch-craft. She was accused in 1616, the charge being brought by some of the people of Leonberg in southern Germany where she lived. These included Frau Reinbold, the wife of Jacob Reinbold, Christopher Frick, the butcher, and his wife, Daniel Schmid, the tailor, and his wife, and Jorg Halley, a day labourer, and his wife. The proceedings that followed, up to and including the criminal trial, lasted for six years.

Kepler unkindly described his mother as 'small, thin, dark-com-plexioned, garrulous, quarrelsome and unpleasant' (he was equally cruel about himself) but even so, when in 1620 Katharina was taken into prison, Kepler moved his entire family to southern Germany and put his career on hold to try and save her. He must have worried that his own heretical views on Lutheranism would damage her chances of survival and likewise that the witchcraft accusation against her could damage his career too.

The charge of witchcraft brought shame on all those surrounding the accused. It also brought danger, since witch-craft was considered to be hereditary, to be imbibed with the mother's milk, to run in families. We know that Kepler and his siblings begged their mother to confess if she had done anything wrong, so as to spare them shame, and also that Kepler's sister Margaretha tried to keep her mother calm by telling her that even if she was stretched on the rack it would only be one bad hour in her lifetime.

In September 1621 Katharina Kepler was ordered to be shown the instruments of torture in the hope they would intimidate her, but Kepler, by now a tiny, fragile, white-haired old woman, was unflinching. She continued to loudly proclaim her innocence and by the end of 1621 the charges against her were dropped. A few months later she died.

Chapter Eighteen
The Magic of Words and Things

Magical thinking was everywhere in those jumpy, excitable, fearful but flamboyant times. Words were magical because just by the sound of them you could change the world. When John Dee and Edward Kelley called down the spirits they did so through prayers – i.e. by the power of words. A century later, the seventeenth-century herbalist Nicholas Culpeper, who inherited John Dee's shew stone, claimed that he had used the stone to cure illnesses but that

> with its use a very great weakness always sets in and lethargy of the body. And further a certain demoniacal apparition, which exercised itself to lewdness and other depravity with women and girls, used to tempt me but by making the sign of the cross and speaking these words: 'Pah Adonai, by thy strength am I fortified, Phorrh!

Phorrh! Haricot! Gambalon!' The apparition used to fly soon or instantly, with noise and evil smell. For these obscenities I have given up the use of the crystal, and to witness these things I have written them on this sheet of the 7th day of March in the year 1651.

And then he signed it 'Nicholas Culpeper, Gentleman Student in Astrology and Physics.'

Things were magical as well. Nothing consisted of just the materials from which it was made; everything took on additional meanings and became infused with magical stories. King Arthur's Round Table and the Holy Grail, the eucharist cup (which you could see in church every Sunday), the relics of saints (in every church) – all these things were imbued with powerful meanings and significance. There were also the strange artefacts that were arriving from the New World. The Spanish brought back head-dresses, cloaks, mantles, priests' apparel, crowns, mitres and shields, many of them made using the feather art at which the Aztecs excelled. All of these things were considered very strange, desirable and beautiful, and when things are considered strange, they also inevitably acquire an aura of magic.

Objects could be dangerous – just the possession of Catholic rosary beads or the Bible in Latin could condemn you to death – and they were also often subversive. The strange artefacts from the New World raised difficult questions concerning chronology, which in those days was not a dull and geeky subject but highly contentious and political because the dates of these antiquities appeared to undermine the Church's dating of our world.

Objects also gained extra magic when they were gathered together to make a museum – and there were many of these in the sixteenth and seventeenth centuries. Back then they were called kunstkammers or cabinets of curiosities and they were imagined to be microcosms of the entire universe. The bigger the museum and the more pieces it contained, the closer it came to reflecting the abundance and fruitfulness of the universe. The magic came from the way they were displayed to reveal the hidden connections and secret affinities between objects that, superficially, seemed to come from many different times and places. Thus, they offered visitors a glimpse into the secrets of the universe, that all things are connected, and reality is one.

Sixteenth-century museums often contained automata, mechanical toys that could apparently move by themselves. Miniature figures that appeared to play musical instruments were especially popular. Rudolf II had many such automata in his museum in Prague and kings and queens across Europe likewise had gardens full of mechanical fountains. And, because there was an old belief that movement was a sign of life, people looked at these machines and wondered whether perhaps, just possibly, in some way they might be alive? (We are back to 'ensouled' statues again and whether it is possible to invest them with the life force.)

There is one of these Renaissance automata in Room 39, the Gallery of Clocks and Watches, in the British Museum. It is a three-masted toy galleon about one metre tall, made of gilded copper and iron, and designed to trundle across the dining table of a wealthy sixteenth-century patron whilst playing organ music and firing off its cannons. On its toy deck are seven miniature men who circle an eighth man on a throne. The seven miniature men are the electors of the Holy Roman Empire, the men who chose the emperor, the eighth man is the emperor himself, Rudolf II, the same emperor who lived in Prague and whom John Dee met. This was a clockwork toy made at a time when clockwork was barely understood and when anything that appeared to move by itself was invested with the magic of life. It is many years since the toy galleon's mechanism, which was the source of its perceived magic, has functioned. Now we have to imagine the clockwork and the magic that accompanied it.

Behind this love for automata is a playfulness that almost certainly goes back to Marsilio Ficino and Neoplatonism.

Some people speculated that perhaps the universe was a museum on a giant scale, which would mean that God was the greatest of all the museum-makers. And again, one of the qualities of the kunstkammers (the early museums) was amusement – because pleasure in artificial creations not guided by usefulness was a sign of God. 'In order for the demiurge' (the old Neoplatonic name for the person who created the world) 'to be able to become the absolute God he had to create something playful and lacking any use...'

Museums were also statements of power. When a king owned a museum, he also owned the universe (albeit in miniature). Thus, the kunstkammers opened up the heady possibility that through them a man could know everything. 'There is no greater pleasure,' wrote Ulisse Aldrovandi, a sixteenth-century Italian who built a natural history museum in Bologna, 'than to know everything.' It is something that any of the wizards might have said.

The Queen's Cabinet of Curiosities

Twelfth Night. The epiphany. The old year nearly done. Downstairs in the Great Hall the candles are guttering, the music fading, the Players tiptoeing away as the old queen drifts into sleep. She dreams with her head on one side and a small dog asleep in her lap, whilst the maids creep in to stack the plates and sweep the floor, and upstairs in the privy chambers the old man and his young son tend to the artefacts in the queen's cabinet of curiosities. Each of them has their head down over their work but the boy keeps glancing up with his big, angry eyes. He is brooding on his father and his mother's death and how his father killed her. Between his fingers he holds a tiny sundial, contrived by the Indians in the New World. 'Son, be careful with that thing,' says the old man gently or at least he thinks he does. He can no longer tell when he speaks and when he doesn't.

They are minor gentry down from Lincolnshire. Back home, they have a house with a gate with stone pillars – because inch by inch the old man's grandfather had pulled his family up above the level of the farmers and fishermen around them – but in the hierarchy of the royal court they are nothing. In fact, they shouldn't be here at all except that when the old man was young and good-looking – and the old queen likewise – he had fallen prey to a new disease. It hadn't existed in his grandfather's time – it was the glamour and the entrancement of the past – they called it 'history' – and the queen had noticed and found it useful. 'You will make me a cabinet of curiosities,' she had told him. 'The queen's cabinet of the strange New World. The king of France and the emperor in Prague – they all have one and I will have one too.'

It wasn't hard. He had gathered up all the curious things that my lords Drake and Raleigh had brought back from the New World – crystals and mirrors and fans and rocks with pearls and stone idols and crocodile teeth and snake skins and soft, flat slippers worn by the natives and a drum covered with deerskin and clay pipes and a knife and sheath and beautiful woven baskets. And so many eyes. Eyes on masks and plates and figurines. A pale green stone vase in the shape of a monkey with amber eyes that laugh at him. A jade mask whose eyes weep downwards at the corners. A serpent with anguished eyes and zigzag teeth snarling up at him. (And the boy's eyes of course, which are just like his mother's.)

It was three weeks ago when the queen summoned him. He had received the letter as he sat in the hall in his old oak chair with a copy of Johnson's *Topographical Study of Lincolnshire* on his lap and his sister beside him, each as silent as the other but very peaceful and companionable because no one else had shared with them their strange, silent childhood.

'The queen has summoned me,' he said.

'Will you take the boy with you?'

'I think so.'

'Brother, you must talk to him. You know he believes you killed his mother.'

'How could he think such a thing?' The old man is pale with shock.

'I've told you already. I heard it from the gamekeeper who heard it from his son. The two boys play together. And Brother, what are you doing about his education?'

But the old man could only keep on murmuring, 'How could he think such a thing?'

So, the old man and the young boy had set out together on that long, dark, midwinter journey, the horses up to their knees in mud, the cold creeping out from the ground to seize them by the ankles, the days so short they hardly saw the white winter sun before it turned red again and slipped back down behind the black trees. The boy wore only a summer jacket. 'I did not kill her,' he tries to say – but what comes out (he thinks) – though it's no more than a murmur – is 'Son, are you warm enough?' and anyway, the boy – with that pure profile – where did he get his beauty from? – rides on ahead without a word.

All day long they've been at work, emptying the shelves and drawers in the cabinet, laying out its contents on the table, cleaning and examining them. A dozen new artefacts have come into the collection. They are a gift from Sir Walter Raleigh, who is always seeking to be first in the queen's favour. One of these gifts is a double-headed turquoise serpent with two red mouths and sharp white teeth. The old man has brought his best books down from Lincolnshire and is now thumbing through them, searching for parallel examples to the turquoise serpent – though there are never parallels for these strange New World things. He has heard that when Christopher Columbus came back from the New World 100 years ago, he brought with him a half-dozen Indians, stunned, speechless people who sickened and died very quickly because they could not live in our air. But who were they? The Bible makes no mention of a fourth continent, let alone these people, so their existence makes no sense.

As he works, the old man broods on his wedding day. Why did the boy's mother marry him? He had heard that her brothers told her not to – 'Why do you want to marry that old man?' – and she didn't have a father of course, because otherwise, surely he would have told her the same thing? He thinks it must have been something about the opposite-ness of it all – he so stern, she so soft – that had appealed to her, had made her believe she could melt him. But she hadn't reckoned on the 'great silence', that gift of never talking which was passed down in his family from father to son, over three, four, even five generations. I should have spoken more to her, he thinks. Yet she had found talking easy and the sound of her words had stirred up a sadness inside him.

Now, she had vanished as completely as whatever people it was who had made these strange things on the table in front of him – which had been before the Spaniard Señor Cortés and his men had ransacked that far-off country, which was back in his grandfather's time.

Son, I loved her, he wants to say, but he's not sure it's true and he will not tell a lie. I didn't kill her, child, I just never spoke to her, he wants to say. But the words won't come out.

All morning the boy has been jumping up and down, going to the window and watching the men bringing in the scenery and the musicians arriving with their lutes and drums. His head is full of everything he's seen: horns and drums and palaces and ships and city gates and soldiers. Down below, he can hear them nailing up the scenery, the musicians tuning up their lutes and the players starting to rehearse. At noon he hears a new commotion and runs across to the mullioned glass to see that a great ship has come upriver on the rising tide. It is one of the ships back from the New World. They arrive three times a week these days, all battered and broken by that continent's storms. One day I will go to the New World and make my fortune, thinks the boy bitterly, because I am an orphan – or as good as – and that's what orphans do. Because he never loved me and maybe he's not even my father? Maybe he kidnapped me? Maybe my real father will come back to claim me? And he turns around to see the old man's white head bent over his work. I will never be like him, he thinks.

In the afternoon the queen's wizard, John Dee, arrives in his long magician's robes and his snow-white beard and with a silver scryer's basin under one arm, with which he hopes to discern who these people were who made these curious things.

'Ah, John,' says each old man to the other – they are both called John. He's aged, thinks one of them. Does he still live in that godforsaken place? thinks the other. Is he still propounding that theory? think both of them.

Meanwhile, the young boy is looking on in amazement. He has heard of Dee, of course he has, and he is thinking what he will tell his friend Jack, the gamekeeper's son back home, and how maybe they will try to do magic together out in the woods where no one can see them. The two boys often spend time together, the one moodily kicking the ground because his mother is dead and he cannot forget it and the other looking on helplessly because he is not gentry, because he is not his friend's equal, because he is only the gamekeeper's son, so what can he say?

This is how their conversation went the last time they met.

'He killed her,' says the boy.

174

'Did he?'

'That's what she said. In my dream.'

And Jack, the gamekeeper's son, thinks, I may not be gentry but everyone knows that demons sometimes come to you in dreams; that you should not trust a dream-spirit.

'Is your father a magician?'

'No, just a historian,' said the boy sadly.

Dee touches the turquoise serpent and turns it over between his fingers. He turns a page of the first book on the pile, then touches the serpent again.

'How old?' he asks.

'Who knows?'

The wizard says, 'You know we have a problem with time. The Good Book tells us that the world is six thousand years old – and how can we doubt that? – but these people kept calendars, stone calendars that you cannot destroy, and they marked off the years and those years go back far beyond six thousand. I have seen them.' The old man said nothing, he didn't catch his son's eye. He thought, Those are heretical thoughts and a wizard may say them but a mere man can't – though maybe a man as silent as him might think them?

It is midnight and the play has finished and the music died away. The old man and the boy fall asleep. It is a night of comings and goings. The boy dreams of his mother although even in his dream he thinks he is awake and that she isn't a dream but a ghost and that this is a memory, or very nearly one. In this dream-memory it is summer and they are out in the garden. She is directing the gardeners whilst he sits on a flowerpot with his knees drawn up to his chest and his face following her like a sunflower follows the sun. In his dream he is thinking, Now

I have five different memories of her – because before he only had four. The sweetness of seeing her squeezes and folds his heart painfully.

The old man dreams that he is sitting at this table and that every drawer and cupboard in the cabinet has been flung open and all its contents, all these strange and wondrous things, have left their places and are lining up in the air overhead. There, they remain quite still, as if a conjuror is holding them aloft. The old man gasps and at that moment the things – the pipes and knives and stone idols and crocodile teeth – begin to fly in the direction of the west-facing mullioned windows that look out towards the New World. They melt through the glass and vanish in the direction from which they came. The last thing to leave is a native's toy doll, wearing a tiny deerskin tunic.

Downstairs in the Great Hall the old queen sleeps. Nobody knows what she dreams of.

Chapter Nineteen
Dangerous Times

The wizards' greatest enemies were the Church and the State.

The medieval Church never liked any kind of belief in fairies – in fact it believed that the fairies were demons – but it also knew better than to overtly challenge them, belief in fairies being far too ubiquitous for that. Come the Renaissance, though, things changed. By the fifteenth century, beliefs about fairies were beginning to fuse with a fear of witchcraft and to incur the Church's implacable hostility. Nor did the Church like the high, learned, bookish magic of men like John Dee and Giordano Bruno – their Neoplatonic talk of spirits and the idea that the earth was a living creature with a soul made the Church deeply uneasy. No doubt it felt that the wizards' magic allowed them to perform a land grab on the power they believed should belong to the Church. In addition to this, from the 1520s onwards, the Church was growing increasingly alarmed by Martin Luther's teaching and so became increasingly intolerant of all heretical beliefs.

The Catholic and Protestant churches disliked all aspects of Renaissance magic – under which capacious heading they placed demons, fairies, witches, ghosts, magical words, angels (one of Luther's particular bêtes noires), the many heretical (though entirely true) astronomical beliefs of men like Kepler and Galileo, and magicians such as John Dee and Giordano Bruno. Thus, the Church lumped science and magic together and condemned them both. They were particularly alarmed by astronomical advances. First, because the heavens were God's house and therefore should not be trashed by the new astronomers' fancy ideas, and second, because, if some of the new astronomers were right and the universe was infinite, how then could men ever find God, or God find men?

After Johannes Kepler, whom Tycho Brahe met in Prague, Galileo was the next great Renaissance scientist. Galileo's restless, ingenious mind moved in many directions. He was a professor of mathematics, first in Pisa and then in Padua, and he believed passionately in testing hypotheses through practical experiments and used this approach to explore mechanics, gravity and magnetic phenomena. He helped to develop the early telescope and turned it on the heavens, discovering that the pale, pure disc of our moon is an illusion, and that in reality it has a pockmarked, mountainous surface. He also discovered that Jupiter has four moons, that Saturn has rings and that Venus appears to wax and wane like our moon.

He was also argumentative, combative and a devoted follower of Copernicus, and so quite soon incurred the anger of the Church. In February 1633 he was put on trial in Rome for his heretical thinking and threatened with torture. He might have been executed, except that he recanted and was instead sentenced to life imprisonment, which afterwards was commuted to house arrest under the condition that he remained silent for the rest of his life and denied what he knew to be true, 'that the sun stands still in the centre of the world and the earth moves', and henceforth 'not to hold, teach or defend it in any way whatsoever'.

It is easy to view Copernicus, Brahe, Kepler and Galileo as shining beacons of Enlightenment rationality in a pre-Enlightenment world, but of course this wasn't the case. None of these astronomers knew where they were going or where they would end up. They were feeling their way in the dark. Sometimes, indeed quite often, they arrived at the right answer through the wrong reasoning and so, for example, Copernicus evokes Hermes Trismegistus in his book in ways that make us wonder whether one reason for him putting the sun at the centre of the universe was not because of what we would call science, but to return to an earlier, purer religion, the one that Hermes Trismegistus believed in, with the sun as the 'visible God'.

There was another philosopher/magician who incurred the Church's wrath and that was the Italian Tommaso Campanella. He was born in Calabria, the bright child of illiterate parents, and was educated by Dominican friars until his subversive nature became apparent, whereupon they threw him out of the order. Like all the wizards he fell in love with the ideas of Plato, Pythagoras, Hermes Trismegistus and the Neoplatonists. He was also, like Giordano Bruno, wildly imaginative, particularly about the heavens, and believed in a 'plurality of successive worlds, their recurrent conflagration, their structure, if not their nature, periodically destroyed and renewed, the resolution of each in the Divine Fire, which afterwards reconstructs it'.

In 1589 Campanella went to Naples where he spent ten years or so writing whilst in and out of prison, until in November 1599 he was arrested in connection with a planned uprising against the Spanish authorities. The prison records describe him as having a black beard and being dressed in layman's clothing: a black cap, a black overcoat, leather trousers and 'a mantel of that wool commonly called cheap Morano' (in other words, Morano shawl apart, the outfit of all revolutionaries, everywhere). He was charged with claiming that sexual liberty, including sodomy, is not a sin, that the Turkish doctrine is better than Christianity, that the mass celebrated by a priest in mortal sin is not valid, that all the existing religious orders are unnecessary, and eternal salvation is possible, even without baptism. Campanella might have been executed, except that he claimed insanity. The authorities tortured him to see if he was only pretending to be mad, but when he passed this test they sentenced him instead to life imprisonment.

Campanella was in prison for twenty-seven years, much of that time in the gloomy Castel Nuovo in the heart of Naples. He was sometimes treated with great cruelty; sometimes with comparative leniency. Whilst in prison he wrote his most famous book, *The City of the Sun*, which was a utopian dream of a better world.

•

The Protestant churches were just as quick as Catholics to condemn magic and early forms of science. Luther, with the Protestant churches behind him, thundered against Copernicus, disliked mystical Neoplatonism and condemned any belief in ghosts on the grounds that the frontier between the living and the dead was sealed for ever and could never be crossed, except once in death.

Protestant thinkers also believed that the Catholic Church was itself inclined to magic – as evidence, they pointed out that the Catholics claimed to be able to turn bread and wine into the body and blood of Christ at mass every Sunday – and it's true that in some ways Catholic thinking was more accommodating of occult ideas. For instance, ghosts might be the dead travelling to or from purgatory, whilst the Protestants, having discarded the idea of purgatory, couldn't use that explanation. But even so, the Catholic Church was no friend to magic. Nor to the activities of the star men.

It was not only the Church that was upset by magical beliefs; so too were Elizabeth's Protestant ministers. They saw magic as subversive because it possessed a kind of power that was a threat and a challenge to Elizabeth's authority. For politicians like William Cecil, it was also associated with Catholicism, the latter being increasingly seen as a dangerously seditious belief and no better than conjuring. As the century went on, Catholicism became increasingly tainted by the dangerous presence in England of Mary Queen of Scots and this also contributed to a backlash against magic in its many forms.

With hindsight, we can see that the Florentine demagogue Girolamo Savonarola, who seized power in Florence in 1494, was only the beginning of the backlash. Even in the more tolerant fifteenth century, Marsilio Ficino had got into trouble for a book he wrote called *De Vita*, in which he speculated whether it was possible to summon celestial forces to bring inanimate objects to life, after which accusations of heresy and black magic began to be whispered against him and it took all of his persuasiveness to get himself out of this trouble.

During the sixteenth century the backlash from the Church and State grew stronger. For the twentieth-century scholar

Frances Yates, who studied both John Dee and Giordano Bruno, the Church's increasing hostility to magic was also a reaction against Platonism and the Renaissance in general. As an example, she cites a book called *De Harmonia Mundi*, written by the Italian Francesco Giorgi, published in 1525 and a copy of which is now in the British Library. Inside it, the censor has written in black ink that this book abounds with the arguments of Platonists and Kabbalists and should be read with caution. (John Dee also owned a copy of this book.)

In 1542 Pope Pius III established the Supreme Sacred Congregation of the Roman and Universal Inquisition, which served as the final court of appeal in trials of heresy. In 1559 the Catholic Church also established the Index of Forbidden Books (the *Index Librorum Prohibitorum*) – to prohibit or censure offensive titles and stop the spread of heresy. The complete works of more than five hundred writers were placed on that first list, including works by the humanist Erasmus. Later, his books were joined by works by Johannes Kepler and, most famously of all, Galileo. Being on the Index of Forbidden Books meant that Catholics couldn't read, quote or discuss your work. Kepler's books were on the Index from 1621 to 1835 and there was a general ban on books promoting heliocentrism until 1758.

Meanwhile in 1542, Henry VIII also passed a law that made witchcraft a capital crime. Confessions could be elicited by torture and if the defendant was found guilty they would be punished by death, usually by hanging, sometimes by being burnt alive at the stake. More laws against witchcraft were passed in 1562 and 1604.

And yet, attitudes towards magic and alchemy were always touched with ambivalence. On the one hand, monarchs disliked alchemy for all the reasons cited above, and because they feared that by multiplication (i.e. making money) an alchemist could undermine the existing currency. On the other hand, many monarchs, Queen Elizabeth included, kept their own alchemist in the hope that they could do exactly that – make money.

To some extent the punishment you received for practising magic depended on whether your magic was considered good or bad. It also depended on the character and gender of the person practising it; men obviously had more latitude than women and prosperous men more than their poorer counterparts. And, it also depended on the degree of anxiety in society at large then, and the extent to which onlookers felt duped and taken for fools.

Through this dangerous world John Dee trod with care. He was only arrested once – in 1555 during Queen Mary's reign when he was accused of using divination to predict the monarch's death. This was considered treason and he was sent to the Tower of London, though he was not there for long. Later in Queen Elizabeth's reign, he was something of a favourite of hers, which meant that he was protected and never again lost his footing in this dangerously magical and political world until he came home from his great adventure in 1589. He was almost an old man then and found that his many enemies had turned against him.

CHAPTER TWENTY
GIORDANO BRUNO

In early summer 1583 there arrived in London – as if blown in on the eastern wind – a wandering, self-styled Italian wizard called Giordano Bruno.

Bruno was a little man, an excommunicated priest, with beautiful dark eyes, a huge imagination, an unshakeable belief in himself and an absolute inability to keep his mouth shut when he was in trouble, which was often.

He had been born on the slopes of Mount Vesuvius, adopted by the Dominican friars (like Tommaso Campanella) and then expelled by them for reading heretical literature. After this, he left Italy and wandered across France and Germany, writing and lecturing on astronomy and philosophy and becoming known for being a witty, opinionated, quick-talking and entertaining dinner guest. Unlike John Dee, he never owned a house or belonged to any one place. He therefore had none of the accoutrements of a wizard that John Dee possessed – the library, the alchemical stills, the collection of magical objects (the wizard's museum?). Nor did he have any of Dee's diplomacy and charm. Instead, he was passionate, vehement, scornful and sarcastic. He also had the wizards' wandering ways.

Like John Dee he was saturated in Neoplatonism and believed that the world has a soul and that everything in the universe is alive, including the planets and stars. He accepted that the planets had intelligence, because how else would they know how to stay on their courses? He thought that every element in the universe was connected and made one living entity that shared a world soul. He also believed that the air was full of demons and spirits, rational beings but with rarified bodies made up of aether.

He believed many other things as well, all of which the Church considered to be heretical. He was not a practising scientist or even a protoscientist. He was more like a philosopher of science, and always strangely intuitive about the nature of the world. This was a time when most people believed that although the universe was huge in comparison to human beings, it nonetheless had edges, it was not infinite and the entire body, the earth and the heavens, was neatly made and dainty enough to sit in the palm of God's hand.

But Giordano Bruno (and a small number of others) dreamt of something very different.

Bruno believed that the stars are numberless and the universe is infinite, that our sun is a star, that all the stars out there are suns with planets travelling round them, that there are many, many worlds and that the universe goes on for ever. The idea of its vastness and abundance entranced Bruno. For him, infinite meant more than the mere absence of limitation. On the contrary, it meant 'the immeasurable and inexhaustible abundance of reality ... Man no longer lived in the world as a prisoner enclosed within the narrow walls of a finite physical universe. He can traverse the air and break through all the imaginary boundaries of the celestial spheres.' And Bruno was right, of course, that the universe is infinite, or at least so vast that we will never know the location of its edges. There was something uncanny about his intuition. How could he know that the universe was like this? It was as if he had torn a rent in the old, medieval cosmos created by the Church and through this tear had broken into our world and brought back news of it the other way.

He also declared that he doubted the Trinity, rejected the cult of saints, believed in transmigration of the soul and that magic could be a good thing, and stated that Christ was a notorious magician, not a god, and that he himself sympathised with Arian heretics. In one of his many stints in prison, the other prisoners claimed that he had looked up at the stars and said that God needed the world as much as the world needed God and that the latter would be nothing without the world, and for this reason God did nothing but create new worlds. Many people believed that Bruno was a wizard or a magician, a man who understood the secret workings of the universe and could bend them to his own desires, both good and evil, but the Church was afraid of him because of his wild and heretical imagination.

Bruno spent several years in Paris, but in 1583 he decided to come to London. He was not the first magician to arrive in the city from the Continent. Seventy years before, in 1510, the German magician Heinrich Cornelius Agrippa (whose book John Dee kept on his desk) had arrived in England to be greeted with great cordiality by John Colet, the dean of St Paul's Cathedral. Yet, those were gentler and more optimistic times. Now, unbeknownst to Bruno, the British ambassador, Henry Cobham, sent a message back ahead of Bruno to Francis Walsingham, Elizabeth's spymaster. It said: 'Doctor Jordano

Bruno Nolano, a professor in philosophy, intends to pass through England; his religion I cannot commend.'

In April 1583, Bruno came to London to the French ambassador's residence in Salisbury Court. He was thirty-five years old and had spent years wandering and living in poverty and although he was still witty, opinionated, bold and quick-talking, he was probably also shabby, irritable and sorely in need of material comforts. Such was his reputation that in the good times, before his fall and despite his penniless upbringing, he could still move in exalted circles. The scruffy Bruno even knew the aristocratic Philip Sidney well enough to dedicate a book to him.

We don't know if the two wizards, Dee and Bruno, ever met, although the dates we have – assuming they are accurate – mean it is possible. If they did meet, we can be sure that they would have squared up to each other with scarcely concealed competitiveness. And, if they didn't meet we can be sure that they would have heard of each other.

Whilst he was in England Giordano Bruno gave two lectures at the university church in Oxford, one on astronomy and the other on the immortality of the soul. In one of his later books, he includes the letter by which he introduced himself to the Oxford professors. 'Salutations from Philotheus Jordanus Brunus of Nola,' he writes, in his usual conceited and big-talking fashion. 'Doctor of a more scientific theology, professor of a purer and less harmful learning, known in the chief universities of Europe, a philosopher approved and honourably received, a stranger with none but the uncivilised and ignoble ... tamer of presumptuous and obstinate ignorance ... whom only the propagators of folly and hypocrites detest, whom the honourable and studious love, and whom noble minds applaud ...' And so on and so on.

His lecture was received badly, as we know from an account of that same event in a book written by George Abbot (who later became Archbishop of Canterbury). The book was published in 1604 though only rediscovered in 1960. Abbot's account begins as follows:

When the Italian Didapper, who entitled himself Philotheus Jordannus Brunus Nolanus, magis elaborate Theologia Doctor ... with a name longer than his body, had in the traine of Alasco, the Polish Duke, seene our University in the year 1583, his hart was on fire, to make himself by some worthy exploite, to become famous in that celebrious place. Not long after returning again, when he had more boldly than wisely, got up into the highest place of our best and most renowned schoole, stripping up his sleeves like some juggler, and telling us much of chentrum & chirculus & circumferenchia (after the pronunciation of his Country language) he undertook among very many other matters to set foote the opinion of Copernicus, that the earth did goe round, and the heavens did stand still; whereas in truth it was his own head which rather did run round and his braines did not stand still.

In this vivid account it is easy to see Bruno rolling up his sleeves, climbing into the pulpit and beginning to speak as if in a trance. Despite his small stature he would have laid down enormous truths, one after another, with absolute certainty: that there are eternal verities (the great Plato tells us this) that lie behind all the confusions of the world as we know it, that the nearer heavens are filled with demons and that the universe is infinite. It is not true that it is made finite by walls of aether as they believed in centuries past. Moreover, it is the case that God has created many worlds, because he needs these worlds far more than the worlds need him and so he can't stop making them (at this, a murmur of shock would have begun in the lecture hall and spread rapidly beyond the doors), that Aristotle is often wrong (more shock) and of course – as Signor Copernicus established forty years ago – the earth goes round the sun (not the sun around the earth), as indeed do all of the planets and to think anything else is to let our minds get pointlessly tangled up in needless complexities.

It was the old Copernican heresy. According to Abbot, a couple of scholars shouted out, 'Leave Aristotle out of this' and the master got to his feet and hurried away to his study where he found a book written by that Italian heretic Marsilio Ficino 100 years before and he came back waving it triumphantly. It was proof that everything the little friar had said was just more of the old foreign heresies, and plagiarism to boot.

George Abbot sided with the Oxford dons and against Bruno and Copernicus, and thus exactly on the wrong side of history. Bruno's references to the same event, in his book *The Ash Wednesday Supper*, are as sarcastic and scornful of his opponents as you would expect. He said of Oxford University that 'a doctor's degree is to be had there as cheaply as sardines'. After causing this uproar, Bruno had to be smuggled out of Oxford, probably by river, and back to the French embassy in London.

CHAPTER TWENTY-ONE
THE GREAT ADVENTURE

In the 1570s you could have looked at John Dee's life and (almost) thought that he was a worldly man. He taught mathematics, attended court and was embroiled in the dramas surrounding the search for the Northwest Passage. He shared his maps, his books and his knowledge with the explorer Martin Frobisher, who was launching expeditions to find the routes to Cathay which were believed to lie to the north of North America. From his first expedition, Frobisher brought home a small lump of black rock from near Baffin Island in the desolate wastes of north-eastern Canada. Soon, word spread round London that the black rock contained gold, and gold fever erupted. A second and a third expedition set sail (with both the queen and John Dee investing in them) and by the time the black rock was officially proven to be worthless, Frobisher's partner Michael Lok was bankrupt.

And yet despite all this, John Dee was never as worldly as this pursuit of gold (albeit misguided) might suggest. He was in fact, preoccupied with dreams about subjects that were even stranger and more spiritual than New World gold.

For years he had tried hard to read the mind of God and to understand what God had created and why. He had tried to understand the universe mathematically and astrologically. He had tried to read the world like a book and had built the finest library in England to aid this process. He had looked at the world through the eyes of the Jewish Kabbalah and the Neoplatonists, had been – in the words of the seventeenth-century scholar Meric Casaubon – 'A Cabbalistical man up to the ears' – but in all this he had failed. And so he had come to believe that the Book of Nature, which was how he thought of the world, was decaying and corrupt and could never reveal its secrets and that there remained only one way to reach the mind of God, and that was by talking to God's angels who had been present when God first created the world. Only thus could we ever understand God's intentions.

As John Dee had searched for the meaning of God's creation, there had been a steady drumbeat of portents – each more momentous than the last if only their significance could be understood. First, there was a new star seen in the constellation of Cassiopeia in 1572, the first new star since the Star of Bethlehem; then a comet seen in 1577; then an earthquake in London early one morning in April 1580; and now in 1583 – most portentous of all – the stars were about to complete a great cycle, more than 900 years in duration, when a conjunction of Jupiter and Saturn re-entered what was called the Fiery Trigon.

The concept of the Fiery Trigon was as follows. The signs of the zodiac, twelve in all, were broken down into four groups of three, called trigons, which were imagined as triangles within the circular edge of the zodiacal wheel. Every thirty years, Saturn and Jupiter lined up in a great conjunction. For about 200 years they lined up within the same trigon, before moving on to a new one. Then every 800 years or so, they lined up in the Fiery Trigon, the one with the sign of Aries in it, which was considered the most momentous of them all. In 1583, this moment was about to occur and it seemed to Dee and others like him to presage vast changes across the world.

So, sometime in the early part of 1583, the same year that Giordano Bruno came to England, Dee began to plan a great adventure. He prepared to leave England and travel all the way across Europe in search of wealthy, powerful patrons, in Krakow and Prague, the latter being where the melancholy philosopher emperor Rudolf II had created a city full of artists, poets and erudite philosophers, all of them book lovers like Dee, all of them inclined towards bookish magic and all of them in search of the meaning of life. Rudolf was nominally a Catholic but in practice he was tolerant of all religions. He also had a fine library and had created the finest cabinet of curiosities (museum) in the whole of Europe – with, amongst many other artefacts, a six-foot narwhal whale tusk, the dried remains of a dragon, mandrake roots, plague remedies and virgins' blood. It was also full of automata – magical clockwork devices.

Dee must have yearned to see all these things, must have believed that such a city would be conducive to his experiments and that having so much magic all around him would ensure his own magic worked.

Yet, because he was both wayward but also domestic and home-loving and yet couldn't give up on his dreams, he decided to take his wife Jane and their three children with him. He must have had reasons, which we can only guess at – maybe trouble at court, maybe the growing conservative backlash against magic or maybe John Dee, like most alchemists, had debts? – which would explain why he devised this plan at this particular moment. And if – as seems to be the case – the angels were encouraging him to go, we might wonder why Edward Kelley also wanted to leave England?

For whatever reason, on 21 September 1583 the Dee family and their friends departed by boat for Eastern Europe. In this group of semi-fugitives were Dee, his wife Jane and their three small children: Arthur, Katherine and the youngest, Roland, who was only nine months old. With them were Edward Kelley and his family. Joanna Kelley was only twenty and her two small children were, respectively, three and two. The Dees also took all of their clothes, their most favoured possessions, the 600 books Dee loved best and his magical equipment, including his scryer's mirror and his Holy Table – all of which had been packed into numerous trunks.

They waited for nightfall and then set off from Mortlake, passing the Lambeth marshes to their right and first the Palace of Westminster and then the Palace of Whitehall on their left. It was approximately a month since Giordano Bruno had been run out of Oxford and they would have passed the water steps that led to Salisbury Court and to the French embassy, where at this moment Bruno was taking refuge. They darted under London Bridge, saw the Tower of London disappearing on their left and followed the river down past Deptford village and the Palace of Greenwich.

As the river widened out they transferred to a bigger boat which took them out into the Thames estuary where two sailing ships were awaiting them. Dee, Kelley, their wives and all the children embarked on the larger of the two ships, whilst the servants and their luggage were stowed away on the second one. Once ready, they headed for the open sea and for Europe. Thus, it transpired that John Dee was no different from all the other wizards – wandering, nomadic, obsessive, unable to give up on his dreams.

•

Dee, Kelley and their families were abroad for six years. First, they went by boat to northern Germany and then by coach, through winter storms and snow and floods, to Krakow, which was then the capital of Poland. From here, they wrote to the emperor in Prague, which was the capital of the Holy Roman Empire. At last, they received an invitation to come to the capital and by August 1584 they reached Prague, a city that was indeed as magical as its reputation suggested. For a while their careers flourished there, until they were caught up in the machinations of the Jesuits and the pro-Catholic movement who saw them as a threat. Eventually in May 1586, the emperor expelled them, ordering them to leave Prague within a week.

From there they went to Třeboň Castle, south of Prague in Bohemia, where they were taken in by Count Rosenberg, a wealthy patron of alchemy, and so they could continue with their angel experiments. But then, in April 1587, John Dee's diaries begin to tell a peculiar story. Dee writes that Edward Kelley says the seven-year-old angel Madimi has offered Dee the chance to understand God's secrets, an offer that Dee is delighted to accept, and yet, in the next breath, Dee also says that Kelley has detected a different and utterly abhorrent meaning in Madimi's words. Very quickly, Dee learns what this meaning is. Madimi is saying that God is instructing the two men 'to use their wives in common', for – she says – 'All things are possible and permitted to the godly. Nor are sexual organs more hateful to them than the faces of every mortal. Thus, it will be: the illegitimate will be joined with the true son. And the east will be united with the west, and the south with the north.'

Dee is shocked. Surely, he says, Madimi must mean spiritually, not carnally, but no, the answer comes back from Madimi: 'I speak of both.' Despite his shock Dee agrees and so afterwards he tells Jane, 'I see that there is no other remedy but as hath been said of our cross-matching, so it must needs be done.' Thereupon, says Dee, 'she fell weeping and trembling for a quarter of an hour and I pacified her as well as I could, and so in fear of God and in believing of his admonishment, did persuade her, that she showed herself prettily resolved to be content for God his sake and for his secret purposes, to obey the admonishment. At length that same night in bed she yielded to do the commanded doctrine and requested that we might all have our lodgings in one chamber that I might not be far from her.'

At this moment the reader's eyes – or at least *this* reader's eyes – are wide open in astonishment, not least because these momentous instructions are coming from Madimi, a seven-year-old girl. Why would you do something so significant on the say-so of a very small girl? One reason (though we will never know for sure) might be the value that Neoplatonism put on the childlike, the idea that the world is a kunstkammer (a museum) made by God where he loves to play, and from there the idea that the truth might emerge from the mouths of children.

Once he has secured Jane's agreement, John Dee writes a covenant that all four of them, the Kelleys and the Dees, sign. It states that they will do God's will and on 21 May, Dee writes in his diary just two laconic words, *Pactum factum.* 'It is done.'

But this is not the end of the revelations in Dee's diary, because the natural question then arises: if Kelley slept with Jane Dee, did John Dee sleep with Kelley's wife Joanna? Sure enough, on the next pages of the diary (and here I am quoting from Edward Fenton's 1998 edition of the diaries), John Dee writes that Edward Kelley claims, in sentences that Dee has crossed out but are still legible, that a horseman has come to him on a great, white horse. The horseman asks, 'Kelley, was thy brother's wife obedient and humble to thee?' to which Kelley answers, 'She was.' The horseman then asks, 'Dee, was thy brother's wife obedient unto thee?' Dee says that she was obedient, and the horseman says, 'Even as you were one obedient to another, even so shall the Lord deal with you.' Then Edward Kelley says that Madimi has come and that she (Madimi) is asking, 'Dee, dost thou lie or say troth, in saying she was obedient?' To which Dee answers, 'I counted her obedient for what she did whereof she thought her obedience to consist; for that she did not come after as I thought she would she might seem in some part disobedient, but if it offended not God, it offended not me, and I beseech God it did not offend him...' This sounds very much as if John Dee slept with Kelley's wife as well, or tried to, but that she slipped away.

The next few pages of the diary are equally strange. In a flood of extravagant language that makes you realise what a great talker Edward Kelley must have been, he claims that a golden woman is appearing to him and saying: 'Few or none that are earthly have embraced me, for I am shadowed with the circle of the sun and covered with the morning clouds. My feet are swifter than the winds and my hands are sweeter than the morning dew. My garments are from the beginning and my dwelling place is in myself. I am deflowered and yet a virgin. Happy is he that embraceth me in the night season. I am sweet and in the day full of pleasure. My company is a harmony of many cymbals. I am a harlot for such as ravish me and a virgin with such as know me not. For lo, I am loved of many, and I am a lover to many. Cast out your old strumpets and burn their clothes, abstain from the company of other women that are defiled, that are sluttish and not so handsome and beautiful as I...' And then a green woman, who is standing next to the golden woman, says, 'Neither shall the things that shall be opened unto you be revealed unto your wives...' All of which sounds very much like a call for free love, at least for the men, but which is to be kept hidden from their wives.

Nine months later, Jane Dee gave birth to a baby boy.

After these tumultuous events, the relationship between the two men fell apart and in the end Kelley went east but Dee and his family came home to Mortlake. There they discovered that Dee's magical library had been trashed and many of the books stolen, along with all his scientific equipment, including the glass equipment that was crucial to his alchemical experiments. The great celestial and terrestrial globes that Mercator had given him had also been taken. In the weeks leading up to Dee's departure in 1583, he had made a catalogue of his books. It is 172 pages long and still exists today, even though the library itself is long since gone.

The destruction of John Dee's library was one of the great tragedies of his life. Even today, no one knows the exact reasons behind it. Until recently, it was thought that the library was trashed by a local mob, outraged by Dee's magic, but more recently the finger has been pointed at high-born book thieves. Dee had left his books in the care of Jane's brother, Nicholas

Fromond, but Fromond, as Dee said angrily later, 'unduely sold it presently upon my departure or caused it to be carried away'. As scholars have traced what happened to Dee's books, they have noticed how often his signature was rubbed out and replaced by another name – usually a certain Nicholas Saunders, who seems either to have been the thief or to have received stolen goods on a vast scale.

After the trashing of Dee's library, the queen sent him north to Manchester to manage Chetham's Library, but he was never happy there and in 1605 Jane and at least two of his children, Margaret and Madinia, died of the plague.

(History records, without comment, that Dee named this second daughter, born abroad, after the seven-year-old spirit girl. We cannot know for certain why he did so, though we can guess that he felt that Madimi, the spirit girl, was his daughter; that she had somehow floated free of her corporeal body and needed anchoring in a child that he and Jane had conceived.)

After this, Dee finally came home to Mortlake, an old and broken man, to die beside the Thames. The old queen was dead, there was a new king on the throne and Dee's reputation as a magician was passing into a half-forgotten legend. All his erstwhile patrons and supporters were dead – Philip Sidney in 1586, Robert Dudley in 1588 and Francis Walsingham in 1590. In Mortlake, Dee lived in poverty, quite quietly, with his youngest daughter Katherine to look after him. He brooded on his many failures, though he still hoped to find the answer to when the world would end and why God had created us.

Story Seven
Wife to Dr Dee

When word got round that the wizard was returning, all those to whom he owed money gathered outside the house at Mortlake. There had been many births, marriages and deaths since the wizard had gone away and many young men and women who had been children when they last saw him were now grown up. Even back then, in his glory days, the wizard had been a fairy tale and a bedtime story and now, even more so. As they waited, the villagers thought about the food they had cooked, the clothes they had laundered and the garden they had tended, all for no pay. They were amazed at how trusting they had been. If he was really such a great wizard how come he hadn't made the money to pay them?

Five children sat on the wall and watched. They belonged to Will Shannon, the queen's under-gardener at the Palace of Richmond, just up the river. Katherine was the oldest. She was twelve, pale and proud and anxious-looking and wanting to be good. Next came Alice, who was nine and who dogged her sister's footsteps with her clever comments – they struggled a lot over who got to tell the other what to do. After that came the twins, who were eight, and last of all their brother Thomas, who was four. He clutched his toy lamb and couldn't even tell the twins apart, but he was still the apple of their father's eye.

With them was Granny, who was a little old woman, bent like a wheel and wearing a tall black hat. She had brought them curd cheese wrapped up in muslin from the cow back in Watlington. When Granny came to stay, she made them say their prayers morning and night, but their father turned silent and Granny would get angry and shout at him: 'I don't know how you can be my son, you're not even house-trained,' and their father would mutter back, 'And nor are you, woman, nor are you.'

'Shush, Granny,' said the children.

After the wizard and his family left, the house had sat as quiet as a mouse, low down in its garden on the riverside, sunlit and silent by day and shrouded in darkness by night. Dr Dee had taken most, but not all, of his magic. The children played as close as they dared to the garden wall. In the second summer the wall began to crumble, and they could see inside to where strange flowers were springing up. Each flower had scarlet petals, the edges of which were twisted into flames. 'Granny, Granny,' they shouted and the old women came and peered at the flowers and measured the height of the wall with her eyes, wondering whether she dared send Katherine in to take a cutting. But the magic even frightened Granny.

After some months, half a dozen men – they looked like the queen's men – arrived with a wagon and servants and broke down the padlock on the iron gates at the front of the house and so got in and came out with armfuls of books. The villagers gathered to watch and the servants scowled at them, but the men took no notice. Those who had seen the wizard leave could affirm that he had taken a boatload of his favourite books with him and yet his library must be of considerable size, because however many books he had taken there seemed an infinite number left behind.

In the second winter, a tinker in the nearby tavern claimed that he had seen a book fly out of the window of the wizard's house. 'Books don't fly,' said one of his audience. 'This one did,' said the tinker.

In the third year, news came back to Mortlake that the wizard and his family had reached the occult city of Prague and that the wizard was cooking up magic there with the Holy Roman Emperor. After that there was silence, until in the fifth year they heard that the emperor and the wizard had fallen out over a magical project to upend every church tower in Prague so that the bells rang underground. And then, in the sixth year, they heard that the wizard was coming home and had in fact reached the City of London with his family (now much larger). Early in the morning a week later they heard that he was loading his family into a carriage and was about to set off from the Strand, and that he would be here within the day. Only half an hour later, however, a man passing by on horseback shouted out that he had seen the wizard on the road where a wheel had fallen off the family's carriage and that they had had to pause to mend it.

By the time the carriage could be seen in the distance, beating its way towards them, a crowd had gathered outside on the green. The carriage drew to a halt and a quiver ran through the crowd. The coachman opened the door and down stepped one, two, three, four little children, all thin and sunburnt and strangely dressed. They stood, dazed and confused, at the bottom of the steps.

Next stepped down a tall, thin, weary-looking woman – the wizard's wife – she had grey hair and carried a small child in her arms. The five children on the wall watched through narrowed eyes. If you counted the child in the wife's arms, these thin, sunburnt, foreign children were the same number as themselves. They also, though strangely dressed, looked richer. They had clearly never gone hungry.

'I wouldn't dress my children like that,' said Granny.

'Shush, Granny,' the children said.

And then at last, scooping up his long robes and lowering himself gingerly out of the carriage, came first the feet and then the legs and then the long white beard and, finally, the face of the wizard, his eyes very remote. He looked like God. A shudder ran through the crowd. They knew what they had done. They waited to see how the wizard would take it.

•

Years later when Jane Dee lay dying in Manchester, she remembered the day of their wedding and how all summer long they had kept open house – it was the custom – and the ladies had come from court to see what it was like to be married to a magician. When they walked up the garden path their dresses were so thickly embroidered with flowers you couldn't tell where their dresses ended and the flowerbeds began. 'Does he do his magic in bed?' the ladies asked.

The local people came too and peered down the steps of his alchemical laboratory, speculating how rich the wizard must be. And my Lord Burghley came, whose pragmatic mind was secretly entranced by occult matters. And so likewise Walsingham, who was not so much entranced as sceptical, but even so, despite himself he loved the wizard. The wizard had a slow, sweet smile. Everyone loved him. She was amazed at how many friends he had.

The wizard was in charge of all their dreams and desires. He knew her desires even before she did.

He was also the most husbandly man she had ever met. In the evenings he liked to sit close to her, whilst she sewed and he read. She thought that with God's blessing it is easy to love, that if God wills it the love will flow forth like honey. There was just one thing. 'No spirits,' she said to him, the day of their wedding. 'I will not have spirits in my house.' 'No spirits,' said the wizard, always compliant.

And she remembered the day that Edward Kelley had arrived. 'I need a scryer,' said the wizard and word must have got out that he was looking for a spirit-medium because, shortly afterwards, the agent Mr Clerkson appeared at the door with a young man beside him. 'You were asking for a scryer,' he said. 'Step forward, Mr Kelley,' and he stood to one side and a tall young man stepped forward into the light. He wore a dark scarf over his ears. He looked about twenty and both petulant and resentful, and yet somehow the wizard grew to love him. 'My dear Mr Kelley,' he liked to say.

She remembered the night they left and that terrible journey to Bohemia, how the children were always crying and how she had left her best dress behind and there were nothing but wearisome days of travelling and thieving inn keepers in towns where nobody spoke English, and a pawn shop in Bohemia where she wept as she parted with her favourite necklaces. 'Dear heart,' said the wizard, 'all these things and much more will be returned to you when God grants us his glory,' but Jane couldn't stop crying. And then they came at last to Krakow – and after that there was never a time when a child wasn't ill – first Arthur, then Katherine, then Roland – and so she was always hanging over a sickbed where a child lay, limp and unprotesting, whilst little Fanny ushered in one shockingly superior and unhelpful foreign doctor after another. One of them said, 'Your husband is a wizard. Let him do magic.' That was when Katherine nearly died.

And meanwhile, the wizard and Edward Kelley were always in some other part of that big house and with much plotting and conspiracy were devising a letter that would capture the attention of the Holy Roman Emperor in Prague. When the house went quiet, she knew they were calling on the angels for advice. Sometimes, she met them in one of the house's many corridors and then the wizard was always solicitous – it lowered his spirits to think that Jane might be cross with him – whilst in the background, Mr Kelley damped down his excitement and tried to look serious.

At last, the letter went off and shortly afterwards a letter came back, ordering Dr Dee and Edward Kelley to attend the emperor in Prague, and so the two men left with much excitement and a carriageload of books. Afterwards, a peacefulness fell upon the house and the children got up from their sickbeds and suddenly their bright eyes (they looked like field mice) were to be seen everywhere, under beds and behind curtains and in the kitchen with their noses in the cooking pots.

And Mrs Kelley too emerged from the bedroom where she seemed to have been hiding. She had dark eyes and was sharp and somehow narrow (narrow shoulders, narrow hips as if made to slip through doors only half-ajar) and had a despairing manner. 'This is Mrs Kelley,' Mr Kelley had said on the first day they met. Later that day, Jane had heard Kelley saying to her husband, 'I cannot abide my wife. I do not love her, I detest her.'

Now, she slipped out of the bedroom, with a book in one hand and her usual half-smile, and sat down next to Jane, who was sewing. Mrs Kelley never sewed. 'What are you reading?' asked Jane and Mrs Kelley said, with another of her vague and rueful half-smiles, 'Oh, it is the story of the world and all us men and women in it.'

Letters, full of news and excitement, came from the wizard in Prague – 'The angels are with us. We are very close to finding the Philosopher's Stone' – and then came another letter asking for the presence of the wives, and so it was that Jane and Mrs Kelley found themselves packed tight into a carriage with the children, crossing a strange landscape of marshlands and sand dunes and deep forests and fishponds, bound for Prague.

And she remembered Prague and what a strange city it was, with its blackened spires and the great clock in the marketplace where a skeleton with a bell rang in the hour, and its taverns called The Unicorn or The Spider or some such strange name, and its whispered stories of a man-monster called the golem. High up on the hill were the castle's gilded towers and weathervanes and between Castle Hill and the town was the great, flat, flowing river, curling like a dragon. Even the children were stunned by its strangeness and stopped falling ill, instead growing quite robust. They were four little English children – three walking and one in the nursemaid's arms – the three arranged in order of height, escorted by herself and the nursery maid, eyes wide open in amazement as they walked to the park each day. In the afternoons she and the wizard went out to tea or received visitors at home. The ladies of Prague came to eye up the English wizard and the local wizards – she was beginning to see that there were wizards in every town in Europe – came to measure themselves against this foreign competitor.

Their fortunes increased and they took on the lease for a fine house owned by the emperor's physician. It had five good bedrooms and a study for the wizard. Their bedroom looked west towards their old house in Mortlake a thousand leagues away, but their breakfast room looked east to where the sun rose on even stranger lands. It had a garden with a fine pear tree and a vineyard and gardener. The winters here were colder but the summers warmer and the garden grew all manner of things that you couldn't grow back home. When the local wizards heard what Jane liked they brought her presents of strange bulbs and cuttings. Distantly, she could remember the young woman in Mortlake, with her sheets washed in scented water, her laundry carefully folded, her sun dial and her knot garden. How very far we have travelled, she thought in amazement. They will not know us back home, she thought.

One day, Jane was outside tending to her pots when Mr Kelley came limping up to her. He stopped to watch her work. She did not like him. He made her mouth pucker up in distaste.

'My magic could make your garden grow better,' he said.

'God's magic is enough for me.' (She was very stiff.)

'Do you mean my magic is not God's magic?' he asked her sharply. How keen he was to set traps for her.

Another day, Jane was summoned to meet the emperor. 'It's a good sign,' said the wizard. 'We are in his favour.'

The emperor lived high on Castle Hill, halfway to heaven. Jane's carriage climbed slowly up the steep and forested road and went in by the west gate where six soldiers escorted her along a tunnel and then by a bridge across the ravine and so into the emperor's garden. She saw gravelled pathways, fountains, statues in apses, lemon and orange trees and flowerbeds with salvias and roses. She could hear the roar of the emperor's lions in their cages at the bottom of the ravine. Far down on the plain she could see the city's church spires.

They came to the emperor's summer house. Inside, a small man with dark, hollow eyes and a lantern jaw stood at a table, planting a flower in a pot. It was the man himself, the emperor of half the world. Jane heard him mutter in German, 'You are late.' A servant whispered in his ear. 'Mistress Jane,' said the emperor, 'I hear that you love gardens.'

So out they went into the gardens. 'Tell me what you think of this,' he said, pointing to a small shrub with shiny leaves in a wooden pot. 'My ships brought it back from the New World. And these' – pointing to great heaps of blowsy blossom – 'are from our Asian lands, and these' – pointing to a flower with tall, sharp petals like daggers – 'the Mohammedans call them Laleh.' All this was said very fast and without so much as a glance in her direction. He's shy, she thought in amazement.

'Now this,' he said, 'is a rose of course, but of a very special kind. It comes from Persia. Do you have roses in England?'

'Yes, but not like these. How do you protect them in winter?'

'My gardeners have many ingenious solutions.'

And then – moving down the terrace – 'Your husband is a remarkable man, Mistress Jane. One day he will open up a road between the worlds and we will walk along it, although...' – and here, he suddenly turned on Jane and fixed her with his dark eyes. His voice was as cold as ice – 'I could wish that sometimes he weren't so ardent.'

Husband, husband, thought Jane in alarm, you must not tell him what to do. He is the emperor of half the world. You must not do it.

Within a week their disgrace was plain for all to see. Suddenly, there were a great number of Jesuit priests in Prague, sent there by the Pope in Rome. 'My enemies have been plotting against me,' said the wizard furiously, but it was too late.

Within two weeks they were expelled from Prague for practising magic and travelling south to Třeboň, the children crying and all the wizard's books piled high in a second carriage. Now there was another castle – they were staying in the residence of Count Rosenberg – and the children were sick again, the doctors unreasonable, the servants rebellious, her husband and Mr Kelley pursuing the angels and oh God, Mr Kelley, with his sharp, sour looks and his eyes that were always following her. The angels had come with them and were more demanding and difficult than ever. Mr Kelley passed on their wishes.

So, the weeks passed until late one night when the children were asleep (although only just and they had taken so long to nod off) her husband and Mr Kelley summoned her to their work room. She was tired and little Michael had a tummy upset and she wanted to send her excuses, but the servant insisted and so she set off after him – through room after high-ceilinged room, fires burning in the hearths, the yellow haze of candle flames – until they came to the great room over the guardhouse where the wizard had his study. Her husband was sitting at his desk, Mr Kelley was standing beside him. They had an air of great excitement. She thought, They've been calling down the angels again. Mrs Kelley wasn't there. The servant said that she was sick.

'Jane, sweetheart,' said her husband, half-rising and reaching out across the desk to take her hand and guide her towards him. There were tears in his eyes. 'Jane, sweetheart, you know the angel Madimi and how she has only ever spoken truth to us. She has been here only an hour ago and she has brought disturbing news...'

'Husband?' she said, puzzled.

More tears came into his eyes. The big man, Mr Kelley, seemed to fade away a yard or two.

'Husband?' she said again.

He drew her to his lap. He wiped a strand of hair from her face. She wondered what was wrong with Kelley's wife Joanna.

'Madimi came to Mr Kelley and myself and said that we are to share our wives.'

'Share?' she said, even more puzzled. 'In what way, share?'

'I asked her that,' he said – and now his voice was trembling – 'and she said, in every way. Spiritually. Carnally.'

'Husband' – she was shocked – 'that is against the law of God.'

He shook his head. 'I fear it isn't,' and then he added in a whisper, 'for then God will reveal all to me and we will know everything,' and she was startled to see the speechless yearning in his face.

She looked up, saw the big man beyond Dee's shoulder, and in his opaque eyes a sudden sharpness. He wants to punish me, she thought.

In the tangled days that followed she sometimes felt her body shake – where had that come from? – and a wetness on her cheeks – tears – she didn't even know that she was crying. He tried to put his arms around her, but she shook him off. She thought that he would relent, that he couldn't ask such a thing of her, but though he was sweet and tentative she saw that ultimately, he had made up his mind, that he wanted this, and he would have it. And then one day she thought that by agreeing to this it would be the fastest way out of the tangle and confusion and so the words came out of her mouth: 'If God asks this of me I will do it,' and 'Sweetheart,' he said with love and relief. After that she tried to put it out of her mind.

Then a night came very quickly – she realised now that he'd been planning it all along – when the fire burnt low in the bedroom grate and the house had fallen quiet because all of the servants had been sent away. The wizard watched as she said her prayers and then she climbed into bed and at some point he must have slipped away, because there she was, alone, whilst the candles guttered and the fire dwindled even lower. And then she wasn't alone, because she felt a sudden weight on the mattress, the big man's body, first lying on the bed beside her and then carefully arranging himself on top of her, his lips close to her ear. 'Mistress Jane,' he whispered, as with one hand he lifted her nightdress and she felt herself freeze with horror. Afterwards she couldn't remember what he had done, only that there was a silence and then in the darkness she felt the mattress shift and change and after what felt like an hour there was another shift in the mattress and the wizard took her hand.

The days that followed were full of black and tangled shame. The servants got to hear of it, of course they did, and looked at her sideways. Her anger struck at her like lightning bolts, then jumped like a lightning storm from her to him. At first, he looked alarmed, and then regretful, but one morning over breakfast she realised he was angry and the thought came to her, with disbelief, that he was telling himself this had all been her idea, that it was she, not he, who had chosen this, that he had only given her what she had wanted all along. At this, her anger flashed again.

Now, he and Mr Kelley were falling out. She heard them shouting around the house. They were trying to work but couldn't. The angels had deserted them. Even Madimi was nowhere to be seen. After a month she realised she was with child and when she told the wizard he and Mr Kelley came to blows and Mr Kelley packed and went eastwards. Nine months later, she gave birth and not long after that she and Dee and all the children came home, and with them a small baby in her arms, and flowing through her such anger at Dee that she could hardly speak.

•

One day, when Katherine was ten and the wizard had been gone four years, Granny proposed that Katherine should climb into the wizard's house and bring her back a book. Granny couldn't read and it pained her that there were things the grand people could do and she could not. She wanted to hold a book, to feel its magic, to see if she could read it, like they could. She had walked the perimeter of the gardens many times, had surveyed the house from all sides, had carefully imagined its inner layout and had deduced the whereabouts of the library – on the west side of the house, to catch the setting sun. Furthermore, she had also identified a small window behind the laburnum bush that would surely let you into the scullery or some such space and from there it should not be hard to find the library. The window was low off the ground, quite accessible. Next, she pondered which of her two granddaughters she could most depend upon. Little Alice was seven and as sure on her feet as an acrobat, but she was also prone to shrieking with excitement when surprised. And so, Granny chose Katherine, who was quiet and steady, although underneath the calm she burned, as Granny knew, with the injustices of life. One day in September, Granny whispered in Katherine's ear, 'I want...' And then she stopped. What did she want? She couldn't find the words, but Katherine knew. 'I'll get you one, Granny,' she said.

That night in bed, after their prayers, Katherine said, 'Granny wants a book.'

'What for?'

'I don't know.'

And so, the next afternoon, when the men were out in the fields, Katherine climbed on top of the wall and saw a sight that she had never seen before – an overgrown orchard, a collection of outhouses and the house itself from an unfamiliar angle – red brick, gabled and with chimneys. She paused in amazement – to think that this strange, new sight had been there all along and she had never known it – and then she slid down onto the open grass, the enormity of what she was doing making her eyes grow very wide. She ran for the laburnum bush. Behind it was a window and, sure enough, the latch was broken. It slid up easily, someone must have entered this way before. It took just a jump to get onto the sill, to turn sideways, to see inside a long-abandoned scullery with old milk pails on a damp stone floor and cobwebs infesting a dried-up sink, and then she dropped her legs and followed them down, onto the floor.

Here, she paused, listened with all her might, heard nothing and so tiptoed to the door and opened it. Beyond, she saw a brown corridor with brown wainscoting on either side and a thick and dusty air ahead. Forwards she went, tiptoe by tiptoe. Her heart grew big inside her. She thought she felt a demon breathing down her neck. She looked behind her. The door to the scullery was still open. The further in she went the harder it would be to escape. She saw a door at the other end of the corridor and moved towards it. She stopped, listened again. Nothing. She reached the door, tapped it gently, watched it creak open.

Inside was a long, low room, white plaster and brown timbers, a window at the far end through which slanted a beam of golden light – the westering sun – and all around her empty shelves.

Perhaps half of the books were gone and the rest lay on the floor like fallen birds – on their backs, spines broken, pages torn and covering the floorboards so thickly that she had to tiptoe between them. 'It's a library,' whispered Katherine in amazement. She'd heard of places like these, where books gathered and fomented a bookish magic, though she'd never seen one. She herself couldn't read. None of them could.

She reached down, picked up a book, turned the pages, looked at the pictures. She saw a sun with a face like a beautiful boy, the locks of hair flowed outwards like flames from every part of his head. She stared in wonder and then she heard a noise – men's voices from somewhere beyond the other end of the library. Panic seized her. She couldn't move, and then she took off like a rabbit, still clutching the book, back through the door through which she'd come, up the corridor and into the scullery. *Close the door behind you, close the door.* And then over to the window. *Stop, stop, is anyone out there?* But she heard nothing and so she hopped over the windowsill and down into the shadow of the laburnum bush.

Here she paused, terrified. She could hear their voices now, at the front of the house. *Suppose they have dogs?* If she ran, they'd see her. If she stayed, they'd find her. She ran. Over the grass towards the wall. She threw the book over in front of her, leapt up the wall and gripped the topmost brick, heaved herself up, swung around and was horribly aware for one moment of how visible she was, then she slid down the other side to where Granny was standing, eyes wide open in horror, the book already in her hands.

Granny shoved the book into a bag, took the girl by the arm and led her through the graveyard behind the church, down to the river by the back path. Here, she made Katherine sit down on the bank and catch her breath. After a few minutes Katherine craned her head round to where she could see the front of the house in the distance. There was a carriage and a wagon with four horses, waiting to be loaded. The men had come back for more books. Katherine turned white. Granny looked guilty. For the first time in her life, Katherine could see the young Granny – *But why can't I have that?*

They walked to the edge of the fields where the woods began and, kneeling down, took the book out the bag and put it on the ground between them, turning its pages in fear and astonishment. They saw a zodiac wheel with a wizard beside it, a dragon with red-tipped wings, a city square where rich men in long robes and round flat hats like dining plates gazed upwards in amazement at a huge glass jar in which a peacock is rising – all in pinks and reds and oranges and golds. 'What does it mean?' asked Granny. Katherine shook her head; she had no idea.

They hid the book in a bush and went back half a dozen times in the hope that it might give up its magic, but it never did. Granny lost interest first – she was offended that, stare as she might, the squiggles would not resolve themselves into recognisable words. Katherine stayed entranced longer but, in the end, she too lost interest. She was afraid her father would find out what they had done and so she buried the book in a nearby wood but soon forgot where she had placed it. Indeed, she forgot about it all together until the day the wizard returned. She was twelve when he returned. She could hardly remember the ten-year-old Katherine.

•

The day the wizard came home he walked slowly and deliberately up the front path, his wife beside him, the four strangely dressed children trailing uncertainly behind them. The crowd held its breath. The five children on the wall stared through narrowed eyes. They felt sorry for the wizard but also strangely elated. They wouldn't have stopped the play for one moment. At his front door the wizard took out a huge black key and the eyebrows of the children on the wall shot upwards and their eyes grew very wide. Then, the family went in, first the wizard, then his wife and then the four children, though the last one – the smallest one – paused and turned to look at the audience before he followed his brothers and sisters.

There was silence. A bird sang. The trees soughed. The river ran on. And then there came a scream. It was like the scream of a cow being slaughtered. 'My books,' the wizard screamed, 'my books,' and the children who only a moment before had been strangely thrilled, now felt their spirits fall, down, down, down.

Chapter Twenty-Two
Magical Shakespeare

There was one more magician in Elizabethan London, perhaps the greatest of them all, and that was William Shakespeare. Words, as we have seen, were magical (as Shakespeare knew well) and there are obvious affinities between telling stories and practising magic. Both of them have a lightness about them, a feeling of enchantment, of stopping time, of stepping out of time, a feeling of freedom which has always been the hallmark of both magic and storytelling, and the sensation of flying. Inventing characters is like raising ghosts and stories and alchemy have always been connected, since both are concerned with the magic of change and transformation. In many ways, stories and magic have always gone together.

Shakespeare, the great storyteller, lived in London for perhaps twenty years; we do not know how long exactly. We know he probably came to London around 1588 and that he lived in the parish of St Helen's, Bishopsgate, a prosperous parish full of migrants in the north-east corner of the city, for at least two years (from 1597 to 1598) and possibly four or five (from 1593/94 to 1598), though where exactly he lived in St Helen's we cannot say. After that, we know that he was living in Southwark in 1599 and that between 1602 and 1604 he lodged in Silver Street near Aldersgate in the house of Christopher Mountjoy, a Huguenot refugee who made women's wigs. This, give or take some details, is all we know about his London lodgings.

Nor do we know much about his everyday life outside the theatre. What we do have, however, are his plays and from these we can see that he was very knowing about his own storytelling profession and its enchantments, and so he was happy to break out of the illusion of the story and accentuate its magic by calling time on it, saying that what you've heard is just a story, albeit a gorgeous one, and that like magic it arrived and like magic it will go. This is exactly what the wizard Prospero says in *The Tempest*:

These our actors,
As I foretold you, were all spirits and
Are melted into air, into thin air,
And like the baseless fabric of this vision,
The cloud-capp'd towers, the gorgeous palaces,
The solemn temples, the great globe itself,
Ye, all which it inherit, shall dissolve
And like this insubstantial pageant faded,
Leave not a rack behind.

In a world which had only just acquired physical theatres and which had no films, streaming, television, novels or comics – or any of the other paraphernalia of storytelling – the great Globe theatre and everything that happened in it must have seemed quite magical.

In 1534, sixty years before William Shakespeare's career took off, Anne Boleyn's sister Mary fell in love with a man called William Stafford, who was of a lower social status than her. Fearing that her family would stop her marrying him she did so in secret without their permission, for which crime she and Stafford were banished from court. In 1536 she wrote a letter to Thomas Cromwell begging him to intercede on her behalf. It is an extraordinary letter, steeped in the magic of romantic love. It reads like something from the free-loving 1960s.

'Master Secretary,' she writes,

Consider that he was young and love overcame reason and for my part I saw so much honesty in him that I loved him as well as he did me ... I thought I could take no better way but to take him and to forsake all other ways and to live a poor, honest life with him ... I might have had a greater man of birth and a higher, but I assure you I could never have had one that should have loved me so well, nor a more honest man ... if I were at my liberty and might choose I assure you, master secretary, I had rather beg my bread with him than to be the greatest queen in Christendom, and I believe verily he is in the same case as me, for I believe he would not forsake me to be king.

Thomas Cromwell, being a worldly man, must have received this letter with a sigh. He would have known quite well the trouble that romantic love could cause, as did William Shakespeare, who, sixty years later, would often make it a theme in his plays.

In *A Midsummer Night's Dream*, Shakespeare brings together romantic love and magic and demonstrates how much they have in common. Both possess the power to entrance us and to lift us out of ourselves but both also have the power to cause havoc and confusion.

In the play, three groups of people collide in the forest outside Athens: first, Oberon and Titania, the king and queen of the fairies, and their entourage, all quarrelling with each other and causing mayhem in the lives of mortals; second, Theseus, Duke of Athens, and his queen, Hippolyta, plus a furious father (Egeus) trying to stop his daughter Hermia loving the man she chooses, as well as two other young people, Demetrius and Helena, who also cannot love where their interests lie or who their elders want; and third, an amateur theatre group trying to put on a play for the king and queen.

It's no accident that Shakespeare only permits love to let loose for one night, the night of Midsummer's Eve, when by convention the strict laws of propriety were relaxed, and also that he places the play's action beyond the city walls in the wilderness of the forest. It is also no accident that at the end of the play Egeus (the father) does not get what he wants – the marriage of his daughter Hermia to Demetrius. Instead, she marries the man she wants – Lysander – whilst Demetrius and Helena, with some help from magic, fall in love with and marry each other. Shakespeare knew that love was a form of magic, and he also knew what his story's ending demanded, that Hermia had to marry Lysander. Love and magic belong together and storytelling, itself being a magical art, knows this and makes love possible.

Some scholars have seen the play as an alchemical drama, with the endless swapping of partners representing the way the world constantly changes as it dances towards perfection. Certainly, the world of *A Midsummer Night's Dream* is an interconnected one with the quarrels of the fairy king and queen causing mayhem everywhere, so that the green corn rots and the moon turns pale with anger.

There is another magical moment in *A Midsummer Night's Dream* when we see Oberon, the king of the fairies, together with his servant Puck. In a recent version of the play (which I saw at the Globe in summer 2023), Oberon, the king of the fairies, is portrayed as tall, lordly and very sexy. When he's on the stage with his servant Puck you feel the difference in social status between them. Oberon is grand, kingly, powerful and educated – every inch the magus – whereas Puck is wild, transgressive, working class and rebellious, and the magic that he gives the audience is the magic of the poor and the rural classes. Oberon is dressed grandly, Puck is dressed in rags. Oberon's magic is hallucinatory ('Once I sat upon a promontory and heard a mermaid on a dolphin's back uttering such dulcet and harmonious breath that the rude sea grew civil at her song...') whilst Puck's magic is mischievous and anarchic. He is Robin Goodfellow, 'a rude and knavish sprite' who makes the milk curdle. His is the rustic magic that existed beyond the doors of John Dee's house at Mortlake.

It feels as if at this moment Shakespeare, pen in hand, is juxtaposing in his imagination the two forms of magic, high and low, and wondering how they will speak to each other.

Chapter Twenty-Three
The Secrets of Mortlake

Magic has always belonged to the old as well as the young. Gandalf the Grey was aeons old and so too was Merlin, and so too was the wizard Prospero in Shakespeare's *The Tempest* and so too was Old Man Dee when finally he came home to Mortlake, an old and broken man.

There is almost nothing left of Tudor Mortlake now – time has taken it all away. The church is the only sixteenth-century building still standing and even that has been much altered. A main road runs between the church and the river, cutting across what would have been John Dee's orchard and gardens. His house, which was next to the church, has vanished under modern flats. It is said that John Dee is buried in an unmarked grave under the nave of the church and so, on the day I visit, that's where I stand, trying to sense whether John Dee is sleeping underneath my feet, wondering if he's waiting – like the wizard Merlin – for his time to come again.

Shortly after John Dee died, William Shakespeare wrote his final play, *The Tempest*. It concerns the old age and last acts of the magician Prospero and is about giving up magic and turning your back on the pleasures of revenge, although even as it turns away from magic it celebrates its power and glories. The play is full of alchemical touches. When Ferdinand staggers in out of the storm at the beginning of the play, Ariel the spirit sings, 'Full fathom five, thy father lies, of his bones are coral made. Those are pearls that were his eyes. Nothing of him that doth fade but does suffer a sea change into something rich and strange.' The reference to coral is a sure sign of alchemy (because coral red was the last colour in the alchemical sequence building up to the appearance of the philosopher's stone). The mention of change, not death, is also characteristic of alchemy because nothing dies in the alchemical universe, it only changes endlessly into something else.

Did John Dee ever go to the Globe to watch one of Shakespeare's plays? We have no evidence to prove this, but it seems likely. And did Shakespeare ever meet John Dee? Again, we do not know for sure though we can assume that he would at least have heard of him. After reading *The Tempest*, some scholars have concluded that John Dee must have been the model for the magician Prospero. When Caliban, Prospero's slave, shouts out, 'Burn his books, without them he is nothing,' Shakespeare may be remembering the destruction of Dee's library. Books are a recurring theme in the play. When Prospero renounces magic in the final act he says: 'This magic I abjure – bury my staff. Deeper than did ever plummet sound, I'll drown my books.'

And so, I like to imagine that one September day, maybe in 1607, the playwright travelled by horse across London Bridge and then turned westwards along the south bank of the Thames and across the Lambeth marshes. That morning, he has bought a piece of land, granted a meeting to a tenant and extended a lease on a house. Now it is late afternoon and the yellow corn is in stocks as he comes to the village of Mortlake and finds Old Man Dee sitting at the end of his garden, looking out on to the river. The tide is low, the water tawny-green, the shadows long on the mud flats. There is a lantern on the bench beside him with a candle burning inside, its light growing stronger as the twilight deepens. The old man looks unutterably old. All that is left of that crowd of children, eight in all, who had once played in the garden at Mortlake is his daughter Katherine and his son Arthur, who is soon to go to Moscow as doctor to the tzar of Russia, and possibly also as the tzar's alchemist.

The playwright sits down. He knows what has happened to Dee, everyone does, how he went east to find the road between the worlds but failed, despite his many promises to the queen, and with a last throw of the dice, prostituted his wife and lost God's favour, for which reason he sits here alone, unloved by both heaven and earth. The old man cannot stop grieving and complaining. The playwright has heard that lately the angel Gabriel has been coming to Dee by means of a scryer called Bartholomew Hickman and that when Dee complains of Emperor Rudolf's neglect of him, the angel says, 'Shush, let it go, let it go, and speak no further of it. The Emperour of all Emperours will be thy comfort...'

It seems that Bartholomew Hickman is a kindly man.

Katherine brings them each a glass of wine.

'Well, old man,' says the playwright jovially.

Dee turns to look at him. 'How's business?' he asks.

'Good enough.'

'You've done well.'

'God has blessed me.'

The old man turns back to survey the river. 'She used to come this way,' he says.

'Indeed,' replies the playwright.

And each man remembers the royal barge and the trumpets, and the brightness of the queen that was so severe it caused them to shield their eyes as she went by.

The playwright is brooding on a fear. It is weeks since a story sprung up in his head, which is longer than it has ever been before, and he is afraid that maybe the storytelling impulse is fading, that it cannot last for ever, that there must come a time when his huge and sympathetic brain can no longer dream up characters, that every storyteller must fall silent in the end. And then he looks at the old man beside him and thinks they are not so different, that they have both tried to do the same thing, because magic and stories are one and the same, and the yearning to find magic, like the yearning for stories, will last for ever.

STORY EIGHT
THE STORYTELLER

The storm is over. It is a day of brilliant blue.

'I won't go,' she says. 'Here I am and here I'll stay.' She is sitting on an old tree stump on the edge of the copse. From here she can see them sweeping up the field towards her, can hear their voices, like seagulls, first loud, then faint, then loud again. 'Ma, ma' – that's Lizzie – and 'Ma' – very faint – that's Mary. They will find her soon because there's nowhere to hide – just this clump of trees, and in front of her the field up which they are swarming – and beyond the field the village, which is just a huddle of houses on the low cliff edge – and beyond that, the sea.

There is a story told round here that once, there was a land out there between England and France, a place of woods and streams and rabbits and deer, and people who hunted and fished and danced and told stories. But then the waters started to rise and the people packed up their wagons and left. Ever since then the waters have not stopped rising – they are rising still – and so year by year this field is getting smaller – more land went in last night's storm – as the clifftop crumbles and the sea moves inwards.

The old woman runs a Dame school for the village children where she teaches them to read and write and count. She also tells them stories – and because she is entranced by everything that's vanished, her tales are always about the drowned land. She says that out there, when the waters rose, the children started to grow fins and were soon leaping from the rooftops into the swirling waters. By the time the waters had risen above the whole of this sunken land the children were entirely transformed into fish and swam away with a flick of their tails. She says that the stories these people told were very light and airy and so when they left the drowned land, they had to pack the stories into boxes, a box for each story, and tie them to their horses. And she says that when the last family was going they left behind one child – she swam away when they weren't looking – and now she's lost somewhere out to sea –and sometimes on still summer nights you can hear her crying. At which point, the children start to cry as well and Ma's own children, and especially Lizzie, tell her off. 'D'you have to, Ma?' she says. 'They're only little. Tell them something to make them smile.' Ma blushes, but the truth is that she likes sad stories, they make her happy.

Almost nobody comes to the village – it's very far from anywhere – and when news reaches them from distant Cambridge or London, it always comes fourth-hand and is as shifting and unreliable as the clouds out to sea or the land under their feet. In the old days, the raree man came twice a year with his magic box strapped to his pony. He would haul it down and invite the children to look into the peep hole and Ma would watch them with a sardonic air, kneel down on her stiff knees and see inside the box a ship with billowing sails and pennants flying. A candle behind the picture cast a moonlit glow, lighting up the devil who is creeping behind the ship, his cloven hooves as light as air on the tips of the painted waves. Ma thinks, It's a good picture but I am a better storyteller.

But now, after three, four, five bad harvests, the end of the world man comes instead, to warn them of the impending end, that comets, dragons and other heavenly prodigies have been seen over London, that the devil himself has been seen in the streets, that all over England people are preparing for the end of days, and so they need to say their prayers and ask for God's forgiveness.

One time, a group of sermon-gadders came this way. It was a Sunday morning and they were on their way to church in Aldeburgh. Lizzie saw them – she was only thirteen. She hid behind the hedge and watched them go past, singing hymns and debating the Book, their faces very bright, their voices rising to a crescendo. Later on that day, she saw them returning, now debating the sermon. Their voices faded away until they vanished into a wood and their voices were lost in birdsong.

And then once a year in the spring comes Lord Audley's factor. Lord Audley lives in Cambridge – he's their landlord – and the factor is his right-hand man. Last year in the autumn floods they sent a message to the factor telling him they needed help, but if he received it he never answered. He will only come once a year – it's all that he is contracted for.

Only three weeks ago a storm tore down the cliff path that leads to the jetty. Ten days later three families lost their barns and parts of their gardens, and all the fields, their own included, have been soaked repeatedly in salt. They have sent another message to the factor but the result will be the same.

Ma says that the people of the drowned land knew more than they do now because they lived closer to the beginning of the world when everything was fresh and new, not faded and confusing like it is now when we are so much closer to the end. The men listened nervously to the old woman's stories. 'Is yer ma a prophet?' one of them asked Lizzie. 'She's talking about the past, not the future. You can't be a prophet about the past,' said Lizzie sharply.

One day before the last storm Ma heard the children talking outside in the barn. Robert had put the wagon up on chocks so that he could examine the front axle and check that the wheels were running smoothly. Lizzie and Mary crowded around.

'We can't stay,' said Robert. 'We can't even plant the fields so what will we live on?'

'She won't leave,' said Lizzie.

'I know, I know.'

'We have to persuade her,' said Mary, and then they saw her outside in the yard. 'Hallo, Ma,' they chorused, suddenly respectful.

'Robert's been mending the wagon,' said Lizzie.

'And touching up the paint,' said Mary. 'Come and have a look.'

But the old woman just stood and stared at them. She's surprised to see them grown so big. Only a minute ago she had seen the small ghosts of their former selves jumping around in the corners of her vision. She is shaking her head with the dazed, half-drowned look of someone coming up for air from deep water. 'Ma, Ma,' they shout – they are flocking around her – 'Are you all right, Ma?'

I was born round here, she thinks. Everything that has ever happened to me has happened on this land. It's where I brought my children up, it's where the ghosts of all their former selves still haunt me.

'It's no good, I won't go,' she says. 'Here I am and here I'll stay.'

One day, Ma saw her long-dead mother walking along the path beside the field towards her. It was a June evening, nearly midsummer, and the sky was green. A fine dust was sifting through the air, and everything was so warm and soft that the birds were still singing although it would soon be midnight. Ma's mother looks young – she can't be more than twenty-five – maybe the age that Ma first remembers her? – and her curly hair is tied back under a handkerchief. Ma stops in shock. 'Mama,' she whispers, but the long-dead woman takes no notice, and walks straight on past her whilst Ma steps hastily out of the way. 'Mama,' she shouts after her – 'You can't go that way, the sea path's gone' – but the young woman keeps on walking until she vanishes behind a hedge.

So much happened in this field. Spring sowing, harvest moons. Springs so hungry they doubt they'll live until summer, summers so hot they think they'll live forever. The woman who sold her child for food, went to Ipswich Market and came home without him. Her brother Samuel with his long legs and white hair – he danced like a prince though he was only a laundress's son. He went to fight the Prussians – she said goodbye to him in this field – but they never heard from him again. And her sister Eliza, who died of the plague because somehow the plague reached them here, though no one and nothing else ever did.

She was born and brought up on this field. Her father died when she was little, her mother brought them up alone just as she has brought up her own children. One day when Ma was eleven, she was driving their three sheep home along the cliff path. She was barefoot, with her skirts hitched up and her eyes narrowed, intent on her job. A group of men stood and watched – though they didn't offer to help. She took no notice. It was six months since her father died and she had a fear – bigger than these men, bigger even than her own hunger – and that is the whispers of witch hunts that have reached their village. *Katherine Lawrett, spinster, bewitched Susan Kynge so that she languished and died. Guilty to hang. Susan Barker, spinster, stole a skull from a grave in Upminster with the intention of bewitching Mary Stephens. Guilty to hang.* Oh Mama, thinks the little girl on the clifftop who was Old Ma. Her Mother is sharp-tongued and not neighbourly. Be careful, Mama, please don't quarrel with everyone.

She married the boy from the next village. He had been popular and well-liked, which she was not. She was growing into her own mother, lonely and difficult, but he loved her and protected her from the whisperers. Every August they threshed the field by moonlight as fast as they could, for fear that the devil would come and steal the harvest. On one of those harvest nights she went into labour and gave birth to Robert out here in the field. He was the first. After him came a second, a third and a fourth, though only three lived. (What will they do when the storms reach the graveyard? Can they dig up their dead and take them with them?) The children are as thick as thieves, always were. When they were little, they used to crouch down together, whispering and talking, their heads close together like the petals of a flower.

And then one day Ma's husband vanishes. The next night Ma stepped out into the field, stretched out her hands and touched the holes in the black night into which he'd slipped away and disappeared. No one ever found out why he vanished. It's just the way things happen. People go out in the morning and never come home. Round here the men still talk about him, put forward two reasons why he went – either he drowned at sea, or he left the old woman because who wouldn't? Sometimes, she sends her mind out searching for him across the darkness of the universe.

A month after he went, little Lizzie, only eleven but very proud, came to her and said, 'Ma, let me cook, I can do it better.' They nearly lost this land when he disappeared. They were only tenant farmers and they had to prove to the landlord and the village that they could manage it without him. Lizzie and Robert begged and pleaded and at last the villagers let them stay and prove it. Since then, none of the children have married. They stick very closely together, as if they've made a secret pact, as if they know something.

All that autumn Ma lay awake at night and repeated her stories, word for word, because she cannot write and so how else will she remember them? And she is doing something else as well. Each time she tells a story she adds in another detail from her own life – the land, the lost baby, how she loved her husband – because how else will she remember all that either?

'In the land beneath the sea,' she tells the children, 'before the waters came the swallows were expert dancers. They danced to swallow music that only they could hear.' That was for her brother Samuel and the last time they danced together.

And 'In the land beneath the sea the Michaelmas daisies grew six-foot tall and had flowers as big as dinner plates and were very, very wise. The drowned baby swam up to them. "I'm looking for my mama. Which way did she go?" and the Michaelmas daisies bent their tall heads together and whispered, "No, no. These are the drowned lands. She went the other way, towards the setting sun."'

The Michaelmas daisies were for the dead baby – a way of remembering her. She died on Michaelmas Day.

Ma thinks, I would like to be remembered.

All through September, Ma watches the children making plans. What will they take with them on the journey? The wagon of course. The sacks of flour, the seeds and plants, tools, clothes and blankets, three live chickens, shoes, a tent in which they'll sleep at night. They'll go west and Robert will find work as a carpenter and Lizzie and Mary will get work on farms until somehow they can persuade a landowner to take them on as tenant farmers. To be landless is a terrible fate. It shames them and makes them nothing. People will shun them for it. They will have to find a landlord who needs more labourers. Nobody mentions the dead baby who will stay behind in the churchyard, as long as the churchyard survives the oncoming waves.

It's obvious what they are doing and the other families come to say goodbye. Ma stands close by and stares until Robert, crouched down beside the wagon, notices and says, 'See, Ma, look how the axle turns, as smooth as butter.' But Ma is picturing the journey west – it could take months – and the cold and discomfort. Beyond the barn she can see the slope of the field. She thinks, It's no good, I will not go. I am tired of being reasonable and I am tired of all the leavings. Here I am and here I'll stay.

But in the end, she had no choice. She couldn't stay without them. And so, one morning she climbed up onto the wagon of her own accord and sat there like a Roman captive queen, riding high with her nose in the air until her children saw her, whereupon they ran around, getting ready to leave as fast as they could. They left with Robert sitting next to her to drive the horse and Lizzie and Mary walking beside them, whilst behind them, following in a train, came all their ghosts: their lost father, their uncle Samuel, the dead baby, the ghosts of all their former selves and the lives they used to lead.

On the second day, they were ten miles in from the coast when they realised that they had never been this far before.

There are heathlands and marshes and scrubby fields and small copses on all sides, and a brown river that brims and swells with new rain as it runs beside them. Over everything is a feeling of freshness and unfamiliarity, because although they have only been travelling for a couple of days they have already passed out of their known world and into this land where everything is new and strange.

That night they camp in a field beside a ruined chapel. The summer vegetation has died back so that they can see a scattering of arches and ruined floors and a broken-down cloister. 'It must have been a monastery,' says Mary. Inside the chapel the pews have gone but there is still an altar and the faint outlines of papist paintings on the mildewed walls. They light a fire of grass and brambles and a thin line of smoke drifts skywards. They eat pancakes and watch the foxes and listen to the hooting of owls and other strange sounds. When it is dark they lie down in the chapel. They have never before slept without the hollow boom of the waves upon the shore.

Sometime in the night, Ma dies. It is Lizzie, sleeping beside her, who wakes in the early morning and sees her mother stiff and cold, the spirit gone, her face turned at an odd angle, the body – without the soul to hold it together – fallen into a jumble of separate pieces.

Her ghost is now walking home towards the field.

The story of the child lost at sea survived Ma. It turned up two summers hence, being told by children up the coast near Lowestoft. And the summer after that it had become a clapping song near Yarmouth. As for Ma herself, when the tide comes in and turns the town of Southwold into an island, the people tell a story about an old woman who wouldn't leave the drowning land but gradually, hour by hour, from her feet upwards, was slowly transformed until, part woman and part story, she was covered by the waters. This story is now older than the oldest man in town, but it shows no sign of dying.

PART TWO
AFTERMATH

CHAPTER TWENTY-FOUR
Tribes

In the last decades of the seventeenth century, fifty years after John Dee died, there came a final flowering of early modern magic. Much had changed since Marsilio Ficino fell in love with Plato's *Dialogues* back in the 1460s – King Charles I had been executed (to the great shock of Europe), the City of London had been destroyed by fire and men now wore flared frock coats and long, curly wigs and high-heeled, buckled shoes – and yet at the same time much seemed the same.

Britain was still full of magic. Elias Ashmole, who founded the Ashmolean Museum in Oxford in 1678, gave large chunks of his life to the study of occult beliefs. He had been the king's astrologer during the civil war and was a learned, scholarly, antiquarian kind of man, as well as – allegedly – an architect of crafty marriages that made him rich. After the king was executed, he retired to the country and produced three books, the first two of which were compilations of old alchemical manuscripts: the *Fasciculus Chemicus* (including works written by John Dee's son Arthur) and the *Theatrum Chemicum Britannicum* (containing works written by the alchemist George Ripley).

Ashmole also befriended a Mr William Backhouse of Swallowfield House in Berkshire. Backhouse was an alchemist and a scholar of the occult and he had a great library with many French alchemical manuscripts that Ashmole copied and translated into English. Backhouse treated Ashmole like a son. On 13 May 1653 Ashmole recorded in his diary, 'My father Backhouse, lying sick in Fleet Street, over against St Dunstan's Church, and not knowing whether he should live or die, about eleven of the clock told me, in syllables, the true matter of the Philosopher's Stone...' though what this true matter was exactly, Ashmole doesn't say.

Elias Ashmole also had an obsession with John Dee and collected his manuscripts and interviewed anyone who might have known him, until one day in 1672 he went to Mortlake. It was a little more than sixty years since John Dee had died. His house had long ago been dismantled and destroyed, along with Jane Dee's orchards and gardens. In their place now stood the prosperous and bustling Mortlake Tapestry Works, which employed dozens of Flemish workers and made tapestries for the king. Very little had survived of old Mortlake, except (as we have seen) the old woman called the Good Wife Faldo.

Then in his old age, Elias Ashmole turned to the creation of the Ashmolean Museum, appointing Robert Plot as his first keeper. Plot was interested in local history, archaeology, antiquities and also in alchemy and its possibilities. He is said to have 'expected to be able to develop in his laboratory what he called the "menstruum"', the elixir of life, a very alchemical-sounding concept.

He also may have had what seem to us rather strange views regarding fairies. In his book *A Natural History of Staffordshire*, he says about fairy rings, 'And as the Devils and Witches do sometimes leave the lively marks of their dancing ... so the little Pygmy spirits that infest the mines of Helvetia and Hungary do sometimes also leave the prints of their feet in the moist land and soft, tenacious earth of the Mines about the bigness of the feet of children of three years old, whence some men may think it probable enough that some few of these circuses' – i.e. fairy rings – '(especially the bare ones that have but little grass) may sometimes indeed be made by the fore mentioned mixt dances of Devils and Witches, and others by those little dwarf spirits which we call Elves and Fairies.'

Meanwhile in Cambridge there was more magic. The great scientist Isaac Newton, founder of modern physics, kept an alchemical furnace burning all through his time in the city, and considered himself one of a select group of men who had been chosen by God to decipher the secret messages of the Bible. Newton owned dozens of Bibles, which he believed to be written in code, and through which he endlessly searched, trying to decipher God's secret intentions.

In Norwich there was also magic. John Dee's son Arthur, whom we last saw as the oldest of the gaggle of small children who climbed down from the carriage at Mortlake when the Dees returned from Prague – this Arthur Dee grew up to become doctor to the tzar of Russia and perhaps also his alchemist. Arthur lived in Moscow for thirteen years until his wife died, whereupon he returned to England and settled in Norwich until his death in 1651. Here, as an old man, he was befriended by Thomas Browne, who also lived in Norwich and was an antiquarian, a philosopher and a writer, as well as a believer in witches and fairies. According to Browne, Arthur Dee remained loyal to his father's legacy to the last. Arthur was, said Browne, 'a persevering student in Hermetical Philosophy ... And confirmed unto his death that he had occularly, undeceivably and frequently beheld it' (i.e. the workings of the philosopher's stone) 'in Bohemia.' In a letter to Elias Ashmole in 1675, Browne also said that he had heard Arthur speak of 'the transmutation of pewter dishes and flaggons into sylver, which the goldsmiths of Prague bought of them' and that 'Count Rosenberg played at quarts with sylver quarts, made of projection' – i.e. the philosopher's stone – 'as before...'

Thomas Browne had a famous museum and library on the shelves of which were some of John Dee's books (perhaps given to him by Arthur Dee). Browne was also friends with Sir Robert Paston, who lived in Oxnead Hall not far from Norwich. Paston employed an alchemist called Thomas Henshaw as his financial adviser and as an assistant in his alchemical laboratory, which was in Oxnead's basement. Arthur Dee, Thomas Browne and Robert Paston were all Neoplatonists.

Magic was even at the heart of the Royal Society, founded in 1660 in London to develop the new scientific thinking. If we look at its early members we can see old magical beliefs mingling with new thinking. All its members believed in the importance of investigation and verifying one's beliefs through experiments and yet many of them also believed in some (to us) strange combination of angels, witchcraft, astrology, second sight and alchemy. (Some were so optimistic about investigative science that they believed it would prove the truth of magic, not debunk it.) They ranged from the extremes of Robert Hooke, who had no time for any kind of supernatural beliefs, to the strangeness of some of Robert Boyle's beliefs, including his speculation that God might be an author who had written us all into existence.

In seventeenth-century England only atheism remained unusual and largely fiercely condemned. Thomas Hobbes was said to be an atheist, a fact that many of his contemporaries found so shocking that some of them believed his atheism must have caused the Great Fire of London. In his book *Leviathan* Hobbes denied that it made sense to talk of immaterial spirits and attributed this belief in spirits 'to vulgar delusions and the misuse of language', but Joseph Glanville called atheism 'that cold and desperate disease' and Robert Boyle feared it mightily, being convinced that it had taken hold amongst young men in the coffee houses of London. It was for this reason that he hoped to make the existence of God more believable by proving the existence of a spirit world. The seventeenth-century scholar Meric Casaubon believed something similar. He said that he could not see how 'any Learned Man, sober and rational, can entertain such an opinion that there be no Devils and Spirits' and that 'it doth concerns Religion in general that we believe in Spirits'.

Chapter Twenty-Five
The Magical Museum of Athanasius Kircher

I n seventeenth-century Rome an old Jesuit priest called Athanasius Kircher created a museum full of marvels and with a reputation for magic in the Collegio Romano. Travellers from all over Europe came to see it and from their accounts we know that it consisted of a tall, echoey stone hall, crammed to its lofty ceiling with strange and peculiar objects. There were stuffed creatures, eagles and lions, and huge skulls and long bones – maybe of giants? There were shelves weighed down with fossils and the busts of ancient men, an organ that played bird song, while another organ appeared to work of its own accord, along with mirrors filled with ghostly spirits and snake stones that were said to be able to draw out a viper's venom.

The museum was also full of automata, especially musical machines that seemed to work by magic. There were also perpetual motion machines, magnetic experiments, models and devices of every kind, all clanking and whirring and spinning, and not a hand to be seen to push or pull them, as if everything moved by itself or the old man had discovered the secrets of eternal movement. He had certainly discovered how to project his voice. He greeted his visitors with a joyful, booming shout of 'Welcome, travellers' from inside some hidden aperture.

Kircher's museum was considered very strange by younger scholars in his own lifetime, and to this day there is no clear consensus on what he meant by it. Some academics have observed that he doesn't appear to believe in magic, at least not in alchemy or astrology or angel magic, as did John Dee. His magic feels more like stage than occult magic, especially when – in his writings – he draws back the curtain to show you how he has achieved it – usually by hydraulics or magnetism or pneumatics. (He writes of 'the astonishment, amazement and wonder of those who witness his machines in action; of how some fear that there might be a demon inside, until he shows them that it is all done by mirrors, magnetism or hydraulic power'.)

On the other hand, Kircher seems to have been a Neoplatonist. His museum's huge, sprawling quality and the way it tried to connect and tell the story of everything feels very Neoplatonic. He does seem to have believed in connections and correspondences between the different planes of the world – the microcosm and the macrocosm – which is also very Neoplatonic. With all his mechanical toys it is easy to imagine Kircher as childlike and absurd, but we should remember that in Neoplatonism childishness is considered a good quality and that games and play are God-like. When Kircher was writing his book about magic lanterns (*The Ars Magna Lucis et*

Umbrae) and how they worked he asked, 'What else is light but the laughter of the heavens?'

It was as if Kircher simultaneously believed and didn't believe in magic.

He also believed that romantic love was a force like magnetism, that it worked by attraction in the way that the sun causes sunflowers to turn their faces towards it or the way that iron filings rush towards the magnet, or the moon pulls on the tides. To us this seems a very strange idea until we remember Marsilio Ficino's concept of love as a magical force that holds the universe together, in which case, of course romantic love could work in the same way as magnetism and sunflowers and the moon on the tides. When we understand one, thought Kircher, we will understand them all.

All museums, even the most apparently rational, have had a faint whiff of magic about them. This is partly because objects themselves easily attract a magical aura (think of magical dancing shoes in fairy tales), partly because – in the case of the big museums – the desire to acquire an example of every type of object there has ever been feels like a magical endeavour in itself and partly because if you believe that God made meaningful patterns and connections between all things, especially between microcosms and macrocosms, then surely the way you organise objects in a museum can endow the museum with magic? Add to this the fact that museums absorb the values of the times in which they are created – and these were particularly magical times – and you begin to understand why so many sixteenth- and seventeenth-century museums would have felt touched with magic.

Athanasius Kircher built his museum at a time when Neoplatonism was beginning to fall out of fashion, not to disappear completely, but certainly to become more private and less mainstream.

As such, Kircher's younger colleagues mocked him roundly for the strangeness of his museum. When Kircher's book *Ars Magnesia* (*The Magnetic Art*) was published in 1642, Evangelista Torricelli reported to Galileo as follows,

> Two bits of news here: the death of Cardinal Pio and the publication of Father Athanasius Kircher's book that has been greatly anticipated for many years. He is the Jesuit mathematician from Rome. The work is a rather thick volume on magnets: a volume rich with a great supply of beautiful engravings. You will find astrolabes, clocks, windmeters, with a handful of most extravagant words. Among other things there are lots of small and large decanters, epigrams, diptychs, epitaphs and inscriptions, partly in Latin, partly in Greek, partly in Arabic, partly in Hebrew and other languages. Amongst the fine things is the score of that music that is said to be an antidote to the tarantula's venom. Enough said. Signor Nandi, Signor Maggiotti and I laughed for quite a long time.

Sometimes, it seems as if there is a thread that runs from Renaissance gardens and fountains, through Athanasius Kircher's museum, to nineteenth-century museums and their influence on circuses and seaside shows, and from them to the slot machines and penny arcades of a 1950s seaside pier. In the best possible way, the seaside pier may be the last remaining evidence of the charm and magic and playfulness of Neoplatonism and the clockwork arts.

CHAPTER TWENTY-SIX
THE COMMONWEALTH OF ELVES AND FAIRIES

K ircher's younger colleagues were baffled by Kircher's museum and in their bafflement we get the feeling that Kircher's world is ending, that faith in Neoplatonism is beginning to fade and that the wizard era is coming to a close.

There is another story from this time that also exudes the feel of an ending. It concerns the Reverend Robert Kirk, who lived in Aberfoyle on the edge of the Scottish Highlands in the late seventeenth century. Robert Kirk was a fairy-scholar and a friend of the scientist Robert Boyle. Both men were ardent Christians, and both believed that if you believed in spirits, you could more easily believe in God. Both were also passionately interested in magical concepts, such as second sight and the fairies.

Reverend Kirk lived in the manse in Aberfoyle and though his home has long since gone we can imagine it – the low, dark, wood-panelled rooms, all well-lit by candles and oil lamps and with fires burning in every hearth; the plain diet – mutton and cabbage – and the God-fearing life, with prayers said twice a day and church twice on Sunday (with Kirk himself officiating) and after church a fire lit in the evenings, around which Kirk and his family would have sat and told stories. Kirk was writing a book about the fairies and so would have spent many hours walking the Scottish Highlands, searching out farms and small hamlets where he could listen to the storytelling.

Robert Kirk's book has survived and is a very strange document. It is a detailed account of second sight and the nature of the fairies, written in the cool, matter-of-fact language of an anthropological treatise. What is striking is that in it, Kirk writes about the wraithlike, vaporous and astral bodies of the spirits and fairies in very similar language to that used 100 years earlier by Neoplatonists like Giordano Bruno. It is as if Robert Kirk is wondering whether he can identify the local fairies with Neoplatonist spirits, comparing them side by side in his mind and asking whether the two ideas are related, if in fact fairies and Neoplatonic spirits are one and the same. It is an idea that would probably only occur to a country clergyman who would have read widely and been on speaking terms with both the gentry above him and his rural parishioners below him.

But where would Robert Kirk have learnt about Neoplatonism? Maybe in the coffee houses of London or the clubs of Edinburgh. Or maybe in a book, because books travel and carry their ideas with them. It is quite possible that one of Ficino's books travelled a thousand miles over several hundred years, from fifteenth-century Florence to seventeenth-century Aberfoyle, perhaps via John Dee's library in Mortlake beside the Thames.

There is a strange and magical postscript to Robert Kirk's life. When he died in 1692 (apparently whilst out walking near a fairy hillock dressed only in his nightgown and nightcap) the story began to circulate that he was not dead at all but had been stolen away by the fairies as punishment for writing books about them and getting them published down in London.

In time, Kirk's book was forgotten but 130 years later, the novelist Walter Scott found a strange document in the Advocates Library in Edinburgh. Scott was the most famous Scottish writer of his generation. He lived in North Castle Street in Edinburgh's New Town where the streets are wide open to the northern skies, but he crossed each morning, walking stick in hand, to the Old Town where he took the many narrow alleyways and flights of steps that run up and down the steep sides of the Old Town until he came to the Advocates Library. Here, one day in 1813, the librarian mistakenly brought him a mysterious document. It turned out to be Robert Kirk's book about the fairies, which had been lost since Kirk's death.

The reverend had died before he could get his manuscript published but somebody else had made a manuscript copy and it was this copy that Scott in turn copied. Scott's version became a printed book but somewhere along the line – in true fairy fashion – Kirk's original manuscript vanished, as did the version that Scott had copied (luckily, since then three more copies of Kirk's original text have turned up).

Then, a generation later, the manuscript fell into the hands of a folklorist called Andrew Lang, who read it and was smitten by it. It was he who gave it its name: *The Secret Commonwealth of Elves and Fairies*. Lang also referred to Robert Kirk as 'Chaplain to the Faery Queen'.

CHAPTER TWENTY-SEVEN
THE IDEA THAT WOULDN'T DIE

Then, during the first half of the eighteenth century, something curious happened. The magical, sparkling, Neoplatonic world, with its beliefs in wizards and fairies and alchemy and angels and in a universe that lives and breathes and dances and has a soul – this early modern world rapidly began to disappear. One hundred and fifty years previously, Giordano Bruno, who was a Neoplatonist to his fingertips, had thought of the cosmos as a 'mother, a nursemaid, a well spring, a light, a love'. Now increasingly, the most widely used analogy was that of a well-oiled and beautifully devised machine that ran of its own accord like clockwork. In this scenario God was the master craftsman who had devised the universe according to his secret laws, but who had now walked away and let it run by itself.

In this new world there were no witches, nor fairies nor spirits. The last witch to be executed in the British Isles was in Scotland in 1727 and after that fairy beliefs appeared to slide away from the mainstream to the periphery, and from the public to the private realm. Fairy beliefs were becoming private beliefs, often living on amongst the poor and the uneducated (although much loved by poets and artists). This process has been called the 'great disenchantment' and it has been much debated. Did it even happen (after all many people still believe in fairies)? Do we believe that fairy beliefs have gone because we want to believe in a myth of progress? And most contentious of all – if magical beliefs have vanished does that connect to the rise of what we would call science? And yet, there is no evidence of a see-saw effect with the rise of science necessarily leading to the decline of magic. Many educated men in the seventeenth century, such as Isaac Newton and Robert Boyle, seemed to be able to believe in both.

The great disenchantment has a curious echo in the persistent story that the fairies are leaving. This story has been around as far back as the time of Chaucer. The concept always comes in the form of a report that someone has seen the fairies departing on their horses, bound in a cavalcade for the coast where they will take a ship to a foreign land and not be seen in Britain again. The story seems to be some kind of lamentation for passing time and for some better world that is currently being lost. For instance, the eighteenth-century Scottish writer James Hogg named a local man, William Laidlaw (born in 1691), as the 'last man of this wild region who heard, saw and conversed with the fairies'.

During the eighteenth century, Dee and Bruno's reputations went into decline, as did Marsilio Ficino's and the reputation of Neoplatonism in general. Philosophy was growing increasingly rational and secular and by the same token the Neoplatonists were appearing increasingly fairy-struck, God-obsessed and confused. Neoplatonism, with its conviction that the universe is bound together by the forces of love and dances to the Music of the Spheres – all these ideas were fading away.

And yet it is also true that neither fairy beliefs nor Neoplatonism have ever disappeared entirely. Many centuries before, the Christian Emperor Justinian closed down the Neoplatonic School of Philosophy in Athens in the sixth century CE (on the grounds that it was full of pagan thinking) but Neoplatonism didn't die. Instead, it spread across Europe and Asia, leaving its mark on music, painting, poetry and architecture, and influencing Arabic and Persian poetry as well as Hebrew poetry in Andalusia in the far West. Neoplatonic ideas have influenced poets and writers, including Samuel Taylor Coleridge, William B. Yeats, Jorge Luis Borges and Robert Graves, ever since. There is something dissident about Neoplatonism which means that artists and writers have always been drawn to it and it has always been popular with the weak in comparison to the mighty. It also appeals to anyone who hopes there might be a place where the walls between the past and the present and between this world and any other grow permeable and thin enough for us to pass through them.

Neoplatonism continues to turn up in unexpected places. One of these is in Philip Pullman's fantasy novel *Northern Lights*, published in the 1990s, which depicts a universe of many worlds, one of which is another Oxford ruled by a harsh theocracy called the Magisterium. Into this alternative Oxford comes the heroine Lyra's father, the Lord Asriel, a frustrated scientist who is convinced that he can straddle the many worlds, go to whatever world he chooses, believe whatever he wants and find God wherever he chooses. In this other Oxford there are daemons

– every human has one – guardian creatures who are perhaps our souls? – whilst the heavens are full of half-seen creatures, such as witches. Meanwhile, the stern and unforgiving Magisterium rules over everything and tries to control what the characters believe, all of which sounds remarkably like the world of Renaissance Neoplatonism, with Lord Asriel based on the bombastic, confident Giordano Bruno – in other words the story you have just read here. It is therefore no surprise to discover that Philip Pullman says he was profoundly influenced by Frances Yates's book on Bruno.

•

The Renaissance Neoplatonists believed that this world and all of nature is infused with God. In the twentieth century, James Lovelock devised the Gaia theory, which suggests that the earth is like a living organism with self-regulating systems. Afterwards, the ecological movement, which is perhaps the spiritual descendant of Neoplatonism, has also often come close to believing that the earth is alive, as claimed by Giordano Bruno. Even as I write, there is a debate online as to whether trees have consciousness. It is also true that if we had continued to believe, as the Neoplatonists did, that the earth is alive and has a soul, and that the planets dance to the Music of the Spheres, we might not have trashed our planet so completely. In Ficino's hands Neoplatonism was a religion of love and kindness. Since then, it has often retained these qualities.

In 1930s America, a funerary poem began to be carved onto gravestones or recited at the graveside by grieving families. Its authorship has been contested but the poem goes as follows:

Do not stand at my grave and weep,
I am not there, I do not sleep.

I am a thousand winds that blow,
I am the diamond glints on snow.
I am the sunlight on ripened grain,
I am the gentle autumn rain.
When you awaken in the morning hush
I am the swift uplifting rush,
Of quiet birds in circled flight.
I am the soft stars that shine at night.
Do not stand at my grave and cry,
I am not there, I did not die.

When we remember the alchemists, who believed that the universe is in endless motion and that nothing dies but is endlessly transformed into something else, and when we remember the genesis myth in the *Corpus Hermeticum*, which says that everything in the universe is our family, that even the stars and the planets are our brothers and sisters and that nature loves us as we love nature, it is clear that whoever wrote this poem was a Neoplatonist to their fingertips.

Chapter Twenty-Eight
Afterlives

And now we should finish Edward Kelley and Giordano Bruno's stories. After the wife-swapping incident, John Dee and Edward Kelley parted. Kelley went back to Prague and for a short while his career as an alchemist seems to have flourished. He worked for both the emperor and Count Rosenberg in Třeboň and his reputation soared so high that it reached Elizabeth and her chief minister William Cecil in England. Cecil began to send letters to Kelley, pushing and prodding him to return to London and reveal his alchemical secrets to the queen – or failing that, to at least send her a sample of the philosopher's stone. For a brief moment, Kelley became the master and Dee the disciple. The peak of Kelley's fortunes came when the emperor knighted him in 1590, but by May 1591 his fortunes had turned and the emperor had him arrested and thrown into gaol. He seems to have stayed there until 1595 when the emperor released him on the condition that he provide him with gold, but when no gold was made he was sent back to prison. One account claims that Kelley injured himself when trying to escape and so was recaptured and died from his injuries, probably at the end of 1597. His wife Joanna and his stepdaughter were with him at the end.

What happened to Joanna Kelley is even less certain. There is an entry in Dee's diaries two months after the wife-swapping episode that simply says, 'A certain kind of reconciliation between our wives. Next day some relenting of E. K. also by my Lord's entreaty.' After that there is nothing, until we hear from other sources that Joanna Kelley and her daughter were with Edward Kelley when he died.

A few years later, Giordano Bruno came to an even more bitter end. After the furore caused by his Oxford lecture, he retreated to London where the French ambassador took him into his house in Salisbury Court. Here he stayed for two years and wrote six books, one of which, *The Ash Wednesday Supper*, caused a scandal so huge that Bruno claimed he could scarcely leave the embassy. (The reason for the uproar might have been his rudeness towards the English – 'England,' he wrote, 'can brag of having a populace that is second to none that the Earth nurtures in her bosom for being disrespectful, uncivil, rough, rustic, savage and badly brought up.') Still, these were probably the best years of his life – and certainly the most materially comfortable.

Even so, in 1585 Bruno left England and went first to Germany and then to Prague (where he almost certainly did not overlap with John Dee) before – and this was the biggest mistake of his life – in 1591 he was tempted to cross the Alps and travel down into Venice at the invitation of a Venetian nobleman named Giovanni Mocenigo.

He hadn't been in Venice long before Mocenigo denounced him to the authorities, saying that he believed that Bruno was possessed by a demon. Bruno was arrested and thrown into a

Venetian prison. From here – in February 1593 – he was taken to Rome, which was by then the heart of the violent Counter-Reformation. He was tortured, recanted and then retracted his recantation. Finally, angry and defiant, he was taken by donkey to the Field of Flowers outside Rome on Ash Wednesday 1600, where he was gagged to stop his protests and burnt alive at the stake. As he died, the clergymen of the Brotherhood of St John the Beheaded gathered in the Field of Flowers and sang hymns and chanted the litany over the noise of the flames.

To this day there is a fierce (and on the part of the Catholic Church, defensive) debate about why exactly the Church murdered Giordano Bruno. There are many possible reasons. It might have been for his cosmological beliefs – his conviction that the universe was infinite. It could have been for his heretical, anti-religious beliefs. We are told that whilst in prison Bruno claimed that Christ was 'a magician and likewise the apostles, and he had a mind to do as much as they, and more ... he wanted to tend to the art of divination, and to draw the whole world behind him'. It could also have been for his magical Neoplatonic beliefs, his view that the universe lives and breathes and has a soul, or it may be that all these reasons – his magical, cosmological and heretical beliefs – lay behind his murder.

•

By 1609 John Dee, as we've seen, was also dying, impoverished and forgotten in his house beside the Thames. It was then that his friend and student John Pontois took him in (even at the end John Dee had friends) to his house in Bishopsgate in the city and there, a few months later, Dee finally passed away, a tall, stooped, white-bearded figure, lost in another age and so old as to be nearly transparent. And yet even now Dee was not completely forgotten, because about five or ten years after his death, the book collector Sir Robert Cotton, acting on a tip-off, sent men with spades to dig up a field close to John Dee's house at Mortlake. We don't know where the tip-off came from, but clearly it was correct because Cotton recovered several manuscripts that had once belonged to Dee and which presumably Dee himself had buried there to keep them secret.

Cotton gave these manuscripts to the scholar Meric Casaubon, asking him to transcribe them before they disintegrated – which Casaubon did and discovered that they were part of John Dee's diaries, including his conversations with angels, and covering those years when he was in Bohemia and hatched the wife-swapping deal with Edward Kelley. They include details of John and Jane Dee's sex life, their everyday activities, their quarrels, their family life and how much John Dee loved his children, with the result that we now have a far more vivid sense of his inner life than we do for most Elizabethans.

Meric Casaubon then wrote a book about John Dee, accusing him of working with the devil – whilst also affirming in the strongest possible terms that spirits, both good and bad, existed. (Casaubon was a member of that old seventeenth-century tribe who – along with the philosopher Thomas Browne and the Reverend Robert Kirk – still believed in angels, witches, fairies and other such spirits.)

A generation later, more of Dee's manuscripts turned up. This time they were rediscovered in 1642 by a certain Mr and Mrs Jones of Lombard Street in London who found them in the secret compartment of an old cedarwood chest that had once belonged to Thomas Woodall, the son of Dr John Woodall who had known John Dee well. These manuscripts are thought to be part of Dee's book, the *Quinti Libri Mysteriorum*. Despite some of these rediscovered manuscripts being lost again (they were used by the Jones's cook to line her pie dishes), a few found their way into Elias Ashmole's hands. The antiquary fell upon them with delight, his obsession with John Dee being already in full swing. Ashmole lived in a time when a growing number of men were obsessed with hunting down the past.

Then, in the late 1830s, two manuscripts were discovered in the Ashmolean Museum which turned out to be more of John Dee's diaries. They were edited by James Halliwell and published in 1842.

Notwithstanding these discoveries, the afterlife of all the wizards was one of forgetfulness and neglect. The Enlightenment put the Renaissance magicians out of fashion. They suffered from a kind of logical-positivist attitude amongst some historians, who believed that if magic isn't real then the history of anyone who pursued magic could not be worth studying. In addition to this, the wife-swapping episode amplified the scandals and embarrassment that clung to John Dee's name.

Yet, neither Dee nor Bruno were ever completely forgotten. They have both been remembered, albeit in unexpected ways, and by the twentieth century their reputations were beginning to be re-evaluated.

A number of book historians, led by Julian Roberts and Andrew Watson – as if moved by John Dee's huge grief at the loss of his library – came together and try and recreate the titles he lost. They used John Dee's own catalogues to hunt down as many of his original books as they could. The books were scattered across the UK. The Bodleian in Oxford, the Royal College of Physicians in London, St John's College, Cambridge and

Chetham's Library in Manchester all have some of Dee's original books. We cannot bring the actual books home to Mortlake, but scholars can list the titles and so recreate a virtual library.

The charisma of the argumentative Giordano Bruno has also spread down through the centuries. The twentieth-century scholar Frances Yates, who most days worked in the Warburg Library, dedicated her life to studying him; everything she wrote is infused with affection for him.

Yates played an important role in keeping the reputations of both Bruno and Dee alive. She believed that their belief in magic was not a maverick one-off conviction, but was symptomatic of ideas that were widespread, even mainstream at the time. She believed that these concepts were not a hangover from the medieval period but flourished in their own right, that the Renaissance was not a forerunner of the rational Enlightenment but a time that glittered with its own beliefs in magic, ghosts and spirits. She believed that the 'dominant philosophy of the Elizabethan age was precisely the occult philosophy, with its magic, its melancholy, its aim of penetrating into profound spheres of knowledge and experience, scientific and spiritual, its fears of the dangers of such a quest and the fierce opposition which it encountered'.

Historians have held many different views on the Renaissance. Some have seen it as the beginnings of the rational Enlightenment world. Others have thundered against its superstitions. Frances Yates recognised and accepted its magical precepts.

Subsequent scholars have modified Yates's conclusions. They have pointed out that there was not such a huge leap from medieval to Renaissance magic and, as well as the influence of the Jewish Kabbalah, they have included the complicated, interwoven story of Arabic magic, thus changing the balance of

Yates's conclusions. But even so, more than forty years after her death, Yates's ideas are still being fiercely debated, which is, in itself, remarkable.

There is something about Giordano Bruno that makes you want to fictionalise him. There have been many imagined versions of Bruno, including in S. J. Parris's crime novels, in which Bruno is the detective-hero. We all have our own Giordano Bruno. For me, he is every big-hearted, big-talking, trouble-making man who rails against the universe that I have ever known.

Chapter Twenty-Nine
Aberfoyle

One day, when I had nearly finished writing this book, I decided to go to Aberfoyle in Scotland to see where the seventeenth-century reverend Robert Kirk had lived (he who wrote *The Commonwealth of Elves and Fairies*).

It was April and I stayed the first night on the castle rock in Stirling, where the grey stones were dressed in green, and the woods were cold and sweet and filled with fluttering birds. From there, I went by bus to Aberfoyle itself, which is still a village under the ridge that divides the Highlands from the south of Scotland. I was looking for Robert Kirk's house, for the woods where he walked, for the roofless, ruined church in whose grave-yard he – or maybe the facsimile of him? – is buried.

I stood by Robert Kirk's grave – if that indeed is where it is – and then walked up into the woods beyond his house. I went to Aberfoyle with no particular magical expectations. In fact, I told myself in a sceptical kind of way that it is not hard to see why Aberfoyle might have acquired its magical reputation: because it is on the Highland Boundary Fault Line and is thus in a liminal space between north and south; because it is at the source of the River Forth, the mightiest river in Scotland; and because it is said that in early times you could find here very beautiful freshwater pearls, some white and some – a very few – an exceptional pale pink. What could be more magical than this?

So, I was taken aback by the atmosphere in those woods, by their strange, dense dreaminess, by their prickly silence and by their sunlit otherworldliness. I passed a few other people, also looking fairy-struck. I was embarrassed by how entranced I must be looking.

I had never planned to fall in love with magic, though it is not hard to see why so many people have done so down the centuries. It is partly because we yearn for the power and freedom that magic gives us, and it is partly because this world – on a good day – already feels full of everyday magic, the magic of music and sunlight and poetry and storytelling and falling in love and the sheer strange fact of being alive, and so it seems but a small jump to believe in the big magic too.

As for Neoplatonism, I never planned to fall in love with that either – I thought I was far too sceptical and twenty-first century. It was Neoplatonism's optimism and its delight in the beauty of the world that seized my imagination. In the bleakness of the pandemic there was something exciting about the idea that the universe is alive, that it lives and breathes and has a soul. I even began to wonder whether it is true – though some days this seems improbable in the extreme – that, as Marsilio Ficino believed, it is love that powers the universe and connects all its bits together.

Maybe it was because of thoughts like these (and because I was spending so much time in the Warburg Library) that there came slipping and sliding through the folds in our bedroom curtains early one morning the very last characters and the very last story...

HE IS NOT DEAD

It is 17 July 1975 and in Brazil a commuter train has just been derailed, in Angola the Portuguese have started evacuating their nationals during a lull in the civil war, whilst overhead in space, the Russian cosmonaut Alexei Leonov and the American astronaut Tom Stafford are shaking hands and making peace. Meanwhile, down in Gordon Square in London the young girls are out with their long, droopy hair and their flowery dresses. They wear sandals made of rope with ribbons that they tie around their legs. Two of the girls have taken off these sandals and are swinging them by the ends of the ribbons whilst pressing their bare feet down onto the soft grass. At the gate to the square, Frances Yates watches in bewilderment. She was born in 1899 into a prosperous Victorian family. Now, she stands here in Gordon Square in July 1975 and thinks she must have taken a wrong turn somewhere in the universe because she feels so utterly lost in time.

She has stood here on this spot hundreds of times before, though the very first time was in the autumn of 1940 and she had not been standing exactly, more like she had fallen to her knees. Throughout the summer that year she and Rosalind had been doing war work, pushing bits of paper around in a big old terraced house not far from Regent's Park. Frances also did ambulance shifts three nights a week. They shared a tiny flat close to Mecklenburgh Square and they often walked home from work and then on to the pub where they smoked Craven A cigarettes and drank until it grew too dark to see their glasses, whereupon they made their way home through the moonlit, starlit streets. The bombing was not too bad that summer, but when September came, they realised that all this had been but a rehearsal, because then the Blitz began in earnest.

It came quite suddenly. One evening – whilst walking to the pub – one of them said, 'That's a beautiful sunset' (pointing to the east) and the other one said, 'But shouldn't it be in the west?' at which the first one said, 'Oh God, it's a fire,' and the other one said, 'They've bombed the docks,' and so it began.

The noise that night and for many nights to come was dreadful – the shrieks and crashes and terrible roar of the incoming bombs – and the sights – when they dared to look out from behind the blackout blinds – redoubled their panic, the flash of guns, the searchlights raking the sky, the parachute flares. They grew used to strange sights. One night, Frances turned into Gower Street and saw a woman and many children running round in circles in their night clothes, the house behind them leaning at a crazy angle. Frances and Rosalind believed it was the end of the world. They thought what terrible luck it was to live when the world was ending, to never get the chance to write the books they wanted to write.

Frances was writing her PhD on the Elizabethan magician Giordano Bruno. She had met him in a book in 1937, whereupon he had taken up residence inside her head and never gone away. Now, he kept her company, which was comforting because he too had lived in dangerous times. One night, Frances and Rosalind were sitting back to back in the air raid shelter waiting for the all-clear. All around them were soldiers and refugees and wardens and firemen. Frances was talking about Bruno.

'Really, I think you are in love with him,' said Rosalind.

'And why not?' said Frances. 'He was a lost cause and I am a lost cause, and I love lost causes.'

Romantic as a boy, thinks Rosalind. 'What will you do if we lose?' she asks.

'What? Now? I don't know. What will any of us do?'

Another night Frances was walking home by herself, past Gordon Square, when she heard the sirens. She looked up, saw the sky cut by a searchlight so that it fell into two halves, felt the roar and the rush of the bomb and saw the flash of guns and the streaks of bullets as they tried to catch it. She should have run for the shelter, but she was mesmerised by the sight of it. She could have sworn she saw a face up there – either it was Bruno's or her brother Jimmy's, she couldn't tell – and so it was only when she felt the rush of the bomb on the nape of her neck that she dived straight into the bushes, just here, just exactly here at the gate to Gordon Square.

And there she lay, she didn't know how long, with her head in the bushes and her legs on the pavement – and she thought about Jimmy and how much she missed him, Jimmy, who had died another lifetime before this, was already twenty-five years dead when that bomb fell. He had died in 1916. This is what she remembered: sitting on the scullery floor of the house in Oxton, her back to the cool stone legs of the scullery sink – reading – she was always reading, when Jimmy came in and saw her and ducked down on the floor beside her. He drew out a cigarette packet.

'You're smoking,' she said. 'Does Papa know?'

He smiled, looked at her quizzically. *What do you think?*

Now she smiled too, didn't say anything either and just took a cigarette, tried an experimental puff. She coughed wildly. He patted her on the back.

'Ugh,' she said. 'Horrid.'

'What are you reading?' he asked.

'Shakespeare. *Much Ado About Nothing.* There are two people in it called Benedick and Beatrice, and they quarrel all the time. When I grow up, I'm going to quarrel a lot.'

'You're a good kid,' he said, dropping a careless kiss on the top of her head. He stood up and brushed down his trousers.

'Be careful, Jimmy,' she said from the floor and then he was gone.

That year, she wrote in her diary, 'I have an awful desire to be famous.'

And she remembered where she was when they heard. It was March 1916 and she had been sitting with her back to the same cool stone legs of the scullery sink – reading – when she heard a scream from the front hall and knew what it was.

Where did all the years go? There was only one entry in her diary for 1922: 'Books read – 97. Including 53 novels.' The following year, she wrote in her diary, 'I am not much good at painting. I am no good at all at music so there is only writing left. So I will write. But in order to write you must have read, and so I am reading like fury.'

Oh, the books I've read instead of living. After Jimmy died there were three of us – me, Hannah and Ruby – and we lived in ruins.

She decided to study history. It was the Warburg that saved her. The old professors in the Warburg Library took her in and so all through the fifties she could pursue Bruno in and out of the book stacks. The professors were mostly Jewish and they had émigré habits and liked to drink tea at four o'clock downstairs in the basement. Sometimes, they were joined by Mr Anthony Blunt, Surveyor of the Queen's Paintings. He was tall and skeletal, twice their height with long, upper-class English legs, and though he wore a threadbare cardigan he breathed an air of ineffable elegance. He was researching the French painter Poussin. The small old Jewish professors looked at him quizzically as if to say, 'We don't understand him,' and then they looked at Frances as if to say, 'He's a gentile, he's one of yours, you explain him to us.' But Frances couldn't, because every inch of Mr Blunt exuded authority and somewhere along the line (where did it come from?) she has picked up the idea that she belongs with these old Jewish professors because, like them, she is an outsider.

Outside the library window, Suez came and went and so did Anthony Eden, and she and Hannah and Ruby never left but continued to live together in the old family house in Claygate. She was growing more prosperous and more highly regarded by other historians, though also squarer and older, her feet bigger, her legs thicker – 'About the size and proportions of a well-made coffin,' she thought, looking at herself in the mirror, though her mind stayed supple and girl-like, touched by poetry, and still moved by the life and death of the little Italian friar. She had never lost the habit of looking up and down the street for him at library closing time.

She grew deft in how she managed men. They were home from the war and so were everywhere in the book stacks, younger than her, good-looking and combative. Not that she minded a fight, and anyway she had discovered how to handle them. Be unreasonable; be a big, unreasonable woman. It confuses them, makes them step back in alarm.

In the late fifties, when she too was in her late fifties, she fell in love. He was less than half her age – a PhD student – it was hopeless and humiliating, and anyway her first loyalty was to Bruno and so she prayed that the boy hadn't noticed. He wore blue jeans and sometimes at night she lay awake and tried to pack him away, blue jeans and all, into a box where she could forget him. At last, he faded out of sight, though for several years thereafter she only had to look at a pair of jeans for the boy himself to spring into solid form, stained in the colours of the past, blue for his jeans, gold for his hair in the sunlight.

Time kept forming new layers and each time she was buried deeper. At first, the sensation was curious, then dismaying, then alarming. She now moved to the metallic sound of hairpins falling from her thick white hair and scattering on the ground. She had discovered that time was not linear, it was circular. One winter evening towards the end of 1959 she looked westwards out of the tall windows on the second floor of the library and saw Tottenham Court Road in September 1940, going up in flames. Sometimes, when she wrote a cheque, she got the date wrong: 1557, not 1957. When she felt gloomy – which was often – she wrote notes to herself, compiled lists, and always at the top was written: 'I must work harder.'

And then just when she had thought the fifties were eternal, they ended and she put her nose outside the library door and sniffed the change. She had to admit that Bruno would have liked this new decade very much, it being so very young and so very, very defiant.

First came the good times, books, reviews, articles, lectures, conferences. She published her book on Bruno, then a book called *The Art of Memory*, and then one on John Dee and the Rosicrucians. For a while she felt like she couldn't put a foot wrong, that her mind would never stop running on ecstatically, that it was like jumping stepping stones across a river, that it was like leaping, like flying. But, as fast as the good times came, they also vanished. If she were Elizabethan, she would have said that the stars had shifted. Her sister Hannah died, whilst her other sister Ruby fell ill and began to have hallucinations. Her own eyes began to fail and her detractors and critics gathered around her, writing unkind articles about her books.

She thought that she had hunted Bruno down, though sometimes she thought it was the other way round and that time and Bruno had hunted her. Sometimes she even thought that the world was a labyrinth and that only once had she ever reached its edge and looked out beyond it. It had been the night the bomb fell near Gordon Square. She had thrown herself down into the bushes and lain quite still and stunned. First she had thought of Jimmy, but then she had thought, 'Oh, he's overhead, he's watching out for me,' and she didn't mean Jimmy, she meant Bruno. She felt how he moved overhead from east to west, the breath of his passing, the touch of infinity, and how in the darkness he tapped the roof of Christ the King with his feet and then was gone in the direction of Tottenham Court Road. And she thought with delight, 'So he did not die, they did not kill him. His skin is still soft and warm, his cheeks are rosy, he is young and tender like asparagus, he is not dead.'

WHO WAS REAL
(AND WHO WAS
NOT)

Heinrich Cornelius Agrippa (1486–1535): German-born scholar, soldier and writer on occult matters. His most famous book – *Three Books of Occult Philosophy* – is infused with Hermeticism, the Kabbalah and Neoplatonism.

Aristotle: the fourth-century BCE philosopher and pupil of Plato. His philosophy became very popular and influential during the Middle Ages.

Elias Ashmole (1617–1692): a scholar, astrologer and alchemist with an antiquarian twist that was typical of the seventeenth century. He founded the Ashmolean Museum in Oxford.

John Aubrey (1626–1697): a seventeenth-century writer with an interest in folklore and archaeology. He records many magical, folkloric beliefs, though – like Elias Ashmole – always with an antiquarian bent.

Robert Boyle (1627–1692): a scientist and an alchemist, as well as an early member of the Royal Society. He discovered Boyle's law on gases. He also believed in spirits and in second sight.

Sophie Brahe (1559–1643): youngest sister of Tycho Brahe and, like him, a talented astronomer. History has rarely accorded her the status that her talents deserve.

Tycho Brahe (1546–1601): a Danish astronomer. He built himself an astronomical observatory on the island of Hven off the coast of Denmark, and – without even the use of a telescope – created the most accurate star map yet invented. He also experimented with alchemy.

Thomas Browne (1605–1682): an English doctor, writer and philosopher, based in Norwich. He was an early member of the Royal Society but saw no contradiction between science and his belief in witches and fairies.

Giordano Bruno (1548–1600): a charismatic Renaissance scholar, reputed in his time to be a magician. He was bold, ironic, brave, sarcastic and opinionated. He was burnt at the stake in Rome by the Catholic Church in 1600.

Tommaso Campanella (1568–1639): born into a poor Calabrian family, he was adopted by the Dominican friars but rapidly got into trouble for his heretical ideas and opposition to Aristotle's teachings. He was first prosecuted for heresy and then accused of being part of an uprising against the Spanish authorities. He served twenty-seven years in prison, during which time he wrote his most famous book, *The City of the Sun*.

Isaac and Meric Casaubon: the Casaubons were father and son and both of them were classical scholars in the sixteenth and seventeenth centuries. Isaac Casaubon dated the *Corpus Hermeticum* to the third and fourth centuries CE, rather than the much earlier date that had been previously believed.

Nicolaus Copernicus (1473–1543): Polish astronomer and mathematician. He came to the revolutionary conclusion that the earth goes round the sun, not vice versa.

Jane Dee (1555–1605): John Dee's third wife. She was twenty-eight years younger than him, the mother of his eight children and followed him on his journeys across Europe. We know of her because she features in his diaries, in which we get a glimpse of the demanding but constrained lives of Tudor women.

John Dee (1527–1608): an erudite and gullible mathematician and expert on navigation whom Queen Elizabeth I employed as her in-house magician. He was obsessed with discovering why God had created the world and believed that he could do so if only he could learn to talk to the angels who had been present at its creation.

Thomas Digges (1546–1595): an English mathematician and astronomer who was the ward of John Dee. He backed the

Copernican system when it was scarcely known and deeply controversial. He also believed that the universe was infinite and in this he predated Giordano Bruno.

The Dudley clan: as a young man John Dee was the tutor of Robert Dudley, who later grew up to be Queen Elizabeth's favourite. The Dudley clan married into the Sidney and Herbert families and became one of the most powerful families in sixteenth-century England, but they never lost their affection for, or feeling of connection to, John Dee.

Marsilio Ficino (1433–1499): an Italian Renaissance philosopher who lived his entire life in or near Florence. He worked for the Medici family, was one of the first European translators of Plato and fell in love with the secret and subversive ideas of the *Corpus Hermeticum*.

Galileo Galilei (1564–1642): the Italian scientist, mathematician and astronomer who made major discoveries in astronomy, the laws of motion and engineering, as well as inventing the telescope.

The Kabbalah: this is mystical teaching from the early history of Judaism which aims to explain the relationship between the eternal, unchanging God and the finite and changing universe.

Edward Kelley (1555–1597): the most important of John Dee's scryers, he accompanied Dee on his journey to Prague and persuaded him that the angels told him they should share their wives.

Johannes Kepler (1571–1630): the child of a poor German Lutheran family who became an astronomer at the court of Rudolf II in Prague. He built on the work of Copernicus and, using Tycho Brahe's data, mapped the movements of the planets. He observed that the further away the planets were from the sun the slower they moved and thus he came close to discovering gravity. His personal life was always hard. He was run out of Graz when the Catholic Archduke Charles began a campaign against the Lutherans, but also (despite being very devout) fell out with the Lutherans over the nature of the eucharist.

Athanasius Kircher (1602–1680): a Jesuit scholar who lived in seventeenth- century Rome and created one of the most extraordinary museums ever invented. He is often misunderstood. He was almost certainly a Neoplatonist, hence his huge sprawling museum that attempts to tell the story of everything.

Robert Kirk (1644–1692): a folklorist and a minister in Aberfoyle in Scotland. He wrote *The Secret Commonwealth of Elves and Fairies*.

The Music of the Spheres: the idea that the journeys the planets traced through the heavens were so harmoniously perfect that they caused a Music of the Spheres that could be heard and felt in men's souls. The idea goes back even before Plato to Pythagoras.

The Neoplatonists: A school of philosophers starting with Plotinus, who lived in the eastern Mediterranean in the third century CE and who set out to interpret Plato and keep his philosophy alive. The Neoplatonists were more mystical (even) than Plato. They have been much maligned over the centuries for their dreamy mysticism, although in the twentieth century their reputation improved.

Paracelsus (1493–1541): Born in Switzerland, he was a doctor and alchemist who lived a wandering, nomadic life. He believed that alchemy could be used to develop medicines and cure illnesses.

Plato (427–348): one of the greatest philosophers that has ever lived. In antiquity he was Aristotle's teacher although during the Middle Ages Aristotle gained a higher standing. Plato's status only recovered with the rediscovery of his writings during the Renaissance.

George Gemistos Plethon (1355–1452): a Byzantine scholar and philosopher who helped to bring about the revival of the ancient Greek classics, and especially Plato, during the early Renaissance. He was said to be a pagan. He was at least seventy-nine when he came west to Florence with Emperor John Palaeologus VIII.

The Renaissance: the Renaissance was a huge cultural movement that impacted art, architecture, literature and science. One key part of it was looking back to classical Greece and Rome, not due to nostalgia but to emulate and surpass the achievements of these civilisations. The rediscovery of Plato was part of all this revolutionary thinking.

Rudolf II (1552–1612): the Holy Roman Emperor, he was known for his interest in alchemy and magic. He made Prague his capital and turned it into a European centre for art, magic and science.

Girolamo Savonarola (1452–1498): an austere Florentine priest and hell-fire preacher who believed that the church needed purging of its vanities and luxuries. He ruled Florence from 1494 to 1498 but made many enemies who ultimately turned on him and in May 1498 they ensured that he was hung.

John Stow (1525–1605): a London-born historian, best known for his *Survey of London*, a ward-by-ward description of London, how it was in his day and how it had been – as far as he could tell – in earlier times. He probably knew John Dee and, like Dee, had an extensive library. For the last half of his life he lived in the parish of St Andrew Undershaft.

The Symposium: Plato's hugely influential dialogue on the nature of love.

Frances Yates (1899–1981): an English historian of the Renaissance, she is associated with the Warburg Library in London (until recently her photograph still hung in the corridor on the ground floor). She was part of a mid-twentieth-century scholarly movement that encouraged us to see the Renaissance not as an early modern version of ourselves nor as a continuation of the medieval period, but as something distinctively different in and of itself.

The other characters –
Grandpa, Grandma and their granddaughters in *The Easterners*,
Cecily, Cassie and their father,
the young woman whose husband vanished with the fairies,
the three young daughters of the man who destroyed books,

the young girl who was an alchemist in Venice,
the old man who made the queen's museum and his son,
the five children of Will Shannon, the queen's under-gardener,
and their granny,
and Ma, the storyteller, and her children –

I invented.

Frances Yates and her respect for Giordano Bruno was entirely real, though whether she ever looked out of the windows of the Warburg Library and thought she was back in 1940 when London burnt, I cannot tell you.

NOTES

The Many Dreams of Robert Boyle, Scientist
Lawrence M. Principe, in his essay 'The Scientific Revolution', says that Boyle once wrote that the world is like 'a well-contrived Romance' and that for Boyle, 'the Creator is the ultimate romance writer, and the scientific investigators are the readers trying to figure out all the relationships and cross-crossing storylines in the world' (*The Scientific Revolution*, Oxford University Press, 2011, p. 25). It was one of those moments – I had them often when writing this book – when it dawned on me just how differently men and women saw the world back then.

Introduction: How I Fell in Love with Magic
For an account of human understanding of the heavens prior to Copernicus (including the idea that the angels turn the crystalline spheres that surround our world) see Max Caspar's book *Kepler* (Dover Publications, 1993, pp. 20ff.).

1. The Wizards
The quote from Henry Agrippa (The word 'magician', said Agrippa, 'does not among learned men signify a sorcerer or one that is superstitious or devilish but a wise man, a priest or a

prophet.') is cited in *Spirituality and the Occult* by B. J. Gibbons (Routledge, 2001, p. 38).

John Dee was not the only scholar at St John's College pursuing angel magic and the philosopher's stone. Glyn Parry also names William Cecil, Richard Eden and John Hatcher. See Glyn Parry's chapter 'John Dee' in *The Occult World* (Routledge, 2015), edited by Christopher Partridge.

Benjamin Woolley, *The Queen's Conjurer* (Flamingo, 2002, p.71), suggests that Christophe Plantin printed the heretical works of Hendrick Niclaes, founder of the Family of Love.

2. Mortlake

The edition of Dee's diaries that I used to write this book was *The Diaries of John Dee* edited by Edward Fenton (Day Books, 1998).

For an exploration of life in the Dees' house in Mortlake, see Deborah Harkness's article 'Managing an Experimental Household: The Dees of Mortlake and the Practice of Natural Philosophy' (*Isis*, Vol. 88, No. 2, June 1997). See also two key books by Deborah Harkness: *John Dee's Conversations with Angels* (Cambridge University Press, 1999) and *The Jewel House* (Yale University Press, 2007).

The quote from Ashmole that Dee's 'great ability in astrologie and the more secret parts of learning (to which he had a strong propensity and unwearying Fancy) drew from the Envious and Vulgar many rash, lewd and lying Scandals' is cited in *Seeing the Word* by Hakan Hakansson (Lunds Universitet, p.10).

3. Magical London

The details about the booksellers around St Paul's Cathedral come from the website www.englandcast.com.

For the museums and collections of sixteenth-century London see the first chapter of Deborah Harkness's book *The Jewel House* (Yale University Press, 2007). Cabinets of curiosities, also known as kunstkammers, were an early form of museum. They were personal creations, not national institutions, and were attempts to replicate the world in miniature and therefore understand it. To us they now seem beautiful, mysterious, credulous and semi-magical.

The Greenwich witch's bottle is in the Old Royal Naval College visitor centre.

The meeting between Cecil and the Venetian alchemist Agnello came about because Cecil wanted his opinion on a mysterious black stone that the explorer Martin Frobisher had brought back from the New World. The meeting is described in Deborah Harkness's *The Jewel House* (Yale University Press, 2007) at the beginning of Chapter 4. Also in Chapter 3 of the same book is an account of London's scientific instrument makers.

For a discussion of the magicians of the poor, see Owen Davies's book *Popular Magic* (Hambledon Continuum, 2007, pp. 4–5).

4. Master Plato

The idea that the earth is alive comes from Plato's *Timaeus*, 30b-d 1.

Guido Giglioni, in his essay on Frances Yates 'Who is Afraid of Frances Yates?' (*Bruniana and Campanelliana*, vol. 20, no. 2, pp. 421–432), said, 'In a universe in which every single thing was deemed to be alive, magic was the discipline in charge of animating objects, such as moving and speaking statues.'

It may be because teachers in the medieval universities, including those who taught astrology, wore long black robes that long robes became the uniform for all magicians everywhere.

For Plato as a counterculture phenomenon, see James Hankins's contribution to the *Routledge Encyclopedia of Knowledge* (rep. routledge.com) under Platonism, Renaissance.

5. Marsilio Ficino
James Hankins's book *Plato in the Italian Renaissance* (Brill, 1990), especially pp. 277 ff, gives an account of Marsilio Ficino's appearance and personality. Anthony Grafton in *Magus: The Art of Magic from Faustus to Agrippa* (Allen Lane, 2024, p. 95) says that Ficino himself believed that his own melancholy character had been formed by Saturn being in the ascendant on the day of his birth.

Ficino's belief that love is magic is cited by Gyorgy Szonyi in 'The Hermetic Revival in Italy' in *The Occult World*, ed. Christopher Partridge, p. 65. And see also David Fideler's *Restoring the Soul of the World* (Inner Traditions, 2014, Chapter 6): 'Love is the cosmic power that circulates through the universe and animates the world ... Love unites those things that are separate and causes like to attract like ... The living, sympathetic interconnections between the different parts accounts for the efficacy of magic and other enchantments.'

Marsilio Ficino's brush with the Counter- Reformation is described in the *Stanford Encyclopedia of Philosophy*, which states that it was the third book of *De Vita* – 'On obtaining Life from the Heavens' – i.e. drawing down celestial forces into inanimate objects – that got him into trouble.

The quote – 'Behold now standing before you the man who has pierced the sky, wended his way amongst the stars and overpassed the margins of the world, who has broken down the imaginary divisions between the spheres – the first, the eighth, the ninth, the tenth, what you will – which are described in the false mathematics of blind and popular philosophy' – is spoken by Theophil (Bruno's spokesman) in the first dialogue of Bruno's *The Ash Wednesday Supper*.

6. The *Corpus Hermeticum*
The creation myth cited here is outlined in the first tract of the *Corpus Hermeticum*. It includes the idea that man and nature made love and from their lovemaking came the world.

The website www.mystai.co.uk is useful on the genesis story in the *Corpus Hermeticum*.

The Origen quote is from *Homilies on Leviticus* 1–16, p. 92.

The information that Ben Jonson and John Milton had copies of Ficino's translations of Plato comes from Ross King's book *The*

Bookseller of Florence (Chatto & Windus, 2021, p. 385). Also, Kristeller's *The First Printed Edition of Plato's Works*, p. 137, which is in *Science and History, Studies in Honour of Edward Rosen*, pp. 25–39.

The quote that 'magic became the most powerful manifestation of the growing conviction that human kind should act out its potential in the free exercise of its power...' comes from page 3 of John S. Mebane's book *Renaissance Magic and the Return of the Golden Age: The Occult Tradition in Marlowe, Jonson and Shakespeare* (University of Nebraska Press, 1989). Chris Gosden's assertion that magic gives you a feeling of kinship with and participation in the universe comes from the first chapter of his book *A History of Magic* (Viking, 2020).

7. John Dee's Library
'My Lord Thresorer' is presumably the lord treasurer, William Cecil. We can guess that Dee feared him because so many of Dee's books concerned the illicit subject of magic.

The probable layout of John Dee's library is explored by Benjamin Woolley in *The Queen's Conjuror* (Flamingo, 2002, pp. 94 ff).

According to Edward Wilson-Lee, *The Catalogue of Shipwrecked Books* (William Collins, 2018, pp. 302–303), chronology – the order in which things happened – was one of the ways in which the new libraries of the Renaissance were starting to be arranged.

On painting book titles (and images) onto the fore edges of books, see the article by Mike Cummings on the artist Cesare Vecellio on the website www.news.yale.edu for 14 March 2019.

8. The Books on John Dee's Shelves

Karen Silvia de Leon-Jones's book *Giordano Bruno and the Kabbalah* (Yale University Press, 1997) is excellent for the influence of the Kabbalah on sixteenth- century intellectuals.

G. Lloyd-Jones's book *The Discovery of Hebrew in Tudor England* (Manchester University Press, 1983) discusses at length how and where Elizabethan intellectuals learnt Hebrew.

The quote about Guillaume Postel comes from *The Occult World*, ed. Christopher Partridge (2015, p. 108).

Benjamin Woolley, *The Queen's Conjurer* (Flamingo, 2002, p. 96), states that John Dee had a copy of Agrippa's *De Occulta Philosophia* on his desk.

Agrippa's visit to London is described in *John Colet* by John Gleason (University of California Press, 1989, pp.145–147). The fact that John Colet had a copy of Marsilio Ficino's *Epistolae*, published in 1475, comes from the same book, p. 47.

That Agrippa believed the discovery of sex brought about the Fall of man is stated in *The Occult World*, ed. Christopher Partridge (Routledge, 2015, Chapter 5, p. 95).

There is a good account of Agrippa's *Three Books of Occult Philosophy* in Anthony Grafton's book *Magus: The Art of Magic from Faustus to Agrippa* (Allen Lane, 2024), especially Chapter 5. The quote that Agrippa was a 'judaising heretic who has introduced into Christian schools the criminal, condemned and prohibited art of the Kabbala' is cited in Grafton's book *Magus*, p. 195.

Martin Del Rio (1551–1608) was a Jesuit demon-hunter. He was part of the Counter-Reformation and a passionate enemy of what he saw as witches, demons and magic. He believed that magic came from the devil and was therefore heretical. He wrote a six-volume work on subject. The story of the demons who got inside Agrippa's house is quoted in Grafton's book *Magus*, pp. 176–177.

9. John Dee and the Women
What little we know about Joanna Kelley is discussed in Susan Bassett's article 'Absent Presences: Edward Kelley's Family in the Writings of John Dee', in *John Dee: Interdisciplinary Studies in English Renaissance Thought* (Dordrecht Springer, 2006, pp. 285–294).

Jane Dee's loving note to John Dee is cited on page 282 of Benjamin Woolley's book *The Queen's Conjurer* (Flamingo, 2002).

10. The Good Wife Faldo's Magic
The observation that John Dee put effort into befriending servants comes from *The Queen's Conjurer* (Flamingo, 2002, p. 93) by Benjamin Woolley. Dee also tried to save the life of his old

nurse Ann Frank, as outlined by Hakan Hakansson in *Seeing the Word* (Lunds Universitet, pp. 31ff).

For the 'old men on Midsummers Eve sitting on the church porch waiting to see the ghosts of those who would die in the following year', see John Aubrey's *Remaines of Gentilisme and Judaisme*, p. 599.

The concept of the 'doubtful spirits', the difference between the responses of the Protestant and Catholics to supernatural beings and the way that Protestants considered Catholics particularly prone to magical thinking all come from Darren Oldridge's book *The Supernatural in Tudor and Stuart England* (Routledge, 2016, p. 40).

The story of Old Shuck, the demonic black dog, is cited in Darren Oldridge's book *The Supernatural in Tudor and Stuart England* (Routledge, 2016, p. 40).

The similarities between the witches' beliefs and those of the Neoplatonists are suggested by J. R. Christianson in his article on Tycho and Sophie Brahe, 'Tycho Brahe in Scandinavian Scholarship' in *History of Science*, vol. 36, pp. 467–484.

11. The Fairies
The suggestion that the fairies were the magic of the poor and the dispossessed is well explored in Owen Davies's book *Popular Magic: Cunning-Folk in English History* (Hambledon Continuum, 2007).

The quote about the Dorset cunning man John Walsh comes from Owen Davies's book *Popular Magic: Cunning-Folk in English History* (as above), p. 70.

The reference to fairies in William Langham's herbal *The Garden of Health* is cited in Darren Oldridge's book *The Supernatural in Tudor and Stuart England* (Routledge, 2016, p. 119).

On 9 March 1582, Edward Kelley offered to introduce John Dee to the fairies. Dee was horrified and appalled by this idea.

Ashmole's papers, including the 'fairy' documents, are in the Bodleian Library, MS Ashmole 1406.

12. Bedtime Stories

There is a good discussion about the intertwining of oral and literary sources for fairy tales by Ronald Hutton in his essay 'The Making of the Early Modern British Fairy Tradition' (*Historical Journal*, Vol. 57, Issue 4, December 2014).

13. Alchemy

There is a good introduction to Renaissance alchemy in Lawrence Principe's book *The Secrets of Alchemy* (University of Chicago Press, 2013), especially Chapter 5. For the alchemists' claim that they could prolong life and restore youth, see Jennifer M. Rampling's book *The Experimental Fire* (University of Chicago Press, 2020, p. 15). Also interesting are two articles by Jennifer M. Rampling, 'John Dee and the Alchemists: Practising and Promoting English Alchemy in the Holy Roman Empire' (2012) and 'John Dee and the Sciences: Early Modern Networks of Knowledge' (2011), which are both available to read on the website www.pmc.ncbi.nlm.gov.

The alchemical steps are listed in www.encyclopedia.com – Alchemy: Renaissance.

The quote concerning Paracelsus ('God was the divine alchemist who created the world, by calcinating, congealing, distilling and sublimating the elements of chaos') comes from Alchemy: Renaissance at www.encyclopedia.com.

The quote that 'a doctor must seek out old wives, gipsies, sorcerers, wondering tribes, old robbers and such outlaws and take lessons from them. A doctor must be a traveller … Knowledge is experience' comes from www.britannica.com.

14. The Golden Age of Alchemy
The fact that Elizabeth kept an alchemist called Millicent Franckwell comes from *Supernatural and Secular Power in Early Modern England* (Routledge, 2016, eds Marcus Harmes and Victoria Bladen, footnote 23, Chapter 1).

The observation that glassworks to make alchemical equipment were scarce in sixteenth-century England comes from Jonathan Hughes's article on Thomas Charnock, 'Base Matter into Gold: The Humanity of Thomas Charnock, a Forgotten Alchemist,' available at The Free Library on the web at www.thefreelibrary.com.

15. Lady Sidney's Recipes
Meredith Ray's book *Daughters of Alchemy: Women and*

Scientific Culture in Early Modern Italy (Harvard University Press, 2015) is an excellent introduction to women and alchemy. The first two chapters tell the stories of, respectively, Caterina Sforza, Countess of Forlì, and Isabella Cortese, both of them Italian women alchemists of the Renaissance.

For a discussion of Sidney's Sonnet 108 and the way that poets have used alchemy as a metaphor for the power of love and transformation, see Jeffrey P. Cain's article 'Sidney's Astrophil and Stella, Sonnet 108', which is available online at www.digitalcommons. sacredheart.edu.

For more on Anna Maria Zieglerin, look at *Anna Zieglerin and the Lion's Blood: Alchemy and End Times in Reformation Germany*' (University of Pennsylvania, 2019) by Tara Nummedal.

16. Brother–Sister Love
For the fact that Tycho Brahe sent a copy of his book to John Dee in 1588, see Chapter One of Deborah Harkness's book *John Dee's Conversations with Angels* (Cambridge University Press, 1999).

The descriptions of Uraniborg on the island of Hven, and of Tycho and Sophie Brahe's relationship, come from an article called 'Tycho Brahe in Scandinavian Scholarship' by J. R. Christianson in the *History of Science*, Vol. 36, Issue 4, 1998.

17. Kepler
That Kepler's sister Margaretha urged their mother to be brave and not fear the rack is stated by Ulinka Rublack in *The Astronomer and the Witch* (Oxford University Press, 2015, p. 199).

18. The Magic of Words and Things

The story of how Nicholas Culpeper shouted out words to frighten the spirit in John Dee's shew stone is cited by John H. Appleby in his article 'Arthur Dee and Johannes Banfi Hunyades' in *Ambix*, Vol. 24, Part 2, July 1977. It is interesting that 'Adonai' might derive from the Hebrew word for God, in which case this could be an example of the magical powers commonly ascribed to Hebrew at this time.

For the wonder with which Europeans beheld the feather art of the Aztecs, see Anthony Alan Shelton's article 'Cabinets of Transgression: Renaissance Collections and the Incorporation of the New World' in *The Cultures of Collecting*, eds John Elsner and Roger Cardinal (Reaktion Books, 1994).

The thread of playfulness that runs through Neoplatonism is well discussed by Horst Bredekamp in his book *The Lure of Antiquity and the Cult of the Machine* (Markus Wiener Publishers, 1995). As Bredekamp says (p. 48 in *The Lure of Antiquity*) automatons and other mechanical toys were 'the most obvious expression of the desire to imitate life by inspiring movement' and (p. 72 in *The Lure of Antiquity*) 'playful pleasure in artificial creation not primarily guided by usefulness was associated with godlike elements'. Playfulness also gets into many aspects of sixteenth- and seventeenth-century creativity, including automatons, garden fountains and museum making. The quote about the Demiurge ('In order for the Demiurge to be able to become the absolute God he had to create something playful and lacking any use') is cited in Bredekamp's book (p. 72) and also the idea that the earth is the kunstkammer (or museum) of God (p. 73).

19. Dangerous Times

Frances Yates wrote about the dislike the Church apparently had for Plato: 'Gradually it became apparent to the Congregation of the Index that the whole of Renaissance Platonism was dangerous, particularly in its combination of Platonism and Cabala.' From Yates's *Occult Philosophy in the Elizabethan Age* in Chapter Seven, 'Reactions against the Occult Philosophy'.

For the way that mathematics was considered akin to conjuring, see Benjamin Woolley's book *The Queen's Conjurer* (Flamingo, 2002, p. 12).

That Galileo and Kepler both read Giordano Bruno, despite the Church's ban on his books, comes from Ingrid D. Rowland's *The Ecstatic Journey: Athanasius Kircher in Baroque Rome* (University of Chicago Press, 2000, p. 16). Also the observation that Kepler was shocked by Bruno's belief in the infinite universe.

That Copernicus cites Hermes Trismegistus in his book is stated by Benjamin Woolley in *The Queen's Conjuror* (Flamingo, 2002, pp. 154–155).

The conservative backlash against Dee, magic and alchemy is well described in *Supernatural and Secular Power in Early Modern England*, edited by Victoria Bladen and Marcus Harmes (Routledge, 2016).

The details here about Tommaso Campanella's life come from John Headley's book *Tommaso Campanella and the Transformation of the World* (Princeton University Press, 2019).

20. Giordano Bruno

Giordano Bruno's personality – witty, talkative, opinionated and conceited – leaps out at us from history. John Bossy's book *Giordano Bruno and the Embassy Affair* (Yale University Press, 1991) gives us one account of what Bruno might have been doing in London during the period from 1584 to 1586. See also P. H. Michel's *The Cosmology of Giordano Bruno* (Methuen, 1973), particularly pp. 21ff, for Bruno's sarcastic, vehement nature.

The quote that for Bruno infinite meant 'the immeasurable and inexhaustible abundance of reality ... Man no longer lived in the world as a prisoner enclosed within the narrow walls of a finite physical universe. He can traverse the air and break through all the imaginary boundaries of the celestial spheres' comes from *The Infinite Worlds of Giordano Bruno* (Charles C. Thomas, 1970, p. 33) by Antoinette Mann Paterson.

Bruno's belief in 'many worlds' may be even more interesting, if – as is possible – he is echoing the beliefs of the third-century theologian Origen, who stated that 'The fact is that prior to this world there have existed others.' For this possibility, see *Burned Alive* by Alberto Martinez (Reaktion Books, 2018, p. 61).

The observation that when Bruno was in prison in Venice his cellmates claimed that he said that God needed the world as much as the world needed God comes from 'Athanasius Kircher, Giordano Bruno and the Panspermia of the Infinite Universe' by Ingrid D. Rowland in the book *Athanasius Kircher: The Last Man Who Knew Everything* (Routledge, 2004, p. 197, ed. Paula Findlen).

The conceited letter that Giordano Bruno wrote to the scholars of Oxford introducing himself is quoted in Part 1, No. V of the Project Gutenberg e-book on Giordano Bruno by J. Lewis McIntyre. The quote about a doctor's degree from Oxford being as cheap as sardines comes from Robert McNulty's article 'Bruno in Oxford' in *Renaissance News*, 1960, pp. 300–305.

21. The Great Adventure
See Benjamin Woolley's book *The Queen's Conjuror* (Flamingo, 2002) for Dee's involvement in the affair of the Northwest Passage.

The quotes from John Dee's diaries regarding the wife-swapping incident and its consequences come from *The Diaries of John Dee* ed. Edward Fenton (Day Books, 1998).

22. Magical Shakespeare
For the observation that *A Midsummer Night's Dream* is an alchemical drama, see *Spirituality and the Occult: From the Renaissance to the Modern Age* (Routledge, 2001, p. 14) by B. J. Gibbons: *A Midsummer Night's Dream* 'can be interpreted as an alchemical drama with the mishaps of the star-crossed lovers representing the dissolution and reconstitution of primal matter...'

Colin McGinn, *Shakespeare's Philosophy* (HarperCollins e-books) is good on *The Tempest* and its emphasis on the power of language to effect magic.

23. The Secrets of Mortlake
The suggestion that Bartholomew Hicks consoled John Dee

comes from Hakan Hakansson's book *Seeing the Word* (Lunds Universitet, pp. 33–34).

24. Tribes
The letters of Robert Plot can be found in R.T. Gunther's *Early Science in Oxford*, Vol. 12 (Oxford, 1920 onwards). Robert Plot's alchemical thinking is described in A. V. Simcock's book *The Ashmolean Museum and Oxford Science, 1683–1983* (Museum of the History of Science, 1984).

Robert Iliffe (*Priest of Nature: The Religious Worlds of Isaac Newton*, Oxford University Press, 2017, p. 13) states that 'Newton shared as many intellectual interests with the fifteenth-century Neoplatonist Marsilio Ficino and the sixteenth-century "hermetic philosopher" Giordano Bruno as he did with Galileo'. Chris Gosden (*The History of Magic*, Penguin, p. 383) says that Newton kept two alchemical furnaces going in his rooms in Trinity College.

Thomas Hobbes (in the *Leviathan*, Part 3, Chapter 34) denied that 'it made sense to talk of immaterial spirits and attributed the belief ... to vulgar delusions and the misuse of language'. Also cited by Robert Iliffe in *Priest of Nature* (Oxford University Press, 2017, p. 240). For Hobbes's philosophical views and what other people thought about them, see Anthony Gottlieb's *The Dream of Enlightenment* (Penguin Books), Chapter 2, 'The Monster of Malmesbury'.

The quote that 'Arthur Dee was a persevering student in Hermetical Philosophy ... and confirmed unto his death that he had occularly, undeceivably and frequently beheld it (i.e. The Philosopher's Stone) in Bohemia' is cited in Tobias Churton's *The Magus of Freemasonry* (Inner Traditions, Vermont, p. 244, Chapter 8: 'The 1650s'). The letter from Sir Thomas Browne in which he spoke of Arthur Dee's memories of pewter dishes turning to silver is at Ashmole MS 1788, art 17.f.151.

The quote from Meric Casaubon ('I cannot see how any learned man, sober and rational, can entertain such an opinion that there be no Devils and Spirits' and also 'it doth concern Religion in general that we believe in spirits') is cited in *Curiosity and Wonder: From the Renaissance to the Enlightenment* (Ashgate Publishing Limited, 2006, ed. R. J. W. Evans, section on atheism).

25. The Magical Museum of Athanasius Kircher

The quote regarding Athanasius Kircher – 'The astonishment, amazement and wonder of those who witness his machines in action, of how some fear that there might be a demon inside, until he shows them that it is all done by mirrors, magnetism or hydraulic power' – comes from Jocelyn Godwin's book *Athanasius Kircher's Museum of the World* (Thames & Hudson, 2009, p. 172).

The playful quality in Neoplatonism has already been alluded to. See note 3 for Chapter 18.

Athanasius Kircher's museum is explained if we conclude that he was a Neoplatonist. Even many contemporary scholars didn't understand him and therefore mocked him. The report by

Evangelista Torricelli to Galileo is quoted by Camenietzki in his article 'Baroque Science between the Old and New World', pp. 322–323 in *Athanasius Kircher: The Last Man Who Knew Everything*, ed. Paula Findlen (Routledge, 2004).

26. The Commonwealth of Elves and Fairies

For more on Robert Kirk's book, see Marina Warner's introduction to *The Secret Commonwealth of Elves and Fairies*, which was first published in the *New York Review of Books*, 2007.

27. The Idea That Wouldn't Die

The quote from Bruno, that the universe is a mother, a nurse, a wellspring, a light, a love etc., comes from Ingrid Rowland's book on Bruno, *Giordano Bruno, Philosopher/Heretic*, p. 174.

The spread of Neoplatonism into Arabic, Persian and Turkish poetry is discussed in *Faces of the Infinite* (Oxford University Press, 2022) by Stefan Sperl and Yorgos Dedes.

In his article on Jorge Luis Borges in the *New York Times*, David Foster Wallace describes him as 'a mystic or at least a sort of radical Neoplatonist – human thought, behaviour and history are all products of one big mind'. From 'Borges on the Couch', *New York Times*, 7 November 2004.

Philip Pullman says that he was hugely influenced by Frances Yates's book *Giordano Bruno and the Hermetic Tradition*. (See the Readers Digest website www.readersdigest.co.uk for 20 November 2017.)

Authorship of the Neoplatonic poem has been ascribed to both Clare Harner (also known as Clare Harner Lyon) and Mary Elizabeth Frye.

28. Afterlives

There's an interesting account of Edward Kelley's final years in Charles Nicholl's article 'The Last Years of Edward Kelley' in the *London Review of Books*, 19 April 2001.

The quote from Frances Yates that 'the dominant philosophy of the Elizabethan age, was precisely the occult philosophy, with its magic, its melancholy, its aim of penetrating into profound spheres of knowledge and experience, scientific and spiritual, its fears of the dangers of such a quest, and the fierce opposition which it encountered...' comes from *The Occult Philosophy in the Elizabethan Age* by Frances Yates, Part II.

There is also something charismatic about Frances Yates, so much so that Marjorie Jones, who wrote Yates's biography, also wrote a series of detective novels with Yates as the heroine.

The accusation against Bruno that he claimed Christ was a magician and that he had a mind to do as much as him and more is cited in *The Book of Magic: Selected by Brian Copenhagen* (Penguin Classics, 2016, p. 392).

The detail that the clergymen of the Brotherhood of St John the Beheaded were gathered at Bruno's execution and sang the litany comes from Alberto Martinez's book *Burned Alive* (Reaktion Books, 2018, p. 75).

John Dee's Library Catalogue, eds Julian Roberts and Andrew G. Watson (Bibliographical Society, 1990) is invaluable in helping us to understand John Dee's library and how and where it was scattered. Dee's copy of Ripley's *The Twelve Gates* complete with his annotations is in the Bodleian, along with Dee's medieval manuscripts which began their life in St Augustine's monastery in Canterbury. The Royal College of Physicians in London has at least 150 books that belonged to Dee, including an edition of Cicero's writings with a beautiful doodle in one of the margins of a galleon in full sail. St John's College, Cambridge has Dee's copy of Marsilio Ficino's translation of Plato's *Omnia Divini Platonis Opera* – also complete with Dee's annotations – and Chetham's in Manchester has five books, including the copy of Gessner in which I saw the beautiful naked young woman in the margin.

Bruno's claim that *The Ash Wednesday Supper* caused such a furore that he could hardly leave the embassy is cited by Ingrid Rowland in *Giordano Bruno* (Farrar, Straus and Giroux, 2008, p. 157). Also cited in this book (in Chapter 18, 'Down Risky Streets') is the quote from Bruno, also from *The Ash Wednesday Supper*, that 'England can brag of having a populace that is second to none that the Earth nurtures in her bosom for being disrespectful, uncivil, rough, rustic, savage and badly brought up.'

29. Aberfoyle
The idea that God's beauty and goodness infuses the world and makes humans loveable is cited in Simon May's book *Love: A History* (Yale University Press, 2012, p.135).

Λcknowledgements

Every book is a journey. There are many places and people who made this journey possible.

Chief amongst the places are four libraries. Firstly, Saffron Walden Library where I spent most of my childhood, lying on the carpet and reading with my nose to the ground and the soles of my feet in their old school plimsoles uppermost. The children's shelves were full of books on magic – including *The Once and Future King* and all the Narnia books. I thought I had grown out of books on magic but it seems I never did.

The second library is Chetham's in Manchester, in one of whose books I first saw John Dee's doodles in the margins and realised that he had not just been a character lost in history but a living human being.

The third library is the Bibliotheca Philosophica Hermetica in Amsterdam, created by Joost Ritman (and also known as the Embassy of the Free Mind), where they let me hold a handsome fifteenth-century copy of the mysterious *Corpus Hermeticum*. (I love old books.)

And the fourth library – which is the library that changed my life the most – is the Warburg Library, near Euston in London. All libraries are a little magical (think of the library in

The Name of the Rose) but the Warburg even more than most. If you want to understand our human yearning for magic, its long, strange history and its enduring fascination, then the Warburg is the place for you. I couldn't have written this book without it.

As well as these libraries I owe a debt to many people. These include Edward Fenton, whose edition of John Dee's diaries remains one of the best, for its clarity and readableness; and Hannah Macdonald and Charlotte Cole of September, as well as the rest of the Duckworth team, who performed the magic of turning a heap of paper into a book. But more than any of these people and places I am grateful to my partner and our two daughters, whose lives have shaped me and without whom I would be a different person writing different books.